Global Economic Prospects

Economic Implications of
Remittances and Migration

2006

© 2006 The International Bank for Reconstruction and Development / The World Bank
1818 H Street, NW
Washington, DC 20433
Telephone: 202-473-1000
Internet: www.worldbank.org
E-mail: feedback@worldbank.org

1 2 3 4 09 08 07 06

ISBN: 08213-6344-1
E-ISBN: 0-8213-6345-X
13-digit E-ISBN: 978-0-8213-6345-4
DOI: 10.1596/978-0-8213-6344-7
EAN: 978-0-8213-6344-7

ISSN: 1014-8906

Library of Congress Cataloging-in-Publication data has been applied for.

Cover design: Naylor Design
Cover photo: Panos

Contents

Boxes

Foreword

For millennia people have migrated in search of economic opportunity. In the nineteenth and early twentieth centuries, technological advances and untapped natural resources drove movements of population from Europe and Asia to the Americas. International migration generated enormous improvements in people's lives. Immigrants enjoyed higher wages, countries of destination profited from increased supply of labor, and countries of origin saw labor market pressures ease.

Current trends indicate that pressures for migration from the south to the north are set to rise again. This movement is driven largely by income gaps and the rising number of young adults in developing countries seeking better opportunities abroad. The economic, social, and political implications that come with the movement of people differ from the movement of goods or money. As a result, the topic of international migration has prompted much political debate in the international community today.

The prospects for migration flows are critical for development. Developing countries benefit through the money that migrants send home to their families (remittances), through reduced labor market pressures, and through contacts with international markets and access to technology.

But migration is not always beneficial. Migrants can be subject to exploitation and abuse, and the loss of highly skilled personnel through migration has hindered development in some countries.

The World Bank's research department, in partnership with others, has launched a program to expand knowledge in an area that deserves greater attention. The program addresses the issues surrounding remittances; migration of high-skilled workers; the determinants of migration; temporary movements of persons; social protection and governance; and the links among trade, foreign direct investment, and migration.

An integral part of this program, *Global Economic Prospects 2006* focuses on policies to improve the developmental impact of remittances. It documents the high level of transactions costs facing migrants sending small remittances to their families, and it outlines the regulatory issues and market imperfections that keep costs high.

Fewer barriers to remittance flows and greater competition among remittance service providers could substantially reduce costs and boost remittance flows to developing countries. *Global Economic Prospects 2006* shows how sound domestic policies and an investment-friendly climate can significantly increase the contribution of remittances and migration to improved living conditions back home.

Migration remains an important force for fighting poverty, the key mission of the World Bank, and it is our hope that this report will contribute to this important debate.

Paul Wolfowitz
President
World Bank
November 2005

Acknowledgments

THIS REPORT WAS prepared by the Development Prospects Group (DECPG). The lead authors of this report were Dilip Ratha and William Shaw, with direction by Uri Dadush. The principal authors of the chapters were Andrew Burns (chapter 1), Dominique van der Mensbrugghe (chapter 2), William Shaw (chapter 3), and Dilip Ratha (chapters 4, 5, and 6). The report was prepared under the general guidance of François Bourguignon, chief economist and senior vice president of the World Bank.

The main macroeconomic forecasts in chapter 1 were prepared by the Global Trends Team of DECPG led by Hans Timmer and including John Baffes, Andrew Burns, Maurizio Bussolo, Annette de Kleine, Betty Dow, Himmat Kalsi, Fernando Martel Garcia, Donald Mitchell, Gauresh Shailesh Rajadhyaksha, Mick Riordan, Cristina Savescu, Shane Streifel, and Shuo Tan. The outlook for the East Asia and Pacific region was carried out with the cooperation of Milan Brahmbhatt and Louis Kuijs. The team also benefitted from in-depth consultations and comments from the regional chief economists and their staff, as well as country economists. The long-term growth and poverty forecasts were prepared by Dominique van der Mensbrugghe, Shaohua Chen, and Martin Ravallion. The companion Prospects for the Global Economy web site was prepared by Andrew Burns, Sarah Crow, and Cristina Savescu, in collaboration with Reza Farivari, Saurabh Gupta, David Hobbs, Shahin Outadi, Raja Reddy Komati Reddy, Malarvizhi Veerappan, and Cherin Verghese.

Maddalena Honorati and Prabal De provided research assistance. Chapter 2 benefitted from collaboration with Hans Timmer and from comments received from seminar participants, notably Lindsay Lowell and Susan Martin. Special thanks are due for the background material provided by Riccardo Faini, Robert Lucas, Julia Nielson, Kathleen Newland, and Irena Omelaniuk for chapter 3; Swaminathan S. Aiyar, Ralph Chami, Neil Fantom, Caroline Freund, Gary McMahon, Irena Omelaniuk, Serdar Sayan, Nikola Spatafora, and K. M. Vijayalakshmi for chapter 4; John McHale for chapter 5; John Gibson, David McKenzie, George Kalan, Dilek Aykut, Nikos Passas, and Jan Riedberg for chapter 6. Ole Andreassen, Jose de Luna Martinez, Raul E. Hernandez-Coss, Massimo Cirasino, and Roger Ballard also contributed background notes for chapter 6. Thanks also to colleagues in the International Organization for Migration who helped collect information on remittance-related government policies (for chapter 4) using their extensive international network, and Bernd Balkenhol of the International Labour Organization for preparing a background paper on forced remittances.

Many colleagues provided excellent comments at various stages of the report's preparation. L. Alan Winters provided comments on the report and guidance throughout its preparation. Luca Barbone, Kevin Barnes, Augusto de la Torre, Shantayanan Devarajan, Mustapha Nabli, John Page, Bryan Roberts, John Whalley, and Dean Yang were peer reviewers at the Bankwide review. Richard Adams, William Easterly, Isaku Endo, Jose Maria Fanelli, Shahrokh Fardoust, Ian Goldin, Daria Goldstein, Yevgeny Kuznetsov, Ali Mansoor, Phil Martin, Maria Soledad Martinez Peria, Fernando Montes-Negret, Nayantara Mukerji, Latifah Osman Merican, Christopher Parsons, Guillermo Perry, Sonia Plaza, S. Ramachandran, and Terrie Walmsley also provided useful comments. Johan Mistiaen and Romeo Matsas provided excellent help in designing and implementing a survey of migrant remitters from Congo, Nigeria, and Senegal residing in Belgium. Maria Amparo Gamboa, Araceli Jimeno, Katherine Rollins, Sarah Crow, and Michael Paul provided invaluable administrative support, including the collection of remittance fee data from all over the world.

The report team held consultations in July 2005 in Accra, Brussels, Geneva, London, and Paris. Thanks are due to Haleh Bridi, Barbara Genevaz, Carlos Braga, Sonia Plaza, Michelle Bailly, and other colleagues in these country offices for efficiently and enthusiastically arranging consultations with several international, academic, financial, and non-governmental institutions. Thanks are also due to the International Organization for Migration for assistance with organizing consultations in Geneva and to the International Labour Organization, the Global Commission on International Migration, the European Commission, and the Commonwealth Secretariat for participating in consultations and providing useful feedback.

This report also benefitted from the comments of the Bank's executive directors made at an informal board meeting on October 20, 2005.

Marilou Uy, Alan Gelb, Jeff Lewis, Amar Bhattacharya, Shaida Badiee, Robert Keppler, and Misha Belkindas provided guidance and encouragement to the team at various stages. Dorota A. Nowak managed production and dissemination activities by DECPG. Steven Kennedy's contribution as an editor is gratefully acknowledged. Book design, editing, and production were coordinated by the World Bank Office of the Publisher.

Overview

THE THEMES OF this year's *Global Economic Prospects* are international remittances and migration, their economic consequences, and how policies can increase their role in reducing poverty. International migration can generate substantial welfare gains for migrants and their families and for the countries involved (countries of origin and destination). The money that migrants send home—remittances—is an important source of extra income for migrants' families and for developing countries: in aggregate, remittances are more than twice as the size of international aid flows. However, migration should not be viewed as a substitute for economic development in the origin country—development ultimately depends on sound *domestic* economic policies.

Over the past two decades, barriers to cross-border trade and financial transactions have fallen significantly, while barriers to the cross-border movement of people remain high. Despite its economic benefits, migration remains controversial and, for some people, threatening. In part, this is because migration, like trade and capital movements, has distributional consequences, whereby net gains for society may mask important losses for some individuals and groups. But migration also sparks resistance because the movement of people has economic, psychological, social, and political implications that the movement of goods or money do not.

This publication has two goals. The first is to explore the gains and losses from international migration from the perspective of developing countries, with special attention to the money that migrants send home. The second goal is to consider policy initiatives that could improve the developmental impact of migration, again with particular attention to remittances. Our focus (for economic purposes) is on international migration from developing countries to high-income countries. Despite their importance, internal migration, migration among developing countries, and the political and social impacts of migration are beyond the scope of this work.

It is important to keep in mind three basic principles. First, migration is a diverse phenomenon, and its economic impact in one location or another depends heavily on the particular circumstances involved. Second, basic data on migration and remittances are lacking, so predicting the impact of policy changes can be problematic. This underlines the need for better data and more research. Third, migration has social and political implications that may be just as important as the economic analysis provided here. These are ably and comprehensively discussed in the recent report of the United Nations' Global Commission on International Migration. For all of these reasons, the analysis and policy recommendations for migration must remain qualified. This report draws conclusions where they can be supported by adequate data and points to an agenda for research where they cannot.

Global economic prospects

The slowdown among industrial economies that began in the second half of 2004 continued in 2005, with GDP growth expected to come in at 2.5 percent, down from 3.1 percent the year before. The pace of the expansion in the high-income countries is forecast to increase slightly over the next two years, with acceleration in Europe offsetting a modest slowing in Japan and stable growth in the United States. Economic activity also slowed in developing economies during 2005. Higher oil prices, domestic capacity constraints, and slower demand for their exports brought GDP growth down from a very strong 6.8 percent in 2004 to an estimated 5.9 percent this year. While GDP growth has remained robust, higher oil prices have sharply slowed real income growth among oil importers from 6.4 to 3.7 percent. Looking forward, continued high oil prices, coupled with inflationary pressures, are expected to restrain growth in most developing countries over the next two years. Nevertheless, GDP in these economies should expand by around 5.5 percent—much more quickly than during the past two decades.

This relatively positive outlook is subject to important downside risks. The outlook for oil prices is particularly uncertain. Low excess capacity has introduced a risk premium into oil prices and will make it more difficult to contain the impact of a future supply shock, should one arise. As a result, a significant supply disruption could slow global growth, with large negative consequences for global economic prospects. The future path of interest rates, which despite recent increases are still low, is another source of uncertainty. Persistent global imbalances, signs of rising inflation, and concerns about the sustainability of government finances in industrialized countries are all factors that could push rates higher and possibly provoke a much more serious slowdown.

The impact of remittances and migration

The impact on migrants
The bulk of the economic gains from migration accrue to migrants and their families, and these gains are often large. Wage levels (adjusted for purchasing power) in high-income countries are approximately five times those of low-income countries for similar occupations, generating an enormous incentive to emigrate. Moreover, to the extent that migrants devote a portion of their income to remittances, the gains are even greater. Essentially migrants can earn salaries that reflect industrial-country prices and spend the money in developing countries, where the prices of nontraded goods are much lower. Migrants, however, incur substantial costs, including psychological costs, and immigrants (particularly irregular migrants) sometimes run high risks; many suffer from exploitation and abuse. The decision to migrate is often made with inaccurate information. Given the high costs of migration—including the risks of exploitation and the exorbitant fees paid to traffickers—the net benefit in some cases may be low or even negative. There are costs, too, for family members left behind—particularly children—although these costs must be balanced against the benefits of the extra income that migrants send back home to their families.

The impact on destination countries
Destination countries can enjoy significant economic gains from migration. The increased availability of labor boosts returns to capital and reduces the cost of production. A model-based simulation performed for this study indicates that a rise in migration from developing countries sufficient to raise the labor force of high-income countries by 3 percent could boost incomes *of natives* in high-income countries by 0.4 percent. In addition, high-income countries may benefit from increased labor-market flexibility, an increased labor force due to lower prices for services such as child care, and perhaps economies of scale and increased diversity.

Nevertheless, there are losers within destination countries. Some workers may see an erosion of wages or employment, although this effect is found to be small in most empirical studies. In the model-based simulation of the impact of increased migration, earlier migrants suffer significant income losses, while the impact on natives' wages is small. (The differential impact is reduced if foreign-born workers are viewed as closer substitutes for natives.) Easing rules that limit labor-market flexibility, and strengthening institutions that provide education and training, will help workers displaced by immigration (both natives and resident migrants) to find work. Note that the simulation results are not intended to incorporate all of the economic impacts of migration, nor do they capture important social and political implications. The goal is not to forecast the overall impact of increased migration, but rather to give us insights into the economic gains that might be expected from changes in policy or circumstances, as well as insights into the channels through which migration affects welfare.

The impact on origin countries

Migration also generates economic benefits for origin countries, the largest being remittances. International remittances received by developing countries—expected to reach $167 billion in 2005—have doubled in the past five years as a result of (a) the increased scrutiny of flows since the terrorist attacks of September 2001, (b) changes in the industry that support remittances (lower costs, expanding networks), (c) improvements in data recording, (d) the depreciation of the dollar (which raises the dollar value of remittances denominated in other currencies), and (e) growth in the migrant stock and incomes. However, records still underestimate the full scale of remittances, because payments made through informal, unrecorded channels are not captured. Econometric analysis and available household surveys suggest that unrecorded flows through informal channels may conservatively add 50 percent (or more) of recorded flows. Several countries with significant migrant populations do not report data on

remittances at all, even those sent through formal channels, or they report remittances under other balance of payments entries.

Despite the prominence given to remittances from developed countries, South-South remittance flows make up between 30 and 45 percent of total remittances received by developing countries, reflecting the fact that over half of migrants from developing countries migrate to other developing countries.

While the impact of remittances on growth is unclear, remittances do play an important role in reducing the incidence and severity of poverty (with no significant effect on income inequality). Remittances directly increase the income of the recipient and can help smooth household consumption, especially in response to adverse events, such as crop failure or a health crisis. In addition to bringing the direct benefit of higher wages earned abroad, migration helps households diversify their sources of income (and thus reduce their vulnerability to risks) while providing a much needed source of savings and capital for investment. Remittances appear to be associated with increased household investments in education, entrepreneurship, and health—all of which have a high social return in most circumstances.

Measuring the poverty impact of remittances is difficult: data are scarce, and calculating the income gains from remittances requires assumptions concerning what migrants would have earned if they had stayed at home. Careful analyses of the available household survey data indicate that remittances have been associated with declines in the poverty headcount ratio in several low-income countries—by 11 percentage points in Uganda, 6 in Bangladesh, and 5 in Ghana, for example. In Guatemala, remittances may have reduced the severity of poverty by 20 percent. Cross-country regressions and simulations also indicate that increases in remittances help to reduce the incidence of poverty.

By generating a steady stream of foreign exchange earnings, remittances can improve a country's creditworthiness for external borrowing and, through innovative financing mechanisms (such as securitization of remittance flows), they can expand access to capital and lower borrowing costs. While large and sustained remittance inflows can contribute to currency appreciation, this outcome may be less severe than it is in the case of natural resource earnings, because remittances are distributed more widely and may avoid exacerbating strains on institutional capacity that are often associated with natural resource booms.

Migration has economic implications for origin countries beyond remittances. The small size of migration flows relative to the labor force suggests that the effects of South–North migration on working conditions for low-skilled workers in the developing world as a whole must be small as well. However, in some countries low-skilled emigration can raise demand for the remaining low-skilled workers (including poor workers) at the margin, leading to some combination of higher wages, lower unemployment, less underemployment, and greater labor force participation. Thus low-skilled emigration can offer a valuable safety valve for insufficient employment at home. In the long run, however, developing country policies should aim to generate adequate employment and rapid growth, rather than relying on migration as an alternative to development opportunities.

High-skilled emigration has more complex implications. Like low-skilled migration, it can greatly benefit migrants and their families and help relieve labor market pressures. However, a well-educated diaspora can improve access to capital, technology, information, foreign exchange, and business contacts for firms in the country of origin. The return of expatriates and the maintenance of close contacts with high-skilled emigrants have played an important role in the transfer of knowledge to origin countries. At the same time, large outflows of high-skilled workers can reduce growth in the origin country for these reasons: (a) the productivity of colleagues, employees, and other workers may suffer because they lose the opportunity for training and mutually beneficial exchanges of ideas; (b) the provision of key public services with positive externali-

ties, such as education and health (particularly for the control of transmissible diseases), may be impaired; (c) opportunities to achieve economies of scale in skill-intensive activities may be reduced; (d) society loses its return on high-skilled workers trained at public expense; and (e) the price of technical services may rise. Highly educated citizens, if they stayed in their countries, could help to improve governance, improve the quality of debate on public issues, encourage education of children, and strengthen the administrative capacity of the state—contributions that would be lost through high-skilled emigration.

It is impossible to reliably estimate the net benefit, or cost, to origin countries of high-skilled emigration because data are limited and a myriad of individual country circumstances enter into the calculus of that benefit or loss. We can only offer two rough observations, which reflect the wide variation in high-skilled emigration rates among countries:

- Very high rates of high-skilled emigration are found in countries that represent a small share of the population of the developing world. Many of those countries have poor investment climates that likely limit the productive employment of high-skilled workers. Of course, the loss of high-skilled workers may aggravate the poor investment climate and limit the potential benefits of economic reform.
- Some countries find it difficult to provide productive employment for many high-skilled workers because of their small economic scale or because misguided educational policies have resulted in a large supply of university graduates for whom no suitable jobs exist.

Policies to improve the developmental impact of remittances and migration

Migration policies

Greater emigration of low-skilled emigrants from developing to industrial countries could make a significant contribution to poverty reduction. The most feasible means of increasing such emigration would be to promote managed migration programs between origin and destination countries that combine temporary migration of low-skilled workers with incentives for return. Temporary programs have several advantages, and some disadvantages, relative to permanent migration. From the perspective of the destination country, managed, temporary migration programs ease social tensions by limiting permanent settlement; they limit the potential burden on public expenditures because immigrants are guaranteed a job and are less likely to bring dependents; and they allow for controlled variation of the number of immigrants in response to changes in labor-market conditions, thus limiting adverse effects on low-skilled native workers. However, temporary migration can be less efficient than permanent migration for firms in destination countries because of high training costs. From the origin-country perspective, managed, temporary migration may be the only means of securing deliberate increases in low-skilled emigration and may raise remittances and improve the skills of returning workers. On the other hand, managed migration programs do not guarantee future access to labor markets (and thus to remittances), because it is easier for destination countries to suspend temporary programs than to expel immigrants. Overall, however, such programs do represent a feasible approach to capturing the efficiency gains from labor migration.

Origin countries that are adversely affected by high-skilled emigration face challenges in managing it better. Service requirements for access to publicly financed education can be evaded and are likely to discourage return; and proposals for the taxation of emigrants to the benefit of the origin country have made little progress. Origin countries can help to retain key workers by improving working conditions in public employment and by investing in research and development. Origin countries can also take steps to encourage educated em-

igrants to return by identifying job opportunities for them, cooperating with destination countries that have programs to promote return, permitting dual nationality, and helping to facilitate the portability of social insurance benefits.

By providing authoritative information on migration opportunities and risks, governments could help avoid unfortunate, costly-to-reverse migration decisions and limit the abuse of vulnerable migrants. Labor recruiters can play a valuable role in promoting migration, but emigrants' lack of information often enables recruiters to capture the lion's share of the rents generated by constraints on immigration and imperfect information. Origin countries with effective public sector institutions might consider the regulation of recruitment agents to limit rents and improve transparency.

Remittance policies

Governments in destination and origin countries can sharpen the developmental impact of remittances through the application of appropriate policies. Access of poor migrants and their families to formal financial services for sending and receiving remittances could be improved through public policies that encourage expansion of banking networks, allow domestic banks from origin countries to operate overseas, provide identification cards to migrants, and facilitate the participation of microfinance institutions and credit unions in providing low-cost remittance services. Remittances, in turn, can be used to support financial products—housing and consumer loans and insurance—for poor people.

A second set of promising policies could improve competition in the remittance transfer market and thereby lower fees. The price of remittance transactions is often unnecessarily high for the small transfers typically made by poor migrants. The *cost* of such transactions is often well below the fees paid by customers. Reducing transaction charges increases the disposable income of poor migrants and increases their incentives to remit, because the net receipts of recipients increase. The overall result would be stronger remittance flows to developing countries.

Competition among providers of remittance services could be increased by lowering capital requirements on remittance services and opening up postal, banking, and retail networks to nonexclusive partnerships with remittance agencies. Disseminating data on remittance fees in important remittance corridors and establishing a voluntary code of conduct for delivering fair-value transfers would improve transparency and reduce prices for remittance transactions. Governments could help reduce costs by supporting the introduction of modern technology in payment systems. Alleviating liquidity constraints by providing a credit line either to the sender or the recipient, based on past remittance activity, would enable senders to take advantage of the lower fee rates available only for larger remittances. Reducing exchange-rate distortions could also lower the cost of remittance transactions. Finally, regulatory regimes need to strike a better balance between preventing financial abuse and facilitating the flow of funds through formal channels.

Several origin countries have attempted to improve the developmental impact of remittances by introducing incentives to increase flows and to channel them to more productive uses. Such policies are more problematic than efforts to expand access to financial services or reduce transaction costs, because they pose clear risks. Tax incentives to attract remittance inflows, for example, may also encourage tax evasion, while matching-fund programs to attract remittances from migrant associations may divert funds from other local funding priorities. Efforts to channel remittances to investment, meanwhile, have met with little success. Fundamentally, remittances are private funds that should be treated like other sources of household income. Efforts to increase sav-

ings and improve the allocation of expenditures should be accomplished through improvements in the overall investment climate, rather than by targeting remittances. Similarly, because remittances are private funds, they should not be viewed as a substitute for official development aid.

Organization of this study

As is customary in this report, chapter 1 reviews recent developments in and prospects for the global economy and their implications for developing countries. Chapter 2 uses a model-based simulation to evaluate the potential global welfare gains and distributional impact from a hypothetical increase of 3 percent in high-income countries' labor force caused by migration from developing countries. Chapter 3 surveys the economic literature on the benefits and costs of migration for migrants and their countries of origin, focusing on economically motivated migration from developing to high-income countries. We then turn to remittances, the main theme of the report. Chapter 4 investigates the size of remittance flows to developing countries, the use of formal and informal channels, the role of government policies in improving the development impact of remittances, and, for certain countries, their macroeconomic impact. Chapter 5 addresses the impact of remittances at the household level, in particular their role in reducing poverty, smoothing consumption, providing working capital for small-scale enterprises, and increasing household expenditures in areas considered to have a high social value. The last chapter investigates policy measures that could lower the cost of remittance transactions for poor households and measures to strengthen the financial infrastructure supporting remittances.

Abbreviations

ADB	Asian Development Bank
AML	Anti-money laundering
AML/CFT	Anti-money laundering/countering financing of terrorism
ARTEP	Asian Regional Team for Employment Protection (ILO)
ATC	Agreement on Textiles and Clothing
BIS	Bank for International Settlements
BoA	Bank of America
BOP	Balance of payment
CECEI	Comité des établissements de crédit et des enterprises, d'investissement
CEMLA	Center for Latin American Monetary Studies (Centro de Estudios Monetarios Latino Americanos)
CEPAL	Economic Commission for Latin America and the Caribbean (Comisión Económico para América Latina y el Caribe)
CES-IFO	Center for Economic Studies at the University of Michigan—Institute for Economic Research
CGAP	Consultative Group to Assist the Poorest
CPI	Consumer price index
CPSS	Committee on Payment and Settlement Systems
DDP	Development data platform
DFID	Department for International Development
DHS	Department for Homeland Security
DPRs	Diversified payment rights
DPS	Deferred payment scheme
ECA	Europe and Central Asia
ECOSOC	UN Economic and Social Council
EU	European Union
EV	Equivalent variation
FATF	Financial Action Task Force against Money Laundering

FDC	First Data Corporation
FDI	Foreign direct investment
FFMC	First Financial Management Corporation
FinCEN	Financial Crimes Enforcement Network
FISDL	Social Investment Fund for Local Development (Fondo de Inversión Social para el Desarrollo)
GATS	General Agreement on Trade in Services
GDP	Gross domestic product
GE	General equilibrium
GTAP	Global Trade Analysis Project
HIV/AIDS	Human immunodeficiency virus/acquired immune deficiency syndrome
HSBC	Hong Kong Shanghai Bank Corporation
HTAs	Hometown associations
IADB	Inter-American Development Bank
IBM	International Business Machines
ICICI	Industrial Credit and Investment Corporation of India
ICMC	International Catholic Migration Commission
IFAD	International Fund for Agriculture and Development
ILO	International Labour Organization
IMF	International Monetary Fund
IOM	International Organization for Migration
IRCA	Immigation Reform and Control Act
IRD	Institut de recherche pour le développement
IRnet	International Remittance Network
LAC	Latin American and the Caribbean
LDCs	Least-developed countries
MCIC	Matricula Consular identification card
MDG	Millennium Development Goal
MIDSA	Migration for Development in Southern Africa
MFIs	Microfinance institutions
MFN	Most-favored nation
MICR	Magnetic ink character recognition
MIDA	Migration for Development in Africa
MIDWA	Migration for Development in Western Africa
MPG	Migration Policy Group
MSB	Money service business
MTOs	Money transfer operators
NAFTA	North American Free Trade Agreement

NBER	National Bureau of Economic Research
NGOs	Non-governmental organization
ODA	Official development aid
OECD	Organisation for Economic Co-operation and Development
OFAC	Office of Foreign Assets Control
OPEC	Organization of the Petroleum Exporting Countries
OLS	Ordinary least squares
PADF	Pan-American Development Foundation
PPP	Purchasing power parity
PRIO	International Peace Institute, Oslo
PROFECO	Procuraduría Federal del Consumidor
R&D	Research and development
SADC	Southern African Development Community
SPV	Special purpose vehicle
TDS	Telephone and data systems
TSG	Technical Sub-Group on the Movement of Persons
UAE	United Arab Emirates
UCSD	University of California, San Diego
UN	United Nations
UNDP	United Nations Development Programme
UNESCAP	United Nations Economic and Social Commission for Asia and the Pacific
UNESCO–ICSU	United Nations Educational, Scientific and Cultural Organization–International Council of Scientific Unions
USAID	United States Agency for International Development
USD	US dollar
WEO	World Economic Outlook
WOCCU	World Council of Credit Unions
WTO	World Trade Organization

1

Prospects for the Global Economy

Following very strong growth, the world economy slowed in late 2004 and into 2005 as output began to push against capacity constraints. High oil prices cut into the incomes of oil importers, but the expansion remained strong, partly because of favorable conditions in financial markets, including still low inflation, interest rates, and interest-rate spreads. Tightness in the oil market, the threat of even higher fuel prices, and the possibility that interest rates may rise pose major threats to the expansion.

Slower but still strong growth

World GDP is estimated to have increased by 3.2 percent in 2005, down from 3.8 in 2004. Growth is projected to be stable in 2006, before strengthening somewhat in 2007. The slowdown that began in the second half of 2004 was experienced throughout the industrialized world, with growth in Europe still underperforming its potential. In contrast, the economies of the United States and Japan, despite having slowed, are expanding at close to their maximum sustainable rates.

Among large developing economies, GDP in 2005 continued to expand rapidly in China and India (in excess of 9 percent and about 7 percent, respectively), but slowed in Russia as growth in oil production weakened. High oil prices, in combination with domestic capacity constraints and slower import demand from high-income countries, are estimated to

have reduced growth among oil-importing developing countries from 6.9 percent to 6.1 percent. In terms of real incomes, the slowdown was much sharper—from 6.4 percent to 3.7 percent. Despite still growing oil revenues, reduced opportunities to expand production in the petroleum sector meant that output growth in oil-exporting developing countries also eased, from 6.6 percent to 5.6 percent.

During 2006 the expansion among high-income countries is projected to be stable, at about 2.5 percent, before picking up a bit in 2007. This reflects a combination of improved performance in Europe and stable growth in the United States and Japan. In the United States, higher oil prices and tighter monetary policy are expected to offset the positive stimulus to growth from past depreciations. The projected pickup in Europe occurs despite a significant drag on growth from high oil prices whose effects are expected to be more than offset by low interest rates, pent up investment demand, and a dissipation of most of the negative consequences following the euro's real-effective appreciation. In Japan, strengthening domestic demand and supportive macroeconomic policies should enable growth to remain close to potential, despite high oil prices.

Growth in developing economies is projected to slow modestly from an estimated 5.9 percent in 2005 to 5.5 percent by 2007. In East and South Asia, the expansion is projected to moderate somewhat but remain very strong, particularly in China and India. In the Middle East and in both North and Sub-Saharan Africa, strong oil revenues should buoy internal demand among oil exporters and partially offset capacity constraints that will slow production growth. The projected easing of growth in Latin America and the Caribbean reflects weaker non-oil commodity prices as well as a return to trend growth in several countries that rebounded very strongly in 2004. In Europe and Central Asia, the waning of the growth bonus following EU accession and capacity constraints in oil-producing countries are expected to contribute to a modest slowing of the expansion.

Tight commodity markets

Weaker global growth should reduce the strain in non-oil commodity markets. Already there are signs of stabilization, and even of decline, in the prices of agricultural products, where supply has responded to high prices. Metals and shipping prices also show signs of easing, although to a lesser extent.

In oil markets, the projected slowdown is not expected to be sufficient to generate a substantial easing of prices. While crude oil supply is growing marginally faster than demand, supply conditions are expected to remain tight. As a result, crude oil prices, which currently embody a large risk premium, are not expected to fall rapidly. The baseline assumes that no major supply disruptions occur and that there will be a gradual decline in oil prices toward $40 per barrel by 2010. This implies an average price of $56 for a barrel of oil in 2006 and $52 in 2007.

Future spikes in oil prices form a potential risk to global prospects. A price hike generated by a sustained negative supply shock would be particularly disruptive, because output would be constrained directly by the reduced availability of oil and petroleum-based inputs. This would be in contrast to the recent past, when prices rose in the context of rapidly growing supply. A supply shock that reduced oil deliveries by 2 million barrels per day could push prices to more than $90 a barrel for more than a year, resulting in a 1.5 percent reduction in global growth by the second year following the shock. The terms-of-trade impact for low-income oil-importing economies would reduce incomes in these countries by more than 4 percent of their GDP (much more than for high-income countries) because their economies are relatively oil intensive, and because a supply shock–induced increase in oil prices is unlikely to be accompanied by higher non-oil commodity prices.

Global imbalances remain an issue

Global current account imbalances and the U.S. current account deficit (which is expected to exceed $750 billion in 2005) remain important medium-term problems. During late 2004 and early 2005 tensions eased somewhat. Rising interest rate differentials relative to European short- and long-term assets made private sector purchases of dollar–denominated assets more attractive. As a result, the dollar appreciated some 2.5 percent in real-effective terms during the first seven months of 2005, and reserve accumulation by foreign central banks became less important in the financing of the current account deficit.

This respite appears to have been short-lived. To some extent, the increased private flows represented a one-off portfolio adjustment toward U.S. assets by investors. Beginning in the second quarter of 2005, the flows diminished, and the dollar faced renewed downward pressure. As a result, foreign reserve accumulation once again became a critical component in the financing of the U.S. current account deficit, restoring the risk that a change in behavior on the part of foreign central bankers could prove destabilizing. Recent decisions by China and Malaysia to widen the range of currencies to which their own currencies are pegged could help ease future pressures, especially if the scope for appreciation included in the regime is exercised in practice. Globally, policy should continue to focus on increasing public and private savings in deficit countries and increasing spending (notably on investment goods) in surplus countries.

Low interest rates are a source of uncertainty

The future path of long-term interest rates and spreads, which have been at historically low levels for an extended period, is an important uncertainty. A number of factors have helped maintain interest rates at low levels, including several years of very loose monetary policy throughout the developed world; increased aging-related savings in Europe; balance-sheet consolidation in the United States and Asia; and a low inflationary environment—thanks, in part, to increased competition following the entry into global markets of China and members of the former Soviet bloc. Most of these factors are temporary and are expected to gradually abate, resulting in a steady rise in long-term rates in the baseline. Indeed, yields on 10-year U.S. Treasuries have risen 50 basis points since September.

However, these temporary factors could continue to hold sway, reversing or bringing to a halt the recent increase in long-term rates (as they have in the past). This would prompt stronger-than-projected demand, but also exacerbate capacity constraints. As a result, oil prices could get pushed higher, which would provoke a more brutal inflationary cycle, and ultimately, a recession.

Alternatively, these forces could dissipate more rapidly, causing long-term interest rates to rise more quickly toward long-term equilibrium levels, which would provoke a more pronounced slowdown. While not the most likely scenario, the recent rise in long-term yields and inflation suggest that a higher interest-rate scenario is a real possibility.

Finally, this environment of slowing growth and global imbalances raises the risk of rising protectionism. In this regard, policymakers need to make a concerted effort to ensure that the Doha round reaches a successful conclusion so that developing countries specializing in the export of agricultural products can benefit from trade liberalization in the same way that other countries have profited from freer trade in the manufacturing and raw materials sectors.

Global growth

The global economy slowed markedly in 2005, but still continued to expand at an estimated 3.2 percent pace, compared with 3.8 percent in 2004 (table 1.1). The slowdown was widespread, reaching virtually every economic region. It was precipitated by higher oil prices, resource-sector capacity constraints, tightening monetary policy in the United States, and in some countries, the maturation of the investment cycle following a year of very fast growth.

Outturns and prospects in high-income countries

Growth among industrialized economies in 2005 is estimated at 2.5 percent, substantially lower than the 3.1 percent recorded the year before. Industrial production and trade flows among high-income countries were particularly weak. Growth rates of the former declined from over 5 percent in mid-2004 to less than 1.5 percent in the middle of 2005 (figure 1.1). High oil prices, rising short-term interest rates, and an unusually disruptive hurricane season[1] slowed growth in the United States to

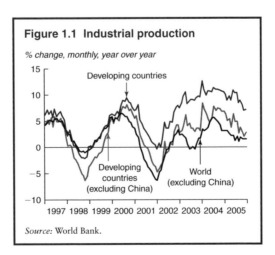

Figure 1.1 Industrial production

% change, monthly, year over year

Developing countries

Developing countries (excluding China)

World (excluding China)

1997 1998 1999 2000 2001 2002 2003 2004 2005

Source: World Bank.

Table 1.1 The global outlook in summary
Percentage change from previous year, except interest rates and oil price

	2003	2004	2005e	2006f	2007f
Global Conditions					
World trade volume	5.9	10.2	6.2	7.0	7.3
Consumer prices					
G-7 countries[a,b]	1.5	1.7	2.2	2.0	1.7
United States	2.3	2.7	3.4	3.0	2.4
Commodity prices (USD terms)					
Non-oil commodities	10.2	17.5	11.9	−5.9	−6.3
Oil price (US$ per barrel)[c]	28.9	37.7	53.6	56.0	51.5
Oil price (percent change)	15.9	30.6	42.1	4.5	−8.0
Manufactures unit export value[d]	7.5	6.9	2.4	2.4	2.1
Interest rates					
$, 6-month (percent)	1.2	1.7	3.8	5.0	5.2
€, 6-month (percent)	2.3	2.1	2.2	2.1	2.8
Real GDP growth[e]					
World	2.5	3.8	3.2	3.2	3.3
Memo item: world (PPP weights)[f]	3.9	5.0	4.4	4.3	4.4
High income	1.8	3.1	2.5	2.5	2.7
OECD countries	1.8	3.0	2.4	2.5	2.7
Euro area	0.7	1.7	1.1	1.4	2.0
Japan	1.4	2.6	2.3	1.8	1.7
United States	2.7	4.2	3.5	3.5	3.6
Non-OECD countries	3.7	6.3	4.3	4.2	4.0
Developing countries in	5.5	6.8	5.9	5.7	5.5
East Asia and Pacific	8.1	8.3	7.8	7.6	7.4
Europe and Central Asia	6.1	7.2	5.3	5.2	5.0
Latin America and Caribbean	2.1	5.8	4.5	3.9	3.6
Middle East and N. Africa	5.2	4.9	4.8	5.4	5.2
South Asia	7.9	6.8	6.9	6.4	6.3
Sub-Saharan Africa	3.6	4.5	4.6	4.7	4.5
Memorandum items					
Developing countries					
excluding transition countries	5.3	6.8	6.1	5.8	5.6
excluding China and India	4.1	6.0	4.9	4.7	4.6

Note: PPP = purchasing power parity; e = estimate; f = forecast.
    a. Canada, France, Germany, Italy, Japan, the UK, and the United States.
    b. In local currency, aggregated using 1995 GDP weights.
    c. Simple average of Dubai, Brent, and West Texas Intermediate.
    d. Unit value index of manufactured exports from major economies, expressed in U.S. dollars.
    e. GDP in 1995 constant dollars;1995 prices and market exchange rates.
    f. GDP measured at 1995 PPP weights.

an estimated 3.5 percent, compared with 4.2 percent the year before. The slowdown was not as marked as it could have been, because low long-term interest rates boosted domestic demand, and the cumulative effect of past dollar depreciations improved net exports.

In Europe, the growth slowdown was less pronounced, but the expansion, at an estimated 1.2 percent (1.1 percent in the euro zone), was much weaker. The relatively low oil-intensity of European economies and relaxed macroeconomic policy stance help explain why the slowdown in Europe was not more pronounced. In Japan, GDP is estimated to have increased 2.3 percent. Rising domestic demand and household incomes, as a result of tighter labor market conditions and reduced industrial restructuring, compensated for much slower Chinese import demand.

Looking forward, the increase in oil prices observed in 2005 is expected to slow global growth by about one quarter of a percentage point in 2006, compared with what it would have been had prices remained stable. In the United States, the pace of the expansion is projected to remain broadly stable, because the negative effects of further expected increases in interest rates and high oil prices will be partly offset by a deficit-financed pickup in post-hurricane investment and additional increases in the contribution of the external sector to growth. In Europe, economic activity is projected to accelerate despite a significant drag on growth from high oil prices, because of low interest rates, pent up investment demand, and a dissipation of most of the negative consequences following the euro's real-effective appreciation. Meanwhile, in Japan, the negative consequences of higher oil prices are expected to be substantially offset by strengthening domestic demand and continued supportive macroeconomic policies.

Developing economy outturns and prospects

Despite a slowdown of almost a full percentage point, growth in developing economies remained very robust, at an estimated 5.9 percent in 2005 (figure 1.2). In part this reflects the strong performance of China and India, where output continued to expand at rapid rates (in excess of 9 percent and about 7 percent, respectively). The slowdown among the oil-importing countries (excluding China and India) was sharper, from 5.6 percent to 4.3 percent.[2] At the same time, dwindling spare capacity in the petroleum sector caused growth in oil-exporting developing countries to ease from 6.6 percent to 5.7 percent, even though oil revenues continued to rise.

High oil prices, rising interest rates, and building inflationary pressures are expected to restrain growth in most developing regions in 2006 and 2007 (figure 1.3). As a group, however, low- and middle-income countries should

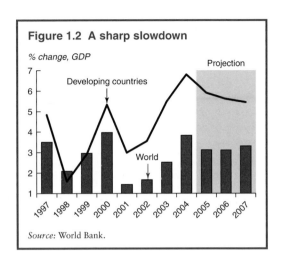

Figure 1.2 A sharp slowdown

% change, GDP

Source: World Bank.

again outperform high-income economies by a wide margin through 2007.

Regional outlooks

Detailed descriptions of economic developments in developing regions can be found in the Regional Outlooks section of http://www.worldbank.org/globaloutlook.

The economies of the **East Asia and Pacific** region continued to expand rapidly in 2005. Regional GDP is estimated to have increased by 7.8 percent, down from 8.3 percent in 2004. Growth in China remained very strong—despite a substantial slowing in both private consumption and investment demand—because exports continued to grow rapidly, and import growth declined by half. China appears to have been a major beneficiary of the expiration of quotas on textiles (see the global trade discussion below), which contributed to rapid export growth in the first half of the year. Since then, the re-imposition of quotas by the United States and the European Union (EU) have attenuated this positive force. For other countries in the region, the slowdown in Chinese imports, weak global high-tech demand, and elevated oil prices have translated into reduced export growth, rapidly rising

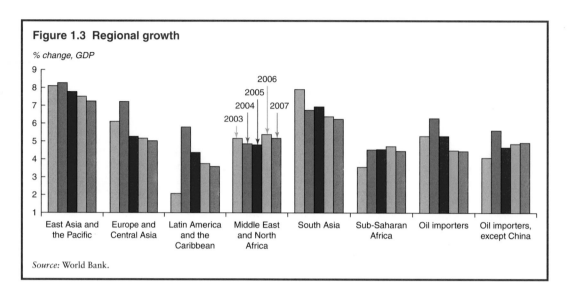

Figure 1.3 Regional growth

Source: World Bank.

producer prices, and a deterioration of current account balances.

Even higher oil prices on average in 2006,[3] the longer-term implications of reduced investment levels of China, and a tightening of monetary policy are expected to slow regional growth to 7.6 and 7.4 percent in 2006 and 2007, respectively. The changes in the currency regimes of China and Malaysia are not expected to have a major impact on growth. Nevertheless, as discussed below, these regimes should improve financial stability both domestically and internationally.

Economic activity in the **Europe and Central Asia** region decelerated sharply in 2005, with GDP growing by an estimated 5.3 percent, down from 7.2 percent in 2004. Slower increases in oil production, a peaking of the investment cycle (especially among economies that recently joined the EU), and less robust world demand for the region's exports contributed to the slowdown, which was particularly intense in a number of the larger economies of the region. Russia decelerated from 7.2 percent to 6.0 percent; Ukraine from 12.1 percent to 4.4 percent; Poland from 5.4 percent to 3.5 percent; and Turkey from 8.9 percent to 4.8 percent.

Higher oil prices constrained domestic demand in oil-importing countries, but oil revenues in oil-exporting countries helped offset much slower growth in the oil sector itself. Reflecting these capacity constraints and the very strong growth recorded last year, inflationary pressures have built up in many countries in the region, notably Russia. Turkey, where improved macroeconomic policy has pushed inflation below 10 percent, represents an important exception. The expected acceleration of demand in Europe, continued high oil prices—which for many countries in the region are a positive factor—and additional gains in European market share, suggest that growth for the region as a whole should remain relatively stable—at about 5 percent in 2006 and 2007, which is close to the region's potential growth rate.

Economic activity in **Latin America and the Caribbean** is estimated to have increased by some 4.5 percent during 2005, substantially slower than the 5.8 percent recorded in 2004 but much faster than the region's 0.4 percent average growth rate during the preceding three years. Supply constraints and tight monetary policy are estimated to have slowed GDP growth in Brazil to some 3.8 percent (down from 4.9 percent in 2004), while in Mexico five fewer working days in 2005 than in 2004 are expected to contribute to a significant slowing.[4] Excluding these countries, regional growth in 2005 is estimated at a robust 5.9 percent, boosted by both strong world demand for the region's exports (particularly oil, coffee, and copper, which account for 65 percent of the regions' commodity exports) and low interest rates. Domestic factors that contributed to the strong performance include past efforts to open the region up to international trade, more responsible budget policy, the introduction of more flexible exchange rate regimes, and lower inflation.

Slower global growth is already easing tensions in the non-oil commodity markets that have driven the recovery in the Latin America and Caribbean region, and this trend is expected to continue. Moreover, while many countries in the region benefit from high oil prices, many others, particularly those in the Caribbean, are heavily oil dependent and face substantial income losses.[5] As a result, regional GDP growth is projected to decline to 3.6 percent by 2007.

High oil prices and strong oil demand continue to be key drivers for the economies of the **Middle East and North Africa,** where GDP is estimated to have increased by 4.8 percent in 2005. Very high oil revenues generated double-digit advances in public spending, which have helped to increase GDP in oil-producing economies by an estimated 5.4 percent. Strong demand from these economies spilled over to the labor-abundant economies of the region through higher remittances and increased intraregional tourism flows. However, weak growth in Europe, high oil bills, and a one-off negative effect from the removal of quotas under the Agreement on Textiles and Clothing (ATC) reduced growth of regional oil-importing countries from 4.6 percent in 2004 to about 4.0 percent in 2005.

Looking forward, high oil prices are expected to continue feeding demand in oil-producing countries, whose economies should expand by 5.4 percent in 2006 and 5.1 percent in 2007. In the oil-importing economies, growth is expected to accelerate to about the same level, supported by stronger European growth and a weaker negative effect from

the ATC. The region's strong performance reflects, in part, past reforms, such as steps to improve transparency in the oil sector in Algeria, as well as banking-sector reform, reductions in customs duties, privatization, and regulatory reform in other Maghreb countries. These efforts, and in particular, the substantial reforms underway in Egypt, help to raise the region's growth potential by improving both infrastructure and the overall investment climate. While heartening, the pace of reform outside of Egypt appears to have waned, perhaps because high oil prices have reduced the sense of urgency attached to reform in oil-exporting countries.

In contrast to the slowdown elsewhere in the world economy, growth in **South Asia** is estimated to have picked up a bit in 2005, coming in at 6.9 percent, compared with 6.8 percent in 2004. This mainly reflects improved performance in Pakistan, where GDP is estimated to have increased 8.4 percent (up from 6.6 percent in 2004), thanks to a broad-based acceleration in the manufacturing and agricultural sectors. Like Pakistan, other countries in the region have enjoyed very strong export performance, in part because of the recent removal of ATC quotas. However, the sharp rise in oil prices and solid regional growth over the past several years have contributed to an acceleration of inflation. Addressing this issue will require a further tightening of monetary policy, which, in combination with rising oil bills, is expected to result in a modest deceleration of economic activity to about 6.3 percent by 2007.

GDP in **Sub-Saharan Africa** is estimated to have increased 4.6 percent in 2005, bolstered by very strong growth among resource-rich countries. Output in South Africa, the region's largest economy, is estimated to have accelerated to 4.2 percent, lifted by high metal prices, strong confidence, low nominal interest rates and the rand's recent depreciation. The economies of oil-exporting countries, including Nigeria (the region's second largest economy), grew an estimated 5.5 percent in 2005, reflecting rapid increases in petroleum production and investment inflows. Growth in some oil-exporting countries may exceed 25 percent in 2006 and 2007, as new oil fields come on stream. However, the pace of the expansion will taper off in other countries as they reach capacity constraints.

In West Africa, strong commodity prices in 2005, improved rainfall, and more vigorous use of insecticides are expected to lift regional growth. In East and Southern Africa the expansion is projected to slow somewhat, partly because the removal of quotas under the ATC will continue to put textile exports under pressure. Political strife and insecurity in Côte d'Ivoire and the Great Lakes region are likely to impact growth there. Countries are increasingly passing higher crude-oil prices through to consumers with the aim of containing budget deficits but will cut into consumer demand and add to inflationary pressures.

The balance of payments and economic consequences of higher oil prices are expected to intensify over the next year as other commodity prices, which have attenuated the terms-of-trade impact of high oil prices, ease. Despite higher oil prices and increased pass-through, inflation is expected to remain in the single digits as a result of lower food prices and prudent monetary policies. Recent economic reforms, and increased donor support—as more countries reach the Heavily Indebted Poor Country (HIPC) completion point—will also help support growth, which is projected to be at or above 4.5 percent over the medium term.

Long-term prospects and poverty forecast

The recent strong economic performance of developing economies and the relatively rapid growth projected for these economies over the medium term owe much to the economic reforms undertaken over the past several years. Improved macroeconomic policies, reflected in lower inflation, trade liberalization (average tariffs have fallen from 30 percent to less than 10 percent since the 1980s), more flexible exchange rate regimes, and lower fiscal deficits have reduced uncertainty and improved the overall investment environment. More microeconomic structural reforms, such as privatization and regulatory reform initiatives, have also played a key role.

Table 1.2 Long-term prospects

Real GDP per capita, annual average percentage change

| | | | Forecast | |
| | | | Medium-term | Long-term |
	1980s	1990s	2001–06	2006–15
World Total	1.3	1.2	1.5	2.1
High-income countries	2.5	1.8	1.6	2.4
OECD	2.5	1.8	1.6	2.4
United States	2.3	2.0	1.8	2.5
Japan	3.4	1.1	1.1	1.9
European Union	2.1	1.8	1.4	2.3
Non-OECD	3.5	4.0	2.0	3.5
Developing economies	0.7	1.5	3.7	3.5
East Asia & Pacific	5.8	6.3	6.4	5.3
Europe & Central Asia	0.9	−1.8	5.0	3.5
Latin America & Caribbean	−0.9	1.6	1.2	2.3
Middle East & North Africa	−1.1	1.0	2.5	2.6
South Asia	3.3	3.2	4.5	4.2
Sub-Saharan Africa	−1.1	−0.5	1.8	1.6

Source: World Bank.

These factors are expected to contribute to better long-term growth performance as compared with past decades (table 1.2). Consistent with recent improvements in economic performance, per capita incomes in developing countries are projected to grow some 3.5 percent a year, more than twice as fast as the 1.5 percent growth rates recorded during the 1990s. Projected future growth rates are higher than during the 1980s and 1990s in every developing region except East Asia, where they are expected to decline somewhat due to an aging population.

Table 1.3 reports poverty projections based on these real per capita income growth rates and the (re)distribution of income within the population. The table indicates that over the next 15 years the share of the population living in extreme poverty is expected to decline in all developing regions.[6]

With the exception of Sub-Saharan Africa, all regions are expected to achieve their Millennium Development Goal of reducing poverty by 50 percent from its 1990 level. In East Asia, the target has already been achieved. Moreover, based on the current long-term forecast, extreme poverty would be almost eliminated by 2015 in both the East Asia and Pacific and the Europe and Central Asia regions. Overall, the number of people living on $1 a day or less will fall to around 620 million, from 1.2 billion in 1990 and an estimated 1.0 billion in 2002.

Despite these heartening prospects, there is no room for complacency. The percent of the population in developing economies living at

Table 1.3 Regional breakdown of poverty in developing countries

| | Millions of people living on | | | | | |
| | less than $1 per day | | | less than $2 per day | | |
Region	1990	2002	2015	1990	2002	2015
East Asia and the Pacific	472	214	14	1,116	748	260
China	375	180	11	825	533	181
Rest of East Asia and the Pacific	97	34	2	292	215	78
Europe and Central Asia	2	10	4	23	76	39
Latin America and the Caribbean	49	42	29	125	119	106
Middle East and North Africa	6	5	3	51	61	40
South Asia	462	437	232	958	1,091	955
Sub-Saharan Africa	227	303	336	382	516	592
Total	1,218	1,011	617	2,654	2,611	1,993
Excluding China	844	831	606	1,829	2,078	1,811

| | Percent of population living on | | | | | |
| | less than $1 per day | | | less than $2 per day | | |
Region	1990	2002	2015	1990	2002	2015
East Asia and the Pacific	29.6	14.9	0.9	69.9	40.7	12.7
China	33.0	16.6	1.2	72.6	41.6	13.1
Rest of East Asia and the Pacific	21.1	10.8	0.4	63.2	38.6	11.9
Europe and Central Asia	0.5	3.6	0.4	4.9	16.1	8.2
Latin America and the Caribbean	11.3	9.5	6.9	28.4	22.6	17.2
Middle East and North Africa	2.3	2.4	0.9	21.4	19.8	10.4
South Asia	41.3	31.3	12.8	85.5	77.8	56.7
Sub-Saharan Africa	44.6	46.4	38.4	75.0	74.9	67.1
Total	27.9	21.1	10.2	60.8	49.9	32.8
Excluding China	26.1	22.5	12.9	56.6	52.6	38.6

Source: World Bank.

or below $2 per day is projected to remain disturbingly high. Moreover, notwithstanding that inroads have been made recently, the incidence of extreme poverty in Sub-Saharan Africa in 2002 was actually higher than in 1990. While current projections suggest 8 percent of the subcontinent's population will be lifted above the extreme poverty line by 2015, some 38 percent of Africans will still be living in extreme poverty. Worse, the absolute number of Africans living at or below the $1-a-day level is projected to increase. And, because per capita incomes elsewhere are projected to grow faster, the continent will continue to fall farther behind the rest of the world—unless steps are taken to greatly improve economic growth in Africa.

International finance

The significant adjustments of international exchange rates over the past several years paused in 2005. In particular, notwithstanding the persistence of the U.S. current account deficit (expected to exceed $750 billion this year), the dollar's trend decline with respect to major currencies came to an end. Initially, the currency appreciated against its trading partners by some 3.5 percent in real-effective terms as of July 2005. It then lost value in August and September, before showing signs of strengthening in October.

The strengthening of the dollar during the first seven months of 2005 is partly explained by rising U.S. short-term interest rates (as the Federal Reserve Bank continued its policy of gradual tightening) and falling long-term rates in Europe (possibly in response to the continent's relatively weaker economic performance). By July, these developments had generated a 300 basis-point swing in the difference between U.S. and European short rates, along with a 75 basis-point gap in favor of long-term U.S. bonds (figure 1.4).

These growing interest rate differentials increased the financial incentive to hold dollar-versus euro-denominated assets, temporarily producing stronger net private sector capital

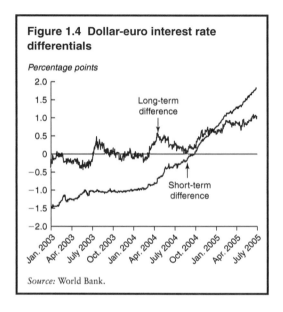

Figure 1.4 Dollar-euro interest rate differentials

Percentage points

Long-term difference

Short-term difference

Source: World Bank.

inflows in the first quarter of 2005 as investors adjusted their portfolios. Not only did these inflows help strengthen the dollar, they also financed a large share of the U.S. current account deficit (figure 1.5). As a result, the dollar was much less reliant on the accumulation of reserves by foreign central banks (foreign official asset purchases) than in 2004.

In the second quarter of 2005, however, private inflows eased, and foreign central banks once again assumed a large role in the financing of the dollar. Moreover, toward the end of July the dollar came under renewed downward pressure and depreciated some 1.7 percent in real-effective terms during August and September. The dollar began to appreciate again only after the long-term interest rate started to rise again. By October 2005, the long-term interest rate differential had widened to about 120 basis points.

The apparent sensitivity of the dollar and the financing of the U.S. current account deficit to interest-rate differentials highlight the problems posed by the large financing requirements of the U.S. current account deficit.

Until global imbalances are resolved, the dollar is likely to continue to come under

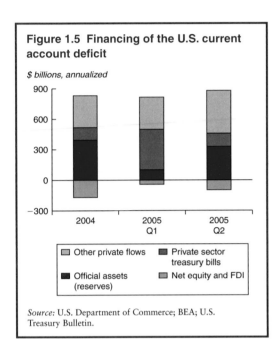

Figure 1.5 Financing of the U.S. current account deficit

$ billions, annualized

Other private flows
Official assets (reserves)
Private sector treasury bills
Net equity and FDI

Source: U.S. Department of Commerce; BEA; U.S. Treasury Bulletin.

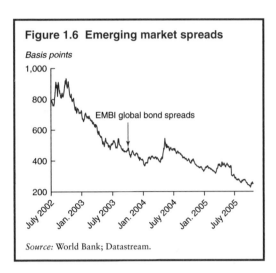

Figure 1.6 Emerging market spreads

Basis points

EMBI global bond spreads

Source: World Bank; Datastream.

downward pressure, unless foreign central banks accumulate substantial quantities of dollars or interest-rate differentials widen further. In the baseline, interest rate differentials are projected to widen further, and the dollar is projected to decline gradually, falling by about 5 percent per year. Should central banks cease to be willing to accumulate reserves at current rates, there could be a disruptive hike in interest rates or a more precipitous fall in the dollar (World Bank 2005).

The recent decision of the Chinese and Malaysian authorities to move from an exchange rate regime linked to the dollar alone to one focusing on a basket of currencies represents a major and welcome move toward a more flexible currency regime. While it will not resolve current account imbalances, it should increase the stability of the renminbi and ringitt with respect to the currencies of their trading partners (other than the United States) and reduce the amount by which the dollar would have to depreciate relative to other currencies to achieve a given level of adjustment.[7] How effective the new regimes will be, depends importantly on how they are

managed. While technically the announced rules could allow the renminbi to depreciate as much as 9 percent per month, similar possibilities for flexibility existed under the former regime but were not exercised.

Interest rates and spreads remain low

The recent period of very low real interest rates has been particularly beneficial to developing economies. Together with narrower risk premia (figure 1.6), low rates have allowed developing countries to reduce their financing costs, restructure their debt, and pursue strong investment growth. Early repayment of Paris Club debt has already reached $22 billion in 2005, and among emerging-market economies, virtually all financing requirements for this year had been met by August.[8]

Short-term rates have been rising, and they can be expected to continue to rise as monetary policy tightens, initially in the United States, but eventually in Europe as well. In contrast and notwithstanding recent increases, longer-term interest rates have remained low longer than expected (figure 1.7), while spreads on more risky emerging market and corporate assets have fallen even further.

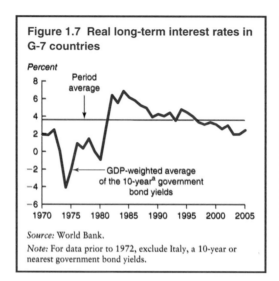

Figure 1.7 Real long-term interest rates in G-7 countries

Source: World Bank.

Note: For data prior to 1972, exclude Italy, a 10-year or nearest government bond yields.

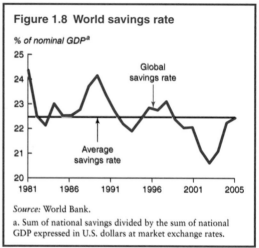

Figure 1.8 World savings rate

Source: World Bank.

a. Sum of national savings divided by the sum of national GDP expressed in U.S. dollars at market exchange rates.

Many reasons for these low interest rates have been proposed (see IMF 2005 for a recent overview), including the following:

- Excess liquidity stemming from an extended period of very low short-term interest rates in almost all developed economies.
- A low inflation environment, thanks to improved credibility of monetary policy, and the disinflationary impact of increased competition following the entry into global markets of China and members of the former Soviet bloc.
- An increase in global savings, due to
  - increased savings in Europe following heightened recognition of the need to prepare for the impending retirement of the baby-boom generation; and
  - increased corporate savings in dynamic East Asia (caused by corporate restructuring following the currency crisis) and in the United States (following the stock market decline in 2000).

However, while global savings have increased recently, this follows a period where they declined substantially, making it difficult to argue that the world savings rate is currently too high (figure 1.8). Rather, investment activity, principally in the developed world, has failed to keep pace with savings as they have returned to historical levels (see IMF 2005).

Most of these explanations for lower long-term rates involve temporary factors, implying that long-term rates will eventually rise toward their long-run equilibrium level[9] (frequently defined as the long-run potential growth rate of the economy). In this context, the question is not so much why long-term rates are low, but how much longer they will remain so. In the baseline, increased investment in Europe and tighter monetary policy result in a gradual rise in interest rates, which will nevertheless remain below recent estimates of the long-term growth potential of the U.S. economy. The final section of this chapter explores some of the economic implications should interest rates stay low for an extended period of time or, alternatively, should they rise more quickly than anticipated.

Signs of rising inflation

Low interest rates have contributed directly to the strong economic performance of recent years. Growth has, in turn, provoked a pickup in inflation in many developing countries. The largest hikes have been in commodity prices (see below). However, producer price inflation has jumped by more than 4 percentage points in some regions and exceeds 5 percent in every developing region except Sub-Saharan Africa.[10]

Consumer price inflation has also been rising (if less spectacularly). Weighted by GDP, aggregate inflation among developing economies increased from 4.0 percent in the fourth quarter of 2003 to 5.4 percent by July of 2005. It has since eased somewhat. Regionally, inflation has picked up strongly in South Asia, Sub-Saharan Africa, and East Asia (figure 1.9). Inflation in developing countries is projected to continue rising in 2005, as growth remains at or above trend rates, and the pass-through from high oil prices continues to exert upward pressure on prices.

In high-income countries, there are only limited signs of rising inflation. In the United States, where output is close to potential, inflation has been rising steadily. It jumped to 4.7 percent in September 2005, but the increase is not expected to be permanent, because it reflects very high gasoline prices that month, which have since declined. Nevertheless, data pointing to rising wages and lower productivity growth suggest that core inflation, which has been more stable, may begin to rise soon. In Europe, high oil prices have limited disinflation despite significant slack and the appreciation of the euro.

These same factors should continue to limit price inflation in Europe. However, in the United States, high oil prices plus the projected further depreciation of the dollar are expected to generate additional upward price pressure.

Low interest rates have resulted in higher prices of interest-sensitive assets in markets with strong financial intermediation—notably in the United States and some European countries—contributing to strong consumer demand (World Bank 2005, IMF 2005). As interest rates rise, housing prices are expected to plateau and even decline, which has already begun in the United Kingdom. As they do so, the rate at which household wealth increases will moderate and its contribution to consumer demand should abate.[11]

Data indicate that house prices have also been rising rapidly in a number of middle-income countries, such as Bulgaria, India,

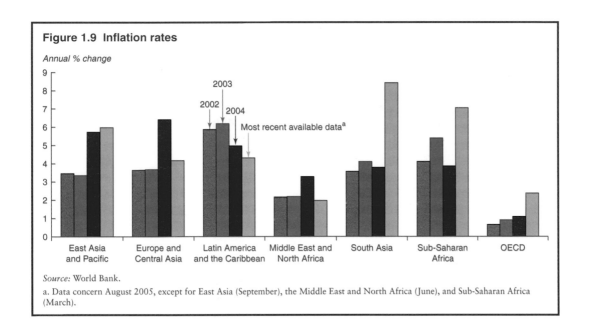

Figure 1.9 Inflation rates

Annual % change

Source: World Bank.

a. Data concern August 2005, except for East Asia (September), the Middle East and North Africa (June), and Sub-Saharan Africa (March).

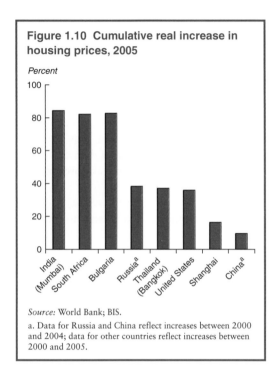

Figure 1.10 Cumulative real increase in housing prices, 2005

Percent

Source: World Bank; BIS.

a. Data for Russia and China reflect increases between 2000 and 2004; data for other countries reflect increases between 2000 and 2005.

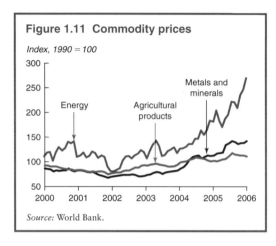

Figure 1.11 Commodity prices

Index, 1990 = 100

Source: World Bank.

Indonesia, Malaysia, and South Africa (figure 1.10). While fast economic growth and changes in the regulatory environment have certainly played a role in these countries, so have low interest rates. Unfortunately, data limitations prevent a thorough analysis of the causes and consequences of rising housing prices in low- and middle-income economies.[12]

Commodity markets

After several years of rising commodity prices, there are indications of a stabilization and even reversal of gains in the markets for agricultural products and for metals and minerals (figure 1.11).

Agricultural prices have been declining most of this year and are down 5 percent since March 2005. However, prices of agricultural raw materials are rising, partly because of higher prices for commodities that are close substitutes for crude oil-based products (for example, natural rubber prices are up 41 percent because of increases in synthetic rubber costs).

Although metals and minerals prices rose during the first months of the year, they have since stabilized, and in October 2005, they were at the same level as in March 2005. Conditions in some metals and minerals markets remain tight, due to low inventories. In the case of copper and aluminum, prices remain elevated (partly reflecting higher energy content in the production of these goods). Demand has weakened markedly for lead, tin, and zinc.

Analysis of past non-oil commodity cycles suggests that this one may have run its course. Already it distinguishes itself from previous episodes by having lasted longer, in part, because energy prices have also been high, which was not always the case during previous episodes. In so far as high fuel prices increase production costs in both agriculture and metals and minerals, they may have reduced the supply response, keeping prices higher longer.

In line with the projected slowdown in global growth and increased supply, prices of agricultural products and metals and minerals are projected to decline somewhat in 2006.

Limited spare capacity to keep oil prices high

In contrast with other commodity prices, oil prices continued to strengthen during the first nine months of 2005. During this period, they averaged some $52 per barrel, a 38 percent increase compared with the average for 2004. These increases occurred despite an easing of conditions in the oil market. Demand growth slowed from more than 3.5 percent in 2004 (the highest growth since the late 1970s) to a 1.4 percent annualized rate during the first three quarters of 2005. As a result, supply is actually increasing faster than demand,[13] and inventories have begun to accumulate, although they remain low.[14]

Rising prices over the first eight months of the year reflected the market's concern that existing spare capacity was insufficient to deal with a major disruption to supply or an increase in demand (figure 1.12). In some sense, hurricane Katrina was the kind of serious shock the market feared. Although oil prices spiked briefly to more than $70 a barrel, they are back below $60, following the release of some 29 million barrels of crude oil from the stockpiles of the International Energy Agency and the U.S. government. Moreover, gasoline prices in the United States have returned to the levels observed before hurricane Katrina, and market concerns have switched from a focus on inadequate oil supply to insufficient

refining capacity, particularly of lower-quality crude oil.

Spare production capacity is now about 2 million barrels per day (mbpd), compared with almost 6 mbpd three years ago, and capacity will remain tight over the near term. This reflects long lags in bringing significant new quantities of oil into production[15] and shorter lags before demand substitution can have an effect.[16] Moreover, approximately half of the expected new capacity is being produced by OPEC, suggesting that the organization will continue to exercise significant market power over the near term.

In this environment, prices are likely to remain volatile, as small events or even minor changes in expectations may provoke significant price swings. As a result, the World Bank has adopted a technical assumption for the future path of oil prices based on a slow decline toward $40 per barrel by 2010. This implies an average price of $56 in 2006 and $52 in 2007, which is somewhat higher than the current consensus forecast. The economic consequences of alternative scenarios, notably a sharp negative supply shock, are discussed in the final section of this chapter.

The impact of oil prices on developing economies

The world economy in general and developing countries in particular have shown considerable resilience to higher oil prices. This reflects increases in non-oil commodity prices and a very robust global economy, which have, until recently, muted the impact of higher oil prices.

The first round of oil price hikes (1999–2000) adversely affected low- and middle-income countries. The price increase was very large in percentage terms (rising from just under $12 to almost $30 per barrel between the first quarter of 1999 and the end of 2000) but smaller than the most recent increases in dollar terms (table 1.4). Current account deficits among low-income oil-importing African countries increased by 0.5 percent of GDP on average.[17] Moreover, government deficits in those countries that did not pass on the price

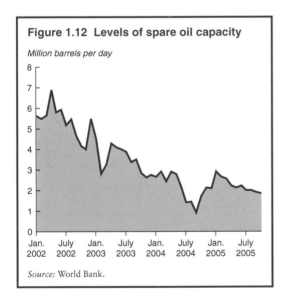

Figure 1.12 Levels of spare oil capacity

Million barrels per day

Source: World Bank.

Table 1.4 Terms-of-trade impacts of commodity price changes

	1999–00	2001–03	2004–05
Cumulative price change			
Oil	120.3	18.9	88.0
Agricultural products	0.3	15.7	8.9
Metals and minerals	25.0	10.2	47.9
Manufactures	−5.0	3.0	10.4
Total terms-of-trade effect (% of GDP)			
Oil Importers			
Low and Middle income	−1.8	−0.1	−0.9
Low income	−3.8	−0.9	−2.9
Sub-Saharan Africa	−2.5	1.4	−1.2
South Asia	−3.9	−1.5	−2.7
Highly indebted poor countries	−4.3	1.5	−3.3

Source: World Bank.

Note: Periods Jan. 1999–Dec. 2000, Dec. 2000–Dec. 2003, Dec. 2003–July 2005.

hikes rose by about the same amount.[18] Among those countries with limited access to international finance, non-oil imports fell by 3.8 percent in 2000, partly because insufficient foreign exchange was available to finance imports at previous levels.

During the second bout of (more gradual) price increases (2001–3) the same countries performed much better. Current account positions actually improved as a percent of GDP, and there were no discernible slowdown in non-oil imports. Part of this improved performance is explained by real exchange rate movements (which diminished the domestic currency cost of the oil-price hike) and by a number of non-oil commodity prices that also increased rapidly during that time, thus providing the necessary foreign currency to meet the additional oil burden without cutting into non-oil imports. On average, high non-oil commodity prices reduced the negative terms-of-trade shock from higher energy costs by more than half.

Drawing from this experience, the impact of the latest hike in oil prices on poor oil importers is a concern, principally because it has not been accompanied by as much strength in

non-oil commodity prices. Indeed, the estimated terms-of-trade shock from price movements since January 2004 is more than three times as large for various groups of low-income countries than the cumulative shock over the preceding three years. As a result, non-oil imports from poor, current account–constrained countries are expected to come under pressure in the coming months. Moreover, the impact on oil-importing poor countries could be significantly aggravated if oil prices remain at or close to current levels and if non-energy commodity prices return to pre-shock levels.

World trade

The expansion of world trade slowed significantly during 2005 (figure 1.13). While merchandise exports were growing at a 16 percent or more annualized pace in the middle of 2004, they subsequently slowed and were expanding at an 8.5 percent pace during the third quarter of 2005.

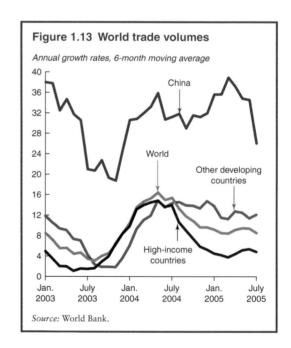

Figure 1.13 World trade volumes

Annual growth rates, 6-month moving average

Source: World Bank.

Most of the deceleration concerned the exports of high-income economies, volumes of which grew by less than 4 percent (annualized) in the first quarter of 2005, before strengthening more recently. Merchandise export volumes of developing countries (excluding China) were relatively robust, increasing at an estimated 12 percent pace toward the middle of 2005. Chinese exports, boosted by the removal of ATC quotas, grew at a 24 percent pace.

Commodity markets have significantly shaped developments in world trade. The merchandise exports of oil-exporting countries, which had been rising at some 5.8 percent in 2004, increased by an estimated 5.2 percent in 2005. The deceleration among developing oil importers (excluding China) was steeper in percentage terms (from 15 percent to 11 percent), but growth rates remained much higher. Growth in the production of non-oil commodities in general is moderating, both because demand is easing and because of supply constraints.

As a reflection of the slowdown already observed, international trade is forecast to slow down relative to 2004 as a whole. Merchandise trade volumes are expected to increase by around 7.7 percent. The goods and service trade is expected to increase 6.2 percent in 2005 before strengthening somewhat in 2006–7.

Exports of developing economies continue to be heavily influenced by developments in the volatile high-tech market. After falling sharply in the third quarter of 2004, global sales of semiconductors and other high-tech products picked up before weakening once again in the second quarter of 2005. This volatility is apparent in East Asian export volumes (high-tech products represent as much as two-thirds of the exports of some economies in this region).[19] High-frequency data suggest a strengthening of demand for these products, implying a pick up in export flows from the region.

Trade growth for some countries was heavily influenced by the removal of quotas under the ATC of the Multifiber agreement in

Figure 1.14 Change in textile exports to the developed world, first half of 2005

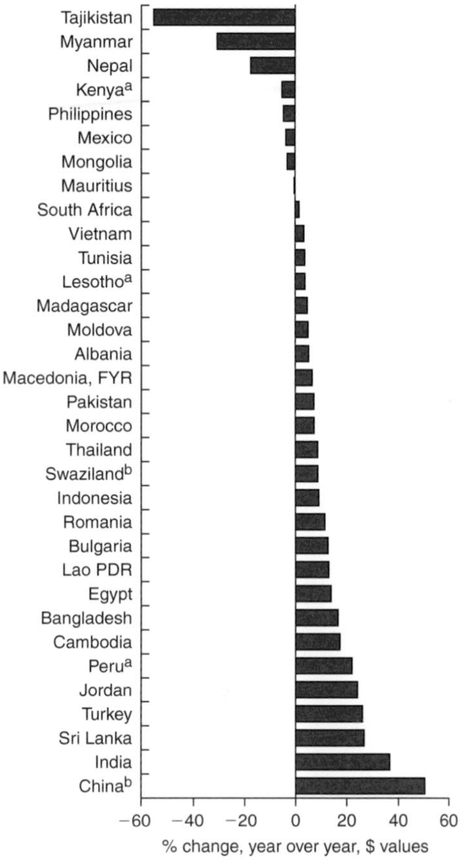

% change, year over year, $ values

Source: World Bank, IMF, U.S. Department of Commerce, and EuroStat.

a. Data refer to the first five months of each year only.
b. Data for China include Hong Kong and Macao.

January 2005 (figure 1.14). While the removal of quotas was done in phases, and ten years of adjustment time provided, backloading of the removal of quotas meant that they were still binding when they were finally removed. As a result, there were significant changes in patterns of trade among affected goods in 2005, most notably in the form of increased exports from China (and other countries, whose market share had been artificially held back under the old quota scheme) to the detriment of

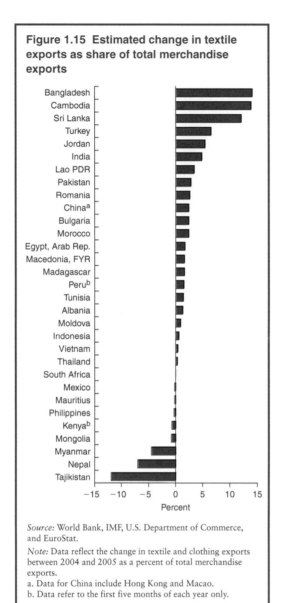

Figure 1.15 Estimated change in textile exports as share of total merchandise exports

Bangladesh
Cambodia
Sri Lanka
Turkey
Jordan
India
Lao PDR
Pakistan
Romania
China[a]
Bulgaria
Morocco
Egypt, Arab Rep.
Macedonia, FYR
Madagascar
Peru[b]
Tunisia
Albania
Moldova
Indonesia
Vietnam
Thailand
South Africa
Mexico
Mauritius
Philippines
Kenya[b]
Mongolia
Myanmar
Nepal
Tajikistan

−15 −10 −5 0 5 10 15
Percent

Source: World Bank, IMF, U.S. Department of Commerce, and EuroStat.

Note: Data reflect the change in textile and clothing exports between 2004 and 2005 as a percent of total merchandise exports.
a. Data for China include Hong Kong and Macao.
b. Data refer to the first five months of each year only.

those exporters that had benefited most from the old quota system.

Using U.S. and European imports of textiles as a proxy for developments in the world as a whole, China,[20] India, Jordan, Peru, Sri Lanka, and Turkey saw the dollar value of their exports increase between the first half of 2004 and the same period in 2005 by more than the 20 percent average increase in high-

income imports over the same period. The textile sectors in Kenya, Myanmar, Nepal, the Philippines, and Tajikistan, on the other hand, saw the dollar value of their exports decline by 4 or more percent.

However, many of these countries are not large exporters of textiles. As a result, these figures may exaggerate the overall economic impact of the relaxation of textile quotas. Expressed as a percent of these countries' total merchandise exports, the biggest gains were experienced by Bangladesh, Cambodia, Jordan, India, Pakistan, Sri Lanka, and Turkey, while the largest losses were those of Kenya, Nepal, Myanmar, Mongolia, and Tajikistan (figure 1.15).

Risks and uncertainties

Low interest rates, moderate inflation, and the robust growth projected in the baseline constitute a relatively benign scenario. However, the outlook is dominated by downside risks.

An oil-market supply shock could cause serious disruption

The most important potential risk comes from the oil market. As global demand and supply are projected to increase broadly in step, excess capacity (currently estimated at 1.9 million barrels per day) will remain very constrained. In this context, the market can be expected to continue reacting to events in a relatively volatile manner. Rather than gradually declining, as in the baseline scenario, prices could remain at current levels, rise further, or even fall.

More fundamentally, with spare production capacity so low, the market is particularly vulnerable to a supply shock. Because no country can easily ramp up production, if output in another producing country were to fall significantly, world supply would fall, provoking a decline in economic activity to the extent that the global economy could not quickly adopt an alternative energy source.[21]

Table 1.5 presents results from a simulation of the impact of a 2-million-barrels-per-day

Table 1.5 Impact of a 2 million bpd negative supply shock

	2006	2007	2008	2009
Price of oil	90	70	44	40
(Change from base line)	34	28	3	0
Change in GDP % of baseline				
World	−1.0	−1.5	−1.1	0.2
High income	−0.7	−1.3	−1.3	−0.3
Middle income	−1.6	−1.6	−0.1	1.4
Large low income	−1.7	−2.8	−1.8	0.7
Impact on inflation rate				
World	2.6	0.6	−0.9	−0.2
High income	1.4	0.0	−1.0	−0.4
Middle income	5.8	2.0	−0.9	0.5
Large low income	2.8	0.9	−0.7	−0.2
Impact on real interest rates (levels)				
World	1.0	0.2	−0.1	0.1
High income	1.0	0.1	−0.2	0.0
Middle income	1.1	0.7	0.2	0.2
Large low income	0.5	0.1	0.1	0.4
Impact on current account balance (% of GDP)				
World	−1.1	−0.5	−0.1	−0.1
High income	−1.1	−0.7	−0.2	−0.2
Middle income	−0.9	−0.2	−0.5	−0.3
Large low income	−1.9	−0.2	1.7	1.0
Impacts on low-income current account–constrained countries (1)				
Terms of trade	−4.1	..	..	
GDP	−0.3	0.1	0.0	
Domestic demand	−2.7	−1.1	0.0	
Current account balance	−1.2	0.9	0	

Source: World Bank.

Note: Impacts on low-income, current account–constrained economies were estimates based on the terms-of-trade impact using a purpose-built VAR model. Other estimates were simulated using the World Bank's macroeconomic simulation model.

negative supply shock.[22] The disruption is assumed to last throughout the projection period, causing prices to rise to $120 for an initial period of three months before easing to $80 for three quarters. Thereafter, supply and demand adjustments result in a gradual decline in oil prices toward $40.

Global output responds to the initial shock by contracting, as compared with the baseline, by 1.5 percent of GDP after two years, while inflation picks up rapidly. On average, the current account position of oil-importing countries deteriorates by about 1.1 percent of GDP. The impact is more severe in large low-income and middle-income countries, both because of higher energy intensities and a greater inflationary impact, which requires a larger contraction to eliminate.

While the impact in terms of GDP for current account–constrained low-income countries is smaller, it is more severe in terms of domestic consumption and investment. Such countries have limited access to international capital markets, and their capacity to pay higher oil prices is limited by their export revenues. If these revenues are stable, they are forced to reduce domestic demand and non-oil imports in order to pay their higher oil bill. As a consequence, when oil prices rise, oil consumption remains relatively constant in volume terms (being generally inelastic in the short run), but the oil bill rises. To compensate, non-oil imports and domestic demand tend to decline in unison—leaving GDP relatively unchanged. For these countries, the terms-of-trade shock of the initial increase in oil prices is estimated at 4.1 percent of their GDP, which would translate into a 2.7 percent decline in domestic demand, with potentially serious impacts on poverty.

The future path of interest rates represents an additional source of uncertainty

Persistent global imbalances continue to be a serious source of uncertainty. The current account deficit of the United States and its financing requirements are very large, and the willingness of investors to finance it is sensitive to both interest-rate differentials and exchange-rate expectations. As net foreign liabilities accumulate, markets will become increasingly sensitive to adverse shocks or changes in sentiment, and the dollar is likely to come under downward pressure once again, which would put upward pressure on interest rates.

Table 1.6 explores the possible implications of higher interest rates. In this scenario, faced with sustained downward pressure on the dollar, investors demand higher returns on U.S.-denominated assets to offset further expected depreciations. This, combined with concerns

Table 1.6 Interest rate scenarios

	2005	2006	2007	2008	2009
A. A 200 basis-point increase in interest rates and in spreads					
Interest rates (change of Q4 level from baseline)					
World	1.8	1.4	−0.6	0.2	1.3
High income	1.7	1.1	−1.1	−0.3	0.9
Low and middle income	2.0	2.7	1.9	2.6	3.1
GDP (% change from baseline)					
World	−0.1	−1.7	−2.9	−1.9	−0.6
High income	0.0	−1.5	−2.7	−2.5	−1.0
Low and middle income	−0.2	−2.4	−3.5	−3.0	−1.5
Inflation (change in inflation rate)					
World	0.0	−0.3	−1.1	−1.1	−0.3
High income	0.0	−0.3	−1.5	−1.6	−0.5
Low and middle income	0.0	−0.3	0.7	1.2	0.9
B. Persistently low interest rates					
Interest rates (change of Q4 level from baseline)					
World	−0.7	−0.5	0.6	0.1	−0.6
High income	−0.7	−0.5	0.8	0.1	−0.6
Low and middle income	−0.8	−0.8	−0.1	−0.1	−0.7
GDP (% change from baseline)					
World	0.0	0.8	1.4	0.3	−0.5
High income	0.0	0.8	1.4	0.4	−0.5
Low and middle income	0.0	1.0	1.4	−0.1	−0.7
Inflation (change in inflation rate)					
World	0.0	0.2	0.6	0.6	0.1
High income	0.0	0.2	0.8	0.8	0.2
Low and middle income	0.0	0.1	−0.2	−0.5	−0.3

Source: World Bank.

about rising debt and pension liabilities in industrialized countries, and a more rapid dissipation of the temporary factors depressing long-term interest rates, causes them to increase by some 200 basis points in high-income countries. Risk premia in developing economies increase by an additional 200 basis points as investors' appetites for risk decline.

The world economy reacts to the substantial tightening of monetary conditions by reducing global growth by half for a period of two years, as higher interest rates cut into investment and consumption demand, both through classic transmission mechanisms and via the impact of interest rates on housing

prices and consumer wealth. Slower growth eases inflationary pressure and global tensions, including in the oil market. As monetary policy loosens in response to increasing output gaps, growth starts to pick up again, bringing output back to the levels in the baseline by the end of the simulation period.

Higher interest rates would also affect financing conditions for developing countries by increasing future borrowing costs. For many countries this will not pose a serious short-term risk, because they have taken advantage of low rates to reduce the share of short-term debt relative to their overall debt and to prefinance some of their future borrowing needs. For others, particularly those with large debt-to-GDP ratios or those that have accumulated large short-term debt positions (figure 1.16), a rapid rise in interest rates

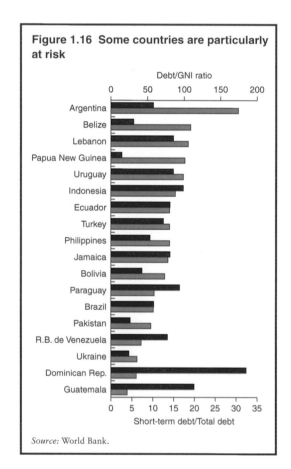

Figure 1.16 Some countries are particularly at risk

Debt/GNI ratio

Source: World Bank.

could pose a real threat—particularly if the rise in base interest rates also provokes a return of spreads to more usual levels.

Alternatively, if excess liquidity and global savings prevent long-term interest rates from rising as quickly as in the baseline scenario, the resulting higher levels of demand could increase tensions in commodity markets, including the oil market. In addition, lower interest rates could cause a number of economies, including the United States, to overheat, generating additional inflation that forces a further tightening of monetary policy. As a result, while growth would be initially higher, the subsequent tightening of policy could provoke a stronger-than-projected slowdown.

The depth of the cycle would depend importantly on the extent of the wealth effect generated by low interest rates on housing prices. The more pronounced, the deeper the cycle. Moreover, because asset prices become even more out of step with their long-run levels, an even longer period of slow growth could be required to re-establish equilibrium.

Policy challenges

Policy can help reduce both the economic severity of such unfavorable outturns and the likelihood that they will materialize.

High oil prices will naturally induce substitution toward alternative energy sources and conservation. In the current context, where the increase in oil prices is expected to endure, countries that have not passed on recent price hikes to consumers (and industry) may wish to revise their policies. Not only are the budgetary costs of such subsidies likely to be difficult to support, but these policies also impede adjustment.

Moreover, countries with restrictive rules concerning the exploitation of oil reserves might wish to re-examine them. Such policies may deny these countries access to technical expertise and financial capital, thereby preventing them from investing in new production to the extent that they might otherwise. This may slow the aggregate supply response and encourage greater conservation and sub-

stitution toward alternative energy sources—to the ultimate detriment of oil-producing countries.

In the developed world, efforts to increase energy efficiency by developing more fuel-efficient technologies, such as hybrid cars, could well pay important dividends. These technologies are already economic in some countries, where gasoline is heavily taxed, and could generate substantial savings in overall fuel demand.[23] In addition to the ecological benefits, making such technology available in developing economies, where the increase in transportation-related energy demand is highest, would be particularly effective in limiting overall demand.

Finally, efforts to improve cooperation between users and suppliers concerning the quality and transparency of oil market data could help reduce unwarranted volatility and perhaps contribute to lower prices by reducing the oil-price risk premia.

To further dissipate the risk from global imbalances, policies need to promote both public and private savings in countries with large current account deficits. Recent measures to tighten fiscal policy in the United States are headed in this direction, but more tightening is required. Tighter monetary policy is helping. Higher interest rates in the United States promote private sector financing of the deficit but also promote private sector saving. In Europe, policymakers should seek to maintain low interest rates in an effort to stimulate demand. As output picks up, fiscal policy (rather than monetary policy) should be used to restrict demand, if necessary. Indeed, given unfunded public pension liabilities in these countries, such a fiscal tightening is necessary in its own right.

Developing economies should react flexibly, seeking to maintain real effective exchange rates in line with their fundamentals, rather than a particular alignment with any one currency. In this regard, recent steps by some countries to adopt an exchange rate regime that reflects their overall trade patterns are positive and could be emulated by other countries. Petro-dollars could help reduce the likelihood of a disruptive resolution of global imbalances if they are recycled into the global economy in a way that reduces tensions. In particular, the financing of investment expenditures both domestically and in other developing countries would help stimulate demand outside of the United States, reducing that country's current account deficit. To the extent that these funds are invested in U.S. financial securities, they could also help finance the U.S. current account deficit.

Finally, global weakness could trigger increased protectionism or a slowing of trade liberalization (which has been the basis for much of developing countries' recent success). The supply disruptions in Europe provoked by the re-imposition of quotas on Chinese imports of textiles, following their liberalization at the beginning of this year, is a good illustration of how trade restrictions work to the detriment of both exporting and importing countries. Not only should countries resist the temptation to intervene in already liberalized domains, concerted efforts need to be made to achieve meaningful liberalization in the agricultural and service sectors in the Doha process. To date, liberalization has largely omitted the politically sensitive agricultural sector, depriving many developing countries of the benefits from trade liberalization that more manufacturing-oriented economies have enjoyed.

Notes

1. The Congressional Budget Office (2005) estimates that hurricane Katrina reduced growth in the United States by 0.4 and 0.9 percent (annual rates) in the third and fourth quarters.

2. The importance of China to aggregate statistics is also visible in the industrial production data. Growth rates for all developing countries showed little slowing, but excluding China, annualized growth rates declined from about 7.5 percent in mid 2004 to less than 5 percent a year later.

3. Although oil prices are projected to decline during 2006, they will be higher, on average, than in 2005.

4. The number of working days each year varies, generally because certain holidays do or do not fall on weekends. Occasionally, these fluctuations can have an important impact on annual GDP growth. While five fewer days corresponds to roughly a 2.5 percent reduction in working time, in general, the actual reduction in production is less pronounced.

5. These losses are estimated at more than 5 percent of GDP for Antigua and Barbuda, Belize, Guyana, Honduras, Nicaragua, and Jamaica.

6. This year's projections differ somewhat from 2004's partly because of a shift in the base year for calculations from 2001 to 2002, which reduces the poverty level of the starting year in all regions that have experienced positive per capita growth. In addition, new survey data was employed for a large number of countries (more than half in the Europe and Central Asia region), including important new household surveys in a number of Latin American countries in the place of labor force survey data used in the past. Finally, revisions to national income estimates of GDP, inflation, and consumption play a role. For more information concerning the changes to the poverty forecast, please visit the Long-term Prospects and Poverty Forecasts section of http://www.worldbank.org/globaloutlook.

7. The extent to which the new regime will contribute to increased stability in world markets will also depend on the extent to which other Asian currencies follow suit, and how much flexibility is permitted in practice.

8. As of August 2005, overall financing for emerging market sovereign debt was already 74 percent funded; this share reached 93 percent for emerging Europe and Turkey, and 100 percent for Latin America.

9. Long-term interest rates tend to be determined by the long-term growth potential of the economy and expected inflation. Historically, temporary factors have caused them to deviate from this measure, sometimes for extended periods of time. However, they have always tended to return to this level.

10. In the first half of 2005, producer price inflation exceeded 15 percent in the Europe and Central Asia region, was more than 9 percent in Latin America and the Caribbean, about 7 percent in the Middle East and North Africa, and around 6 percent in both East and South Asia.

11. The stock of housing in the United States is estimated by the Federal Reserve Bank to be equal to $15.2 trillion, or about 138 percent of GDP. A 10 percent change in the value of that stock would represent 13.8 percent of GDP, or 19 percent of consumption. Econometric estimates suggest that the long-term marginal propensity to consume from housing wealth is 0.05 (see, for example Catte and others 2004 and Benjamin, Chinloy, and Jud 2004), implying a reduction in consumption of 1.35 percent.

12. Very few low- and middle-income countries have housing data similar to the data available in high-income countries; and what does exist tends to be limited to wealthy neighborhoods in single cities. Moreover, there is little information on home ownership ratios, and mortgage-market completeness—all critical components in determining housing-market wealth effects.

13. The U.S. Department of Energy estimates that both oil and gasoline consumption fell by 2.5 or more percent in September 2005.

14. In the second quarter, stocks equaled 54 days worth of consumption versus an average of more than 58 days during the first half of the 1990s.

15. Some oil fields can be brought into production within 1 year, but others would take as long as 10 years. Three to five years would be needed to bring in two million barrels per day over and above expected increases in demand.

16. Opportunities for demand substitution may be less plentiful than in the 1970s because of the substantial conservation steps undertaken then. Nevertheless, use of fuel-efficient cars and less intensive use of existing cars can have substantial impacts on overall demand.

17. Simple average of 32 oil-importing Sub-Saharan economies.

18. Among countries that did not pass prices through fully, fuel subsidy spending rose substantially, for instance in the Central African Republic, Guinea Bissau, Malawi, and the Seychelles.

19. In 2003, high-tech products represented 13 percent of Thailand's exports, but more than 50 percent of Taiwanese, Malaysian, and Philippine exports.

20. China here is taken as the sum of Hong Kong, Macao, and China, based on the assumption that prior to liberalization some of the exports from Hong Kong and Macao had actually originated in China, and therefore, the changes in their market share reported in official statistics are exaggerated.

21. During the 1980s (and before), OPEC acted as a swing producer, stepping up production in response to shortfalls elsewhere. With its spare capacity now measured at less than 2 million barrels per day, its capacity to act as a swing producer is limited.

22. Beccue and Huntington (2005) estimate that the probability of such a disruption occurring during the next 10 years is high (70 percent for one lasting 6 months and 35 percent for one of 18 months).

23. In the United States, for example, hybrid cars currently offer approximately an 80 percent improvement in fuel efficiency. Were these vehicles to gain a 10 percent share of new car sales, new energy demand would be reduced by about 12 percent (c. 0.3 percentage points) per year for about seven years.

References

Beccue, Phillip C., and Hillard G. Huntington. 2005. "An Assessment of Oil Market Disruption Risks." In *Final Report EMF SR 8*. Energy Modeling Forum. October.

Benjamin, J.D., P. Chinloy, and G.D. Jud. 2004. "Real Estate versus Financial Wealth in Consumption." *Journal of Real Estate Finance and Economics* 29(3): 341–54.

Catte, P., N. Girouard, R. Price, and C. André. 2004. "Housing Markets, Wealth and the Business Cycle." Economics Department Working Paper 394. OECD, Paris.

Congressional Budget Office. 2005. "Macroeconomic and Budgetary Effects of Hurricane Katrina." Report. September 6. Washington, DC.

Huntington, Hillard G. 2005. "The Economic Consequences of Higher Crude Oil Prices." In *Final Report EMF SR 9*. Energy Modeling Forum, October.

International Energy Agency. 2004. *World Energy Outlook*. Paris.

IMF (International Monetary Fund). 2005. *World Economic Outlook*. Washington, DC.

OECD (Organisation for Economic Co-operation and Development). 2004. *Economic Outlook*, no. 74. Paris.

World Bank. 2005. *Global Development Finance 2005*. Washington, DC.

2

The Potential Gains from International Migration

International migration can generate substantial welfare gains for migrants, their countries of origin, and the countries to which they migrate. The main focus of this report is on gains from the remittances that migrants send home (discussed in chapters 4–6); chapters 2 and 3 address the economic costs and benefits of migration and the impact of migration on poverty. In this chapter, we use an economic model to estimate the size of the welfare gains resulting from migration from developing to high-income countries.[1] It must be recognized at the outset that the model fails to capture some known costs and benefits of migration; that the results are dependent on the specification of the model and its key parameters; and that the model cannot incorporate social or political considerations.[2] The results of this simulation do not provide a precise forecast of the likely impact of migration; instead, they provide a consistent framework that offers insights into (a) the economic gains that can be expected from changes in policy or circumstances, and (b) the channels through which migration affects welfare—and both are difficult to measure in reality. The conclusions drawn from the model are supported by several empirical studies, and they hold up well under various alternative assumptions for model specification and parameters.

In chapter 3, we complement this model-based approach to measuring the gains from migration with a review of the economic literature, which covers the implications for migrants and for their origin countries. Here we can refer to a broader range of economic issues than are captured by the model, although without the ability to quantify that the model-based simulation provides.

Starting from the base-case forecast of economic activity described in chapter 1, we introduce an additional increase in migration from developing to high-income countries sufficient to raise the labor force of high-income countries by 3 percent over the period 2001–25. The assumed increase, roughly one-eighth of a percentage point a year, is close to that observed over the 1970–2000 period. We imply no judgment concerning whether such an increase is likely or politically feasible, but rather view the rise in migration as an exogenous shock. As discussed in chapter 3, pressures to migrate are likely to rise over the next few decades, but the actual size of the migrant flows will depend heavily on political decisions in destination countries. This exercise presents us with the following key findings.

The expected decline in the labor force in high-income countries will increase dependency ratios, which could add to the benefits from migration. However, such increases in migration are unlikely to be large enough to have a significant impact on dependency ratios in high-income countries.

Under the assumptions adopted in this modeling exercise, the rise in migration—small relative to the labor force of high-income countries, but large relative to the existing stock of migrants—would generate large increases in global welfare. Migrants, natives in destination countries, and households in origin countries would experience gains in income, although migrants already living in high-income countries would see a decline in wages relative to the base case. Estimates of these gains and losses are particularly sensitive to assumptions about the degree of differentiation among workers (between natives and migrants and between old and new migrants), the impact of migrants on fiscal balances, and the extent of remittances.

Empirical studies of the impact of migration on natives' wages have had mixed results. In this simulation exercise, the rise in migration leads to a small decline in average wages in high-income countries relative to the baseline, which one would anticipate from a labor supply shock. But the decline has a barely perceptible impact on the long-term growth rate for wages.

Native households in high-income countries enjoy a rise in income, on average, as returns to capital increase, offsetting the mild decline in wages. The impact on developing countries is nearly the reverse, with wage income rising as labor-market conditions for workers improve, while returns on capital decline with the smaller supply of workers. In developing countries the gain from increased remittances greatly exceeds that from changes in factor returns.

The economic benefits for high-income economies could be even larger than those predicted by the model, due to several factors: the model excludes the increased productivity of migrants (and the benefits to their offspring) over time; investment levels could increase substantially in response to higher returns to capital; labor-force participation could rise among natives with the greater availability of migrant labor (for household help, for example); the labor market would become more flexibile, and diversity would increase.

The costs of adjusting to increased migration and the gains from migration depend, in part, on the investment climate. Adjustment costs as a result of migration will be lower if more flexible labor markets and more efficient capital markets in high-income economies reduce transitional unemployment and the cost of replacing capital as economies adjust to the rise in immigration. Similarly, developing countries with strong investment climates will be able to use increased remittances more efficiently, and enable workers who do not migrate to respond to improved labor market conditions. The cost of adjustment may also be lower if migration is spread over time rather than concentrated in spurts.

A principal conclusion from this exercise is that migration can generate significant economic gains for migrants, origin countries, and destination countries—but migration also can have important political and social consequences. For example, natives in destination countries may become concerned about maintaining cultural identity in the middle of a growing diversity, which also has implications relative to minority languages and other issues surrounding the integration of migrants. To some extent, opposition to migration is driven by these concerns, and not by an economic calculation of the gains and losses.

We begin with a discussion of recent trends and discuss how migration to high-income countries has grown over the past 30 years. We then turn to the prospects for migration, including the intense pressures generated by demographic changes. We describe the base-case scenario for migration and the model-based analysis of the welfare gains from increased migration. We conclude with issues that the model does not consider.

International migration trends

Migration to high-income countries has accelerated

The United Nations (UN) estimates that migrants account for some 3 percent of the

Table 2.1 Growth in international migration by destination, 1970–2000

Percent change per year in stock of migrants

	1970–80	1982–90	1990–2000
World	2.0	4.4	1.3
High-income countries	2.4	2.9	3.1
Developing countries	1.8	5.5	–0.1
Excluding former USSR	1.9	2.1	0.0
Former USSR	0.5	25.0	–0.3

Source: United Nations.

world's population, or about 175 million persons.[3] The stock of immigrants to high-income countries increased at about 3 percent per year from 1980 to 2000, up from the 2.4 percent pace in the 1970s (table 2.1). At that rate of growth, the share of migrants in high-income countries' population almost doubled over the 30-year period, and population growth (excluding migration) fell from 0.7 percent per year in the 1970s to 0.5 percent in the 1990s. Immigration has had a particular impact on population growth in several high-income countries. For example, without immigration Germany, Italy, and Sweden would have experienced a decline in population in the past few decades (OECD 2005; IOM 2005). By contrast, migration to developing countries rose by only 1.3 percent per year from 1970 to 2000. With rapid population growth, the share of migrants in developing countries' population (excluding the former Soviet Union) fell (figure 2.1).[4]

Most high-income countries saw immigration rise by at least 2 percent per year from 1980 to 2000.[5] This increase reflected, in part, increased demand for services accompanying rising incomes, global competition for highly educated workers as technological advances boosted the premium for skills, the growth of networks of immigrants in high-income countries that facilitated new immigration, and increased refugee movements. Almost 70 percent of the increase in immigration is accounted for by the United States and Germany, which together make up less than 40 percent of the population of the high-income countries. In the United States, the Immigration Reform and Control Act (IRCA) of 1986, which provided permanent status to 2.7 million migrants, facilitated further immigration through rules governing family reunification and may have encouraged further irregular immigration (Passel 2005) by encouraging expectations of future amnesties.[6] Germany saw a large inflow of ethnic Germans following the breakup of the Soviet Union (Dustmann and Glitz 2005), as well as an increase in temporary migration under bilateral agreements.

Though the stock of migrants has accelerated sharply relative to the population in the industrial countries, in some respects the composition and patterns of international migration have exhibited continuity over the past few decades. The share of female migrants has remained almost unchanged (47 percent

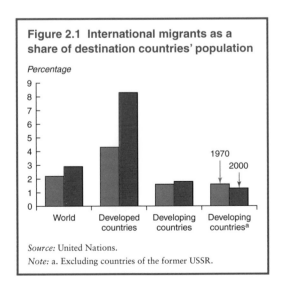

Figure 2.1 International migrants as a share of destination countries' population

Percentage

Source: United Nations.

Note: a. Excluding countries of the former USSR.

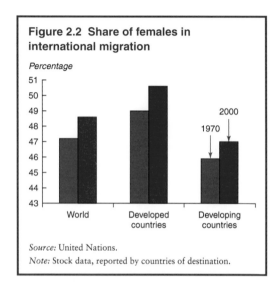

Figure 2.2 Share of females in international migration

Percentage

Source: United Nations.
Note: Stock data, reported by countries of destination.

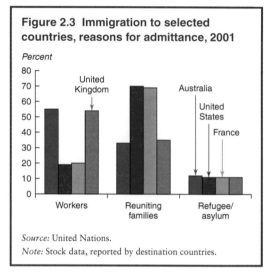

Figure 2.3 Immigration to selected countries, reasons for admittance, 2001

Percent

Source: United Nations.
Note: Stock data, reported by destination countries.

of global migrant populations in 1970, compared with 49 percent in 2000—figure 2.2), although women are the great majority of migrants from some countries. More women today are migrating as independent wage earners, rather than to accompany their husbands (IOM 2005). Migration continues to be heavily determined by geographic proximity (from Mexico to the United States, from North Africa to Southern Europe, and from Eastern to Western Europe), as well as by colonial ties (from Latin America to Spain and from a number of Sub-Saharan African countries to Belgium, France, Portugal, and the United Kingdom—OECD 2005). The major countries of destination continue to admit the largest share of permanent immigrants for family reunification (or, in the case of the EU countries, for humanitarian or refugee resettlement), although some countries are refocusing their migration policy toward economic (largely skilled) immigration (figure 2.3).[7] But international migration is also changing, particularly in the direction of flows. For example, more Asians are today seeking work in other Asian countries rather than in the Middle East (Wickramasekera 2002; OECD 2005; IOM 2005), while more Latin Americans are turning to Europe for work opportunities, in addition to North America.

It should be emphasized that the migration data on which these judgments are based tend to be unreliable and incomplete. Many countries and international agencies do not distinguish between regular and irregular migration or among types of temporary migration. Some record migrants' country of birth; others their nationality (OECD 2005). National estimates of the number of migrants can be vastly different depending on whether "migrant" is defined as foreign born or of foreign nationality.

Migration is set to increase

It is likely that the number of people who wish to migrate from developing to high-income countries will rise over the next two decades. About 31 percent of developing countries' population is below the age of 14, compared with 18 percent in high-income countries. We can thus anticipate a large influx in the age categories most suitable for emigration, as lifetime earnings from migration tend to be largest for those emigrating early in their working life. The surge in immigration since the 1980s has established large diasporas in high-income countries, which help to reduce the costs and risks of migration (see chapter 3). The demand for immigrant services in high-income countries will also rise as the aging of the population shrinks the workforce and increases demand for services that immigrants can supply (such as nursing care). As income standards rise, the demand for other services that employ migrants (such as household and restaurant help) should grow rapidly. The intensifying competition for skilled workers may also draw migrants, especially from countries with strong systems of higher education.

Policies in destination countries can affect migration

Forecasts of migration flows remain problematic. But with the underlying demand for and supply of migrants likely to increase in coming decades, the number of migrants will depend on policy decisions governing admittance and the effectiveness of efforts to police borders and enforce workplace rules. Opposition to immigration may grow as the number of migrants increases, as it did in major countries of destination before World War I. But it is likely that the main policy issue will be how best to manage and live with increased migration. In the simulations that follow, we explore the impact of an increase in migration to 2025 in line with recent historical experience.

The demographic challenge

The labor force in the high-income countries is set to decline

A key driver in the demand for international migrants over the next 20 years will be slowing growth, and then decline, of the labor force in high-income countries. The age group that supplies the bulk of the labor force (15–65 years old) is expected to peak near 500 million in 2010, and then fall to around 475 million by 2025 (figure 2.4). In Japan this age group has already begun to shrink, while in Europe the peak will be reached in 2007–08. In the other high-income countries, the peak will occur later—around 2020 for the United States and 2015 for the rest. As-

suming no change in labor-force participation rates, the high-income countries may lose about 20 million workers by 2025, relative to peak employment.[8]

The expected decline in the labor force is accompanied by a rise in the overall dependency ratio, defined as the ratio of nonworkers to workers. For the high-income countries as a group, this ratio is forecast to remain at just under one through 2009. However, by 2025, 100 workers will be supporting 111 dependents, largely reflecting the increased number of the elderly (also, in most countries the number of children under 15 will fall). The largest rise in the dependency ratio will be in Europe. If we focus more narrowly on the number of elderly per worker, every 100 European workers now support 36 elderly people; by 2025 they will have to support 52. In Japan 100 workers will support 60 elderly in 2025.

In the developing countries the labor force will expand

Developing countries show considerable diversity in demographic trends, but overall the bulge of youths born over the last two decades is now entering the labor force, the number of elderly is as yet still rising slowly, and the number of births is falling rapidly. Thus developing countries are forecast to add nearly one billion workers to the world's labor force by 2025, again assuming no change in the labor-force participation rate, and dependency ratios are expected to fall.

The expected expansion of the labor force in developing countries, coupled with large wage premiums in high-income countries, means that migration could help reduce dependency ratios in high-income countries. However, increases in immigration sufficient to have a noticeable impact on dependency ratios would have to be very large. The scenario discussed below envisions an increase in the labor force in high-income countries of 3 percent through migration, or a hike of nearly 50 percent in working migrants in high-income countries. Even if migrants come with no elderly, the dependency ratio in the host coun-

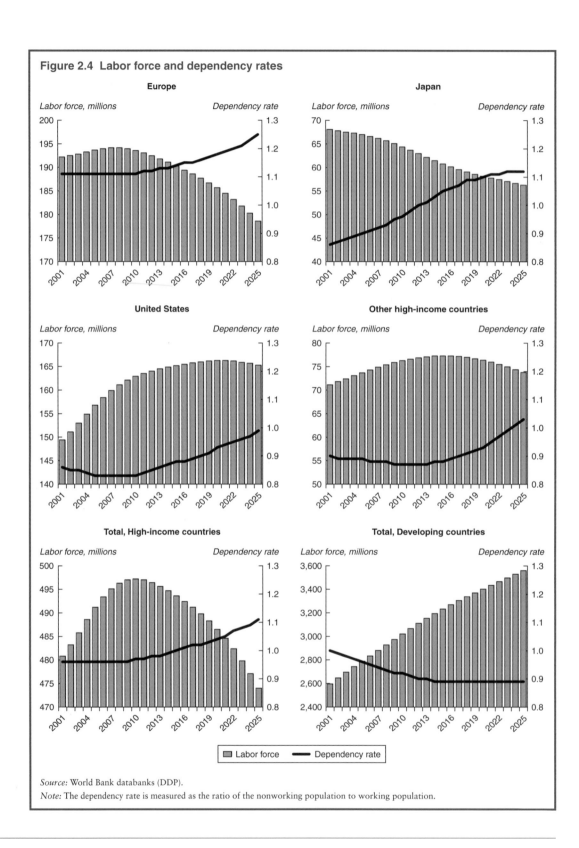

Figure 2.4 Labor force and dependency rates

Source: World Bank databanks (DDP).

Note: The dependency rate is measured as the ratio of the nonworking population to working population.

tries would fall by only about 3 percent under such a scenario. In the case of Japan, it would lower the number of elderly dependents in 2025 from 60 per 100 workers to 59 per 100 workers—barely a dent. Nevertheless, as discussed in more detail below, selective migration—for example, of experienced and skilled workers—can help mitigate the transitional costs of financing pension benefits for rapidly aging populations in high-income countries.

Migration and its development impact

To illustrate the potential gains from increased migration, we compare the base-case forecast for output and consumption in chapter 1 with an alternative scenario, in which the stock of migrant workers is allowed to increase in the high-income countries so as to raise the overall stock of workers by 3 percent (a movement of 14.2 million workers from developing countries to high-income countries by the year 2025). A first approximation of the global gains from such a scenario is simply to calculate the income gains accruing to the new migrant workers—this will reflect the gains to the global economy, because it approximates the increase in global productivity derived from equipping the migrants with more and improved capital and technology. This back-of-the-envelope calculation yields an increase in gross wage income of $772 billion in 2025.[9] As we will see later, when corrected for differences in prices that migrants face in high-income versus developing countries, and taking into account other impacts of migration (on prices, for example) as calculated by the model, global gains fall to $356 billion—an 0.6 percent increase in global income. The scenario is particularly beneficial to developing countries relative to high-income countries. The aggregate percentage gain to developing countries (including the new migrants) is 1.8 percent, whereas the gains to natives in high-income countries amount to 0.4 percent relative to baseline income. These

numbers hold up well as an approximation of the gains to global output, regardless of various assumptions made about taxes, non-wage income distribution, key model parameters, and other factors.

Our modeling exercise uses a global general equilibrium model to measure the impact of migration (box 2.1).[10] One of the purposes of the global model is to verify the basic intuition described above—that migration produces a sizeable global gain. But it also is a powerful tool to evaluate distributional impacts—between skilled and unskilled workers, between native- and foreign-born workers, between capital and labor, and across regions—and to show how these distributional impacts vary with policy choices and parameters (for example, the role of fiscal policies or the propensity to remit).

The assumption is that migrants as a share of population remain constant in the baseline scenario

We begin with a base case for global economic activity (outlined in chapter 1), demographic trends (described at the outset of this chapter), and for migration. For the base case, the proportion of migrants in each region remains the same over time—somewhat contrary to the trends of the last two decades. This does not imply that gross migration is stagnant, or even declining. The stock of migrants in any year will equal the previous stock of migrants, plus new migrants, less the attrition through death and return migration. We chose a relatively neutral assumption because of the difficulty in forecasting these complex processes. For some countries—for example Japan and those in Europe—the assumption results in an absolute decline in the stock of migrant workers. This decline parallels the overall decline in the European and Japanese labor forces.[11] For the high-income countries as a group, the stock of migrant workers would increase by some 760,000 between 2001 and 2025, just a small increment from the estimated 27.8 million in 2001. The main issue, however, is not the base case,

Box 2.1   The model used in this study

The underlying analytical framework used in this chapter is the World Bank's standard global general equilibrium model—LINKAGE—which has been used in previous reports for trade policy analysis. It has been modified to differentiate between migrant and native workers and to incorporate remittances. The model is based on release 6.0 of the GTAP database (base year 2001), developed by the Global Trade Analysis Project (www.gtap.org), a global network of researchers and policymakers engaged in the quantitative analysis of international policy issues. It is supplemented for use in our model with a new database developed jointly by GTAP and the University of Sussex (Parsons and others 2005). That database contains a comprehensive estimate of bilateral stocks of migrants for 226 countries and territories.

While the new migration database is undergoing constant improvements as new data become available and obvious errors are corrected, its developers have done a remarkable amount of detective work, largely in national data sources. The GTAP center has used this underlying migration database to build a bilateral migration database for the 87-region level of aggregation of the main GTAP database—

including estimates of population and the stock of workers, both skilled and unskilled (Walmsley, Ahmed, and Parsons 2005).[a] World Bank data (described in more detail in chapter 4 of this report) was used to provide the total level of remittances, and the bilateral stock of migrants was used to estimate the bilateral remittance flows subject to the overall total flows.

The standard horizon for the LINKAGE model has been 2015. For the work described here, the model horizon has been extended to 2025, in part because demographic dynamics play a more important role over the longer-term horizon, and in part to allow for more time to phase in the increase in migration.

---

[a]The 87 regions of GTAP have been aggregated into 21 regions for the purposes of this study. Six of these are high-income regions using World Bank definitions—the European Union and the European Free Trade Area, Canada, the United States, Japan, Australia/New Zealand, and the newly-industrializing economies. The fifteen developing countries/regions include China, the Philippines, India, Russia, Turkey, South Africa, and Mexico as individual countries, plus 6 regions that represent the remaining countries in each geographical area.

---

but rather the impact of deviations from it—although significantly different base assumptions could affect the deviations as well.

According to the base-case scenario, migrant workers would make up about 6 percent of the labor force of high-income countries in 2025, though with sharp differences across regions and skills (table 2.2). The vast majority of migrant workers are unskilled—some 25.3 million migrant workers out of a projected total of 28.5 million, or 7.8 percent of high-income countries' labor force. Skilled migrants, on the other hand, represent just 2.2 percent of the total skilled workforce on average.

There are welfare implications if migration rises significantly

The alternative scenario involves a rise in migration sufficient to increase the labor force

of high-income countries by 3 percent, phased in from 2010 through 2020.[12] As migrants make up about 6 percent of high-income countries' labor force, a 3 percent rise in the labor force (through migration) implies a 50 percent increase in the number of migrant workers. This may seem like a large change, but the resulting stock of migrants in Europe, Japan, and the United States would remain a far smaller share of population than current levels in some high-migration countries. (In Australia, for example, about a quarter of the population are migrants, in Canada 19 percent, in Kuwait 50 percent). The percentage increase in migrants is large in Japan (as the baseline share of migrants is relatively low), and lower in the United States. The increase corresponds to an annual growth rate of about 1.9 percent, somewhat slower than the

Table 2.2 Labor force structure in the base case and after increases in migrants

In millions except where noted

	Baseline		Migration shock	
	2001	2025	Change in millions 2001–25	Change in percent 2001–25
High-income countries				
Total labor force	480.8	474.0	14.2	3.0
Developing-country migrant workers	27.8	28.5	14.2	49.9
Unskilled	24.6	25.3	9.8	38.6
Skilled	3.1	3.2	4.5	137.9
Developing-country migrant workers				
as share of total labor force, percent[a]	5.8	6.0		8.8
Unskilled, percent	7.4	7.8		10.5
Skilled, percent	2.1	2.2		5.0
Developing countries				
Total labor force	2,596.2	3,561.0	−14.2	−0.4
Unskilled	2,395.9	3,294.3	−9.8	−0.3
Skilled	200.4	266.7	−4.5	−1.7

Source: Initial 2001 data from migration database under development by GTAP/University of Sussex (Parsons and others 2005 and Walmsley, Ahmed, and Parsons 2005). Scenarios based on World Bank assumptions.
Note: a. The percentage of migrant workers as a share of the total labor force is assumed to be the same for each individual region of the model throughout 2001–25, but the share averaged across all developed regions will change through aggregation effects.

average increase over the period 1980–2000. Moreover, the growth rate is unbalanced, with an annual increase of only 1.5 percent in unskilled workers, but 3.8 percent in skilled workers. A number of additional assumptions are critical to the results.

First, the high-income countries' labor force of *both skilled and unskilled workers* increases by 3 percent.[13] As the share of skilled workers among migrants is much smaller than the share of skilled workers among high-income country natives, the shock results in a much larger percentage increase for skilled migrants. The number of unskilled migrant workers increases by 39 percent, while the number of skilled migrant workers rises by 138 percent.[14]

Second, the share of migrants by region of origin remains constant; in other words, the new migrants reflect the same allocation by region of origin as existing ones. Thus if Mexicans constitute 30 percent of foreign migrants in the United States in the base case, they maintain the same share after the increase in migration. This assumption is made to simplify the analysis, although it does fail to

reflect the likely migration pressures implied by large differences in demographic trends in sending regions (for example, Sub-Saharan Africa versus Latin America).

Third, foreign workers are assumed to bring family members in proportion to the dependency ratio in their home country. As a result, the total number of migrants in high-income countries increases from 65 million (6.5 percent of high-income countries' population) in the baseline for 2025, to 93 million (9 percent of population) after the shock. This assumption can change the average dependency ratio of the host country. It can also have other implications not modeled explicitly—including fiscal impacts, because the families of new migrants may require additional public services (such as schooling), not fully compensated by the taxes paid by the new migrants.

Fourth, remittances are assumed to be a fixed proportion of migrants' labor income, equal to the level in the base year. The average for developing countries is 17 percent, although the level varies with the migrant's origin and destination countries. New migrants are assumed to send remittances to their home country at the same rate (relative to income) as existing migrants.[15]

Returns to households

The gains from increased migration are large

With the labor force moving, it is best to assess the effects on real income in terms of households as opposed to the national level (as is typically done in analyses of trade reform). Households are broken down into four groups. First are the native households in high-income countries.[16] Second are previous migrants from developing countries now living in high-income countries, that is, those who were in place in the baseline scenario. Third are native households in developing countries—households that do not migrate.[17] And finally, we have the households of the new migrants. Each household's welfare is broken down between the change in private consumption and the change in the consumption of public services.

Natives in high-income countries gain $139 billion in real income, or 0.4 percent of the baseline, as a result of the rise in migration (table 2.3). Nonmigrating households in developing countries see a rise in real income of

nearly 0.9 percent from baseline levels.[18] A significant portion of the increase is due to the remittances from the new migrants, with some improvement in labor-market conditions for remaining workers. Those who are likely to lose—in the absence of any compensatory mechanism—are the existing migrants in high-income countries, who are relatively close substitutes for the new migrants. Their private consumption would decline by over 9 percent and overall consumption (including public services) by 6 percent compared to baseline levels.

New migrants and their countries of origin reap benefits (through remittances)

The main gains come from the higher incomes the new migrant workers can earn in the destination country relative to what they would have earned in their country of origin. New migrants earn $481 billion in real (after-tax) income in 2025 over the base case. However, the dollar increase in income overestimates the welfare gains for migrants. Essentially, an additional $1 spent in the high-income countries does not provide the same amount of welfare as an additional $1 spent in the home country, because prices are higher in high-income countries. Whereas the prices of

Table 2.3 Change in real income across households in 2025 relative to baseline

	Real income			Real income adjusted for cost of living		
	Private	Public	Total	Private	Public	Total
	Change, $ billions			Change, $ billions		
Natives in high-income countries	139	−1	139	139	−1	139
Old migrants in high-income countries	−88	0	−88	−88	0	−88
Natives in developing countries	131	12	143	131	12	143
New migrants	372	109	481	126	36	162
World total	554	120	674	308	48	356
	Change, %			Change, %		
Natives in high-income countries	0.44	−0.01	0.36	0.44	−0.01	0.36
Old migrants in high-income countries	−9.41	−0.02	−6.02	−9.41	−0.02	−6.02
Natives in developing countries	0.94	0.44	0.86	0.94	0.44	0.86
New migrants	584	607	589	198	203	199
World total	1.20	1.15	1.19	0.67	0.45	0.63

Source: World Bank model simulations.

traded goods (for example, cars and electronics) are the same worldwide, at least in principle, the prices of nontraded goods and services (for example, housing and haircuts) are much higher in high-income countries.

A simple example may clarify the idea. Take a household of two persons living in their home country. One works and earns $200. The other does not work. Each spends $100, half on tradable goods (each priced at $1) and half on nontradable goods (likewise priced at $1). Now the worker moves to a high-income country and earns $700. Assume that spending patterns do not change. The worker remits $200 back to the home country, so the income (and welfare, in money terms) of the other doubles. The new migrant buys the same goods—50 units of tradable goods and 50 units of nontradable,[19] but the price of the latter is now $9 and not $1. The migrant thus spends $500, but welfare is unchanged, because the basket of purchased goods is identical.

Welfare evaluations are of course more complex than this simple example illustrates. For one thing, new migrants will have to adjust their spending patterns to deal with their new environment. Heating oil and warm clothes are necessities that will not boost a migrant's welfare above what it was in the home country. For another, the decision to migrate is not taken for simply static reasons; there are significant dynamic reasons for migrating—for example, better opportunities for one's children that are not captured in this simple framework. Nonetheless, the difference in purchasing power illustrated in the example is a strong motivation for migrating, even on a temporary basis. The more wage income earned in high-income countries that can be spent in lower-income countries, the greater will be the welfare benefits. Box 2.2 provides additional detail on the computation and interpretation of global welfare gains from migration.

To account for the change in prices faced by the new migrants, their "new" consumption in the destination country is adjusted to account for differences in the cost of living,

using purchasing power parity (PPP) exchange rates from the World Bank's database.[20] Thus instead of an increase of $481 billion, the rise in welfare for new migrants is $162 billion.[21]

Table 2.3 shows the change in these components for the four household groups and the world. Measured in national accounting terms, that is, with no adjustments for the difference in the cost of living for the new migrants, global real income rises under the model by 1.2 percent relative to the baseline, or 0.6 percent with the cost-of-living adjustment. Global private consumption increases in real terms by $308 billion in 2025 (with the cost-of-living adjustment), with real government expenditures increasing by an additional $48 billion. The total real gain—with equal weight for high-income—and developing-country gains—is $356 billion, with just under half accruing to the new migrants, though natives in both high-income and developing countries also are better off. In percentage terms—where relative weights between high-income and developing countries are irrelevant—the scenario clearly indicates that the relative gains are much higher for developing-country households than high-income country households, rivaling gains from global reform of merchandise trade.

Obviously, global income and global gains would also be larger if expressed in PPP terms. As the percentage increase in welfare for migrants living (originally) in developing countries is larger than the percentage increase for those living in high-income countries, a switch to PPP measures would also increase the global gains as a percentage of global income. If in the migration scenario presented here the gains are PPP-adjusted, the global gains would amount to 0.9 percent of global income in the baseline, instead of 0.6 percent using the EV aggregation. This scenario illustrates that migrants living (originally) in developing countries gain the most from migration in percentage terms.

The impact of higher migration on prices is mild in aggregate in high-income countries, with a small decline in the average price of

Box 2.2   Calculating and interpreting global welfare gains from migration

Two sets of issues arise with respect to the so-called global gains from a policy shock. First, how should the gains of specific groups be evaluated and how do the gains compare with traditional measures, such as GDP or national accounting standards? Second, how should the gains be aggregated over groups and countries, and how should the aggregated gains be interpreted?

Evaluation of the welfare gains of specific groups. In standard applications of general equilibrium (GE) models, the welfare impacts of specific groups are evaluated using a concept from welfare theory called equivalent variation (EV). The concept is relatively straightforward. Welfare changes as a result of changes in nominal income and changes in prices. EV calculations summarize this welfare change in terms of an equivalent change in income alone, showing by how much income at original prices would have to change to achieve the same change in welfare as observed in a simulation.[a]

For most households, the standard notion of the change in real income, that is, the difference in nominal income adjusted by the change in the CPI, is a good approximation of EV.[b]

This is not the case for new migrants, however. There is no standard price index that can be used as a deflator for the change in the nominal gains for the new migrants, since the prices they face in their new host country have no linkages to the prices they paid in their home countries. GE and macro models typically calibrate base-year prices in each region to one (or unit value) by choosing corresponding volume units.[c]

This approach does not allow one to take into account the price increases that new migrants face as a result of their migration. In the simulations, the macro PPP exchange rate (as an approximation of the rise in prices faced by migrants from developing to high-income countries) has been used to adjust the gains to the migrants—although this is just an approximation of the true welfare gains.[d]

Because of the cost-of-living adjustment to the welfare gain of new migrants, the real gain reported is no longer equal to real income gains of countries—and real output gains—measured using

national accounting standards. However, the standard real income measure is still a good approximation of the welfare gains for the other households in the model.

To the extent that new migrants remit part of their income to their country of origin and that income is spent in that country of origin, the increase in the cost of living that new migrants face is not relevant. Therefore, the EV measure of remittances is larger than the same nominal income spent by the new migrant in the host country. This difference illustrates the incentive for new migrants to remit income home.

Aggregation. The second issue relates to the interpretation of the "global" gains. Typically, to derive aggregate or global gains, EV (expressed in a common currency, typically the U.S. dollar) is summed across all households. For individual persons or homogeneous groups this EV aggregation, expressed as a percentage of original income, is a good approximation of the change in welfare (or more precisely, it is a good indication of the change in welfare).[e]

However, no clear link exists between global welfare and the aggregation of EV across heterogeneous groups, because we do not know how to weigh individual welfare across heterogeneous groups (a particularly difficult issue in aggregating across countries at very different stages of development, as is done here). For example, while most groups gain from migration in the scenario discussed in the text, some lose. The fact that the change in global welfare (expressed as the aggregation of EV across groups) is positive does not mean that the welfare gains of the winners are considered more important than the welfare losses of the losers. Thus, global gains as expressed in aggregate EV should not be interpreted as a value judgment on how to weigh individual or local welfare gains.

The aggregation of EV across groups does, however, have a useful interpretation, which is linked to the notion of compensation and Pareto optimality. As long as the global gains are positive—using the standard practice of adding up EVs across households—then it is possible through redistribution to compensate households that lose (so that no one is worse off relative to the baseline scenario),

Box 2.2 *(continued)*

when some households are better off. In that sense *the global gain can be compared with an equal rise in global output plus redistribution.*

In this report we maintain this standard practice of reporting EV aggregates, making the gains comparable to global gains in many other studies.

An alternative approach to calculating global gains would be to add up changes in income measured in PPP terms. The rationale for that alternative is that because prices of nontraded goods are lower in developing countries, the addition of a dollar to a developing country would enable the purchase of a larger amount of goods and services than in an high-income country. In that case, both base income and gains for new migrants and for those who remain in developing countries would be roughly three times as large as reported here. This is true for all gains, whether they come from migration itself, from remittances, or from changes in wages and prices in developing countries. As a result, the share of those who live (originally) in

developing countries in global aggregates would increase in the measurement of both global income levels and global welfare gains. However, the percentage increase in income for developing countries would not be affected.

---

[a] One of the advantages of the EV measure is that it transforms the ordinal concept of welfare into a cardinal concept of income. While it is impossible to measure how much one welfare level differs from another (one can only conclude that one level is preferred to another), the corresponding increase in income can be measured, and the size of the increase has a clear meaning.

[b] For example, in trade-reform scenarios, the change in the price index is a relatively good approximation of the welfare impact, since the new price is approximately the old price less the tariff.

[c] There are exceptions. For example, in the case of climate-change models, it is necessary to know the relative prices of the different fuels to accurately determine the carbon tax.

[d] See Timmer and van der Mensbrugghe (2005) for more details.

[e] The size of the change in individual welfare is undetermined, since welfare is an ordinal concept.

---

absorption (private consumption, private investment, and government spending) of 0.1 percent. However, prices of some key nontradables decline by larger amounts—0.8 percent on average for public services (including health-related services) and 0.2 percent for construction and recreational services. These price declines will be even sharper for specific subsectors where migrant workers are concentrated (for example, household help), for which we currently have no comprehensive data.

The allocation of the gains across developing countries depends on various factors, including the skill loss and the resulting impact on production, the locations to which migrants move and the relative wage differential, and the propensity to remit. By developing region, the gains to households under the model vary from 0.6 percent for Europe and Central Asia to 1.1 percent for South Asia and Latin America and the Caribbean (table 2.4).

For the new migrants, the real income gains—cost-of-living adjusted—increase by nearly 200 percent. There are large differences across regions, with the highest gains (in percentage terms) accruing to migrants from Sub-Saharan Africa (619 percent) and the lowest to migrants from the Middle East and North Africa and Europe and Central Asia. The main reason for the disparity is the relative differential between wages in origin and destination countries. Variations in wages paid to migrants from different regions in destination countries are minor, whereas there are very wide variations in wages in countries of origin. For example, the average wage for a migrant in Europe in the base year is about $16,500—with only minor variation across migrants. However, the average wage in Sub-Saharan Africa is only $470, whereas in the Middle East and North Africa it is $2,700. Thus, the migrant from Sub-Saharan Africa

Table 2.4 Real income impacts across developing regions

Change in 2025 relative to the baseline, adjusted for differences in cost of living

	Natives in region		New migrants from region	
	$ billions	Percent	$ billions	Percent
Total developing	143	0.9	162	199
East Asia and Pacific	37	0.7	32	215
South Asia	21	1.1	2	175
Europe and Central Asia	14	0.6	25	138
Middle East and North Africa	18	0.9	11	134
Sub-Saharan Africa	7	0.9	7	619
Latin America and the Caribbean	47	1.1	85	224

Source: World Bank model simulations.

will gain much more in both absolute and percentage terms than one from the Middle East and North Africa.

The impact of migration on trade would be mild

Whether migration and trade are substitutes for each other is an old debate. For example, in the discussions leading up to the signing of NAFTA—the free trade agreement among the United States, Canada, and Mexico—one of the key arguments was that trade would replace migration and reduce the pressure for Mexicans to migrate to the North. Likewise, allowing for increased migration—for example of unskilled workers—could reduce trade, because it would enable the high-income countries to continue producing low-skill-intensive products at competitive cost.

Evidence of the link between trade and changing the comparative advantage emerges in the migration scenario described here. For example, the largest gains in export revenue for high-income countries come in agriculture, clothing, other manufacturing, recreational services, and public services—all labor-intensive sectors, the first four being relatively intensive in unskilled workers and the last in skilled workers.

Change in comparative advantage has only a mild impact on trade flows in this scenario, however, as migration affects trade through several channels, some of which increase, and others that decrease, trade flows:

- First, the rise in incomes due to migration produces a small rise in global trade flows, with regional differentiation (because income gains differ considerably among regions). In addition to higher incomes, the rise in migration changes the size of regional economies, with implications for their demand for imports and ability to export.

- Second, the nature of the shock assumed in our model differs from the standard debate over trade and migration. The share of skilled workers in total migrants is larger in the shock than in actual migration over the recent past. A large proportion of skilled workers will find employment in nontraded sectors—for example, as doctors and nurses—rather than in producing traded goods. This will have general equilibrium effects to the extent that the price of nontraded goods will decline by more than the price of traded goods. Thus there will be a relative shift to nontraded goods and a potential reduction in demand for imports of traded goods. Overall, the larger share of skilled versus unskilled workers does tend to reduce trade flows.

- Third, the increase in remittances provides an opportunity for developing countries to import more and export less, as their current-account balance will increase by the size of the remittances ($98 billion in net terms). The model results show that total imports into developing countries would increase by $58 billion in 2025 (1.1 percent relative to the baseline), as aggregate exports decline by $40 billion (0.7 percent).[22] The change in remittances leads to an appreciation of the real exchange rate and therefore a loss in relative export competitiveness.[23] For instance, the output price index in developing countries rises by 0.6 percent on average, whereas it declines by 0.1 percent for high-income countries.

In summary, the scenario provides evidence that changes in comparative advantage due to migration do influence trade flows. However, overall migration and trade are not substitutes for each other, because migration has many other economic effects that have more power to stimulate or reduce trade. One implication of this finding is that migration policies should not be pursued because of their specific impact on trade flows. Likewise, in trade policies the impact on migration should not be a main focus.[24] Trade and migration policies should be evaluated on their own merits.

Migrants' impact on government fiscal accounts is broadly neutral

The assumption concerning the level of consumption of public goods and services by new migrants has important implications for individual gains, and global gains, under the modeled scenario. We assume that the new migrants' level of consumption of public goods and services equals the amount they pay in taxes, that is, their impact on the public budget is revenue-neutral. This is broadly consistent with the available evidence (box 2.3). To provide some sense of how different approaches would affect the scenario results, we present two alternative assumptions regarding the distribution of public goods and services to the new migrants (table 2.5). The default assumption had a largely neutral impact for existing residents in the host country. Under another assumption—new migrants pay taxes but receive no benefits from public goods and services—existing residents, native and migrant, enjoy a rise in real incomes of $126 billion ($117 billion for natives and $9 billion for existing migrant households). Note that the global welfare gains increase as well, since the income accruing to natives (and existing migrants) is not adjusted for the differences in the cost of living between developing and high-income countries.[25] A second extreme

Table 2.5 Impact of different assumptions on the consumption of public goods and services by selected groups in 2025

Change in cost-of-living-adjusted real income in 2025; billions of dollars

	Private	Default assumption— "New" migrants receive benefits equal to their taxes		"New" migrants receive no public benefits but pay taxes		"New" migrants receive per capita average benefit	
		Public	Total	Public	Total	Public	Total
Natives in high-income countries	139	−1	139	117	256	−85	54
Old migrants in high-income countries	−88	0	−88	9	−79	−6	−94
Natives in developing countries	131	12	143	12	143	12	143
New migrants	126	36	162	−18	108	75	201
World total	308	48	356	120	428	−4	304

Source: World Bank model simulations.

Box 2.3   The impact of immigrants on fiscal balances

Immigrants' net contribution to fiscal revenues is usually considered to be small. The net fiscal impact of immigration on the United States has been minimal (Coppel, Dumont, and Visco 2001; Auerbach and Oreopoulos 1999). The U.S. Binational Study on Migration (1997) found that irregular migrants did impose a significant fiscal burden on state and local government. However, school expenses accounted for the bulk of these costs, and (as the authors note) education is an investment that may readily be recovered in greater future productivity. Moreover, Lee and Miller (2000) found that the overall fiscal consequences of altering the volume of immigration to the United States would be quite small. Gott and Johnston (2002) and Sriskandarajah, Cooley, and Reed (2005) estimated that immigrants made a positive contribution to public finances in the United Kingdom. Gustafsson and Osterberg (2001) found that new immigrants to Sweden generated a net fiscal cost, but this turned into a positive contribution after a few years. Nana and Williams (1999) found that immigrants to New Zealand had a positive fiscal impact. Bonin, Raffelhuschen, and Walliser (2000) found that the net fiscal contribution of immigrants to Germany could be significant if the government selects for skills.

Calculations of the net fiscal cost of immigration are fraught with difficulties, for several reasons.

First, the computation at any point in time depends heavily on the methodology used, what expenditures and revenues are included, which public services should be regarded as pure public goods (and the extent of economies of scale in expenditures), and whether households or individuals are considered.

Second, static calculations of the current net fiscal impact fail to take into account the age structure of the immigrant population. Smith and Edmonston (1997) found that immigrants arriving between the ages of 10 and 25 years produced fiscal benefits under most scenarios, while immigrants arriving in their late 60s generally imposed a long-term burden. Studies that follow immigrants over time generally conclude that in net-present-value terms, immigrants and their descendants tend to contribute more in terms of tax revenues than they absorb in expenditures, but the orders of magnitude are typically small (OECD 1997). Intergenerational models are sensitive to the discount rate used and assumptions concerning the allocation of the fiscal burden over future generations.

Third, the computation will depend on the level of skills, experience, education, and fertility of immigrants. Rowthorn (2004) calculates that skilled migrants to the United States typically make a large positive contribution to the fiscal balance, whereas unskilled immigrants cost more on average than the taxes they pay. Storesletten (2000) calculates that the net-present-value contribution of the average high-skilled immigrant to the U.S. budget is $96,000; the medium-skilled immigrant's contribution is −$2,000; and low-skilled immigrant's contribution is −$36,000.

The results may change over time, as migrant characteristics and government policies change. The probability that an immigrant to the United States will receive public benefits has risen since the 1970s, probably due to an increasing share of immigrants from poorer countries (Gustmann and Steinmeier 1998).

An issue of particular concern has been the impact of migration on government-financed pensions. Likely increases in immigration can make only a small net contribution to strengthening the financing of pensions in the United States (Fehr, Jokisch, and Kotlikoff 2004), although selecting immigrants for working age and high skill levels could improve the picture (Storesletten 2000). By contrast, increases in immigration could make a significant contribution to financing pensions in Germany (Bonin, Raffelhuschen, and Walliser 2000) and Spain (Collado, Iturbe-Ormaetxe, and Valera 2004).

assumption is that new migrants receive the same amount in public benefits as the average household in the destination country. This would imply a net positive transfer to the new migrant households, since they would receive more in public benefits than they paid in taxes.[26] In this case natives in high-income countries would lose $85 billion in aggregate public goods and services, although this amount would not translate one-for-one into a benefit for new migrants due to the cost-of-living adjustment. These simulations underline the effect of public policy on the distribution of gains from migration.

Additional gains from migration can be substantial

The gains for migrants from this scenario essentially provide the same message as earlier estimates. In their seminal paper, Walmsley and Winters (2003) estimate that a relaxation on the movement of temporary workers on the same order as that modeled here—that is, 3 percent of the labor force of the high-income countries—would yield global income gains of $150 billion (using a 1997-based comparative static model). The result from our scenario that is roughly comparable to their figures (that is, global gains before adjustment for cost of living and measured relative to 2001, rather than 2025) are more than double their results.[27] However, our figures are comparable with the more recent work done by Walmsley and her colleagues.[28] One of the key reasons for the increase in the global welfare impact is a reevaluation of the assumed wage differential between the home and host country. In their initial work, Walmsley and Winters had assumed that new migrants made up 50 percent of the difference between the home and host country's wages. Their new assumption (used in our model as well) is 75 percent, based in part on the fact that the migrants are permanent rather than temporary. Hamilton and Whalley (1984) and Moses and Letnes (2004) have shown that removing all restrictions on labor movement, admittedly not a realistic scenario, would yield a huge increase in world output. Overall, these papers suggest that labor-market restrictions are imposing a much larger burden on the global economy than are trade restrictions. The World Bank's trade model suggests that removing all remaining merchandise trade barriers would yield $287 billion in global real income gains in 2015. For the purpose of comparison, when the gains from the two different scenarios—

those from an increase in migration, and those from global trade reform—are scaled to the same reference year, 2001, the gains from trade reforms are $155 billion versus $175 billion from the migration scenario.[29] This leaves little doubt that easing restrictions on the movement of labor could provide a significant boost to the global economy. Moreover, in comparison with the most recent work on global merchandise trade reform, the gains from an increase in migration are more balanced toward income increases for developing countries relative to developed countries. In a study by Anderson, Martin, and van der Mensbrugghe (2005), the gains to high-income and developing countries are 0.6 and 0.8 percent, respectively, relative to baseline income. In the scenario modeled here, the income increases are 0.4 percent for native households in high-income countries and 1.8 percent for developing countries (including the new migrants).

Returns to factors of production

Four critical factors determine the distribution of gains from migration among skilled workers, unskilled workers, and owners of capital: (a) the size of the increase in migration; (b) the distribution of nonwage income (profits); (c) the degree of substitution between workers by region of origin; and (d) the degree of substitution or complementarity between workers and capital. We have already posited that the increase in migration is large, with an average increase in the migrant labor force of around 50 percent over a 20-year period, and comparable (if somewhat less) to the rise in the share of migrants in high-income country population over 1970–2000. In the absence of any specific data on the source of migrant income, we assume that migrants—both existing and new—receive no nonwage income. In essence, their real income will be driven by changes in wages. The effects of this simple assumption on the distribution of gains are significant, and the implications of relaxing it are discussed below.

Substituting between migrant and native workers determines who gains

The key issue of who reaps the benefits involves the degree of substitution among different workers. The allocation of demand for workers assumes differentiation among workers from different regions. This is done in two steps. First, "similar" workers are bundled together into "native" workers and "foreign-born" workers.[30] In the second step, these two bundles are decomposed into labor demand by region of origin. We assume that there is more differentiation between a native and a foreign-born worker (that is, a lower substitution elasticity) than between two workers from different countries of origin within each of the two aggregate bundles. For example, in the case of the United States, employers see a greater difference between a U.S. worker and a generic immigrant from a developing country than between a Mexican and a Salvadoran worker. The implication is that a rise in the supply of migrants has a greater impact on old migrants than on native workers, which plays a key role in the distributional outcomes of the increase in migration. The assumption of labor demand differentiation operates for both skilled and unskilled labor in the model.

In the default case, we assume that wages are flexible, with a substitution elasticity between unskilled migrants and natives that is roughly comparable to that implied in the conclusions of the meta analysis in Longhi, Nijkamp, and Poot (2004); they conclude that a "one percentage point increase in the proportion of immigrants in the labor force lowers wages across the investigated studies by only 0.119 percent." (See box 2.4 for a review of empirical studies of the impact of migration on wages.) In the scenario described here, the 50 percent increase in the stock of migrants raises their proportion of the labor force by about 3 percentage points, producing a 0.5 percent decline in the wages of natives.[31] We also assume perfect substitution between new and old migrants (the large majority of both categories being unskilled). The

empirical evidence of the extent to which migrants are substitutes for natives or for existing migrants is sparse. Thus in addition to exploring the implications of the assumptions made, we also devote attention to alternative assumptions.

Finally, in a departure from previous work but in line with a developing consensus, we assume that skilled workers are near complements with capital (meaning that they are more productive, and thus earn higher returns, when used together with capital), whereas unskilled workers are substitutes for capital and skilled labor.[32] This specification has important consequences for the distributional impacts of increased migration. Whereas investment rises with increased income, the overall increase in the stock of capital is modest, so that the rise in the supply of skilled workers is not matched by an equivalent increase in capital. Thus the marginal productivity of additional skilled workers declines, provoking a decline in the wage of skilled workers (by more than the fall in the wages of unskilled workers).

Increased migration can generate substantial changes in income distribution among workers and owners of capital

The change in factor returns is depicted in figure 2.5. In the high-income countries only

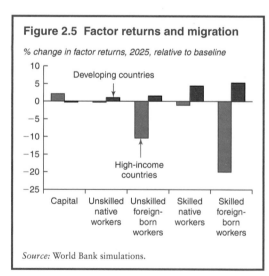

Figure 2.5 Factor returns and migration

% change in factor returns, 2025, relative to baseline

Source: World Bank simulations.

Box 2.4   Empirical studies of the impact of immigration on wages

Most cross-sectional studies find that immigrants have no impact, or a very limited impact, on the wages or employment of natives (LaLonde and Topel 1997 and Borjas, Freeman, and Katz 1997 for the United States; Pischke and Velling 1994 for Germany). However, cross-sectional approaches relate wage differences across local labor markets to the share of immigrants in each market. If immigrants are attracted to high-wage areas, which is likely, it is difficult to identify the exogenous impact of immigrants on wages.[a] Studies of sudden, politically driven inflows of immigrants likewise fail to detect a significant impact on natives' wages or employment in affected areas.[b] However, native workers may adjust to large, sudden inflows of immigrants by moving to other areas (or through reduced inflows from other areas), again obscuring the relationship between immigration and labor-market outcomes.[c]

This problem has encouraged the use of panel techniques that can discern the combined effects of time and cross-sectional effects. Some panel studies have found a significant impact on the wages of unskilled natives, who in addition have suffered declines in wages due to skill-biased technical change and increased trade. Borjas (2003a), analyzed the impact of immigration in the United States across different levels of skills and experience and estimates that immigration reduced the wages of native high-school dropouts in the United States by 8.9 percent from 1980 to 2000. Jaeger (1996) finds that immigration lowered the real wage of U.S. high-school dropouts by as much as 3.6 percent in the 1980s. DeNew and Zimmermann (1994) find that a one percentage point rise in the share of migrants in the labor force reduces the wages of blue-collar workers by almost 6 percent. By contrast, Dustmann and others (2003) find that immigration has little impact on native wages (or employment) in the United Kingdom, including for the low-skilled.

Where wages are relatively inflexible, an inflow of migrants may affect employment levels rather than wages. Angrist and Kugler (2002) find that increased immigration in Europe is associated with a significant decline in native employment, particularly for the low-skilled. Hunt (1992) finds that a one percentage point rise in the share of immigrants in the French labor force (following Algerian independence)

increased the unemployment rate by 0.2 percentage points. This shows more adjustment through employment than through earnings compared to U.S. studies, which may be due to French rules governing wages (Dustmann and Glitz 2005). The comparison underlines the importance of the investment climate, and in particular, labor-market flexibility, in the efficient absorption of migrants. Some studies show that immigration reduces native unemployment in the long term (Poot and Cochrane 2004), presumably because increased consumption demand from immigrants raises the demand for labor.[d]

Thus some articles support the view that unskilled immigrants are relatively close substitutes for native workers (without attempting to distinguish between the effects on native workers and old migrants). However, the share of low-skilled native workers in destination countries is falling. The share of U.S. adults with less than a high-school education declined from 47 percent in 1970 to 22 percent in 1998 (Massey 2000). About 90 percent of new native entrants to the U.S. labor force in 2004 had completed high school (U.S. Labor Survey 2005). By contrast, the average migrant from rural Mexico has six years of education and does not speak English (Mora and Taylor 2005). Many low-skill immigrants may have such limited education and language skills that they do not compete with native low-skilled workers at all, but instead take jobs that natives are unwilling to do. In this view, the rise in immigration in high-income economies since 1980 has been accompanied by increases in native educational levels; essentially natives moved out of certain kinds of jobs, creating a demand for immigrant labor.

---

[a]The researchers do attempt to correct for endogeneity by using instrumental variables.

[b]Examples include the Mariel boatlift from Cuba (Card 1989), the repatriation of Algerians of European origin to France (Hunt 1992), the inflow of workers to Austria after the breakdown of the communist regimes (Winter-Ebmer and Zweimuller 1999), and the return of Portuguese from Africa in the 1970s (Carrington and de Lima 1996).

[c]Still, Card (2001) finds no evidence that immigration into an area leads to offsetting net outflows of workers.

[d]See Gross (1999) for this result for France.

capital enjoys an increase in returns under the model—with wages declining for all labor categories, skilled and unskilled, native and foreign-born. With essentially only a labor shock, the scarcity value of capital increases. The negative impact on unskilled native wages is small, at around 0.3 percent, depending on the assumed elasticity of substitution between migrant and native workers.[33] The greater impact is felt by existing, unskilled migrants, whose wages decline by more than 10 percent.[34] At least two factors mitigate that decline. First, labor markets are not completely segmented, so that part of the adjustment falls on native workers. Second, other general equilibrium effects are at work, such as a relative shift in the demand for unskilled workers as the price of capital (combined with skilled labor) rises and a relative shift in demand toward goods that use unskilled labor intensively, raising the relative demand for unskilled workers.

The impact of the shock on the wages of skilled workers is greater than for unskilled. Wages decline by 1.1 percent on average for skilled natives, significantly more than for unskilled natives. Old skilled migrants suffer a wage decline of 20 percent, which is double that of old unskilled migrants. The impact on skilled workers is larger than for unskilled because skilled workers are assumed to be near complements with capital; with capital increasing only slightly, this would tend to drive down skilled wages. And the impact is largest on old skilled migrants because the rise in migration of skilled workers is large relative to the stock of old skilled migrants, and the new migrants are assumed to be closer substitutes for skilled migrants than are native workers.

The greater impact of migration on skilled than unskilled wages is not at first sight consistent with the limited evidence available. In those studies that find any significant impact of migration on native wages, the largest impact tends to be on unskilled wages (see above). Our seemingly contrary result arises for three reasons. First, unskilled immigration to high-income countries has been much

larger than skilled migration, so that the wage impact of unskilled migration is easier to detect in empirical work. Second, the shock modeled here represents a one-time increase in skilled migration that is larger than the existing stock, which has built up over time. And third, the model assumes little change in the capital stock, while increased investment in response to migration would dampen the fall in skilled wages, a point to which we return in the conclusion to this chapter.

The impact in developing countries is nearly the reverse. Capital returns suffer and labor returns improve, with larger improvements for skilled workers than for unskilled workers. The magnitudes differ because the relative size of the shock differs. For example, the decline in unskilled workers in developing countries is only 0.3 percent, versus 1.7 percent for skilled workers.

Assuming that all capital income accrues to native households, native households in high-income countries are on aggregate better off after the shock, with real incomes increasing by 0.4 percent. That is, the increase in capital income more than offsets the loss in wage income. Part of the old migrants' 6 percent decline in real income is due to the assumption that they own no capital, so enjoy no nonwage income.[35] An alternative, extreme assumption is that on a per capita basis, old migrants receive the same amount of nonwage income as natives. This alternative would reduce old migrants' loss to 3.4 percent of base real income.

To summarize, the new migrants are clearly the large winners, particularly in percentage terms. Under the assumptions of the model, existing migrants are likely to be losers—though the extent of their loss will depend on their degree of substitutability with native workers and their share of nonwage income. Native households in both high-income and developing countries are better off. The sources of their gains, though, are very different (figure 2.6). In the high-income countries the gains are generated by higher returns to capital—somewhat offset by

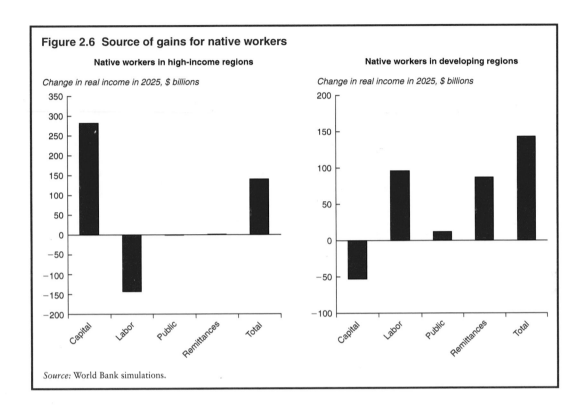

Figure 2.6 Source of gains for native workers

Native workers in high-income regions

Change in real income in 2025, $ billions

Native workers in developing regions

Change in real income in 2025, $ billions

Source: World Bank simulations.

lower wages. The gains for natives in high-income countries would be lower if we assumed a more even distribution of capital (toward migrants) and a greater degree of labor substitutability. In developing countries, the gains to natives essentially are generated by higher wage income and higher remittances—somewhat offset by lower returns to capital. These gains would be lower should the propensity of the new migrants to remit be lower than average.

If migrants are viewed the same as natives, then increased migration reduces natives' wages

The degree of labor-market differentiation plays a critical role in determining the effect of the increase in migration on native and foreign households. An alternative scenario—maintaining the same increase in migration—assumes that employers are perfectly indifferent to hiring native workers versus foreign-born workers.[36] This empirical issue is

linked to real-world dynamics since, over the long run, differences in labor characteristics could fade as migrants adjust to their new environment and as employers cease to see them as different.[37]

The impacts of the alternative scenario on factor returns are shown in figure 2.7. The most notable impact is that native wages (for skilled and unskilled workers) decline by more when natives and migrants are viewed as perfect substitutes for each other, while the wages of the foreign-born decline by significantly less.[38] For skilled workers, the average decline becomes negligible; the burden of adjustment is spread out more evenly between native and foreign-born workers. For the given shock, and depending on the assumed elasticity of substitution between foreign and native workers, the impact on native wages ranges from a slight increase to a decline of 1 percent (box 2.5).

Because increasing migration constitutes a clear labor-supply shock, one would expect it

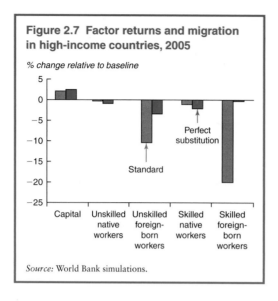

Figure 2.7 Factor returns and migration in high-income countries, 2005

% change relative to baseline

Source: World Bank simulations.

to affect wages (or employment, where movement in wages is constrained). But it is important to view these changes in dynamic terms. First, assuming differentiation between native and foreign-born workers, the impact on native workers' wages in high-income countries is slight even in absolute terms (–0.04 percent for unskilled workers and –0.4 percent for skilled workers). More important, in dynamic terms, these changes alter the rate of growth of wages over the next two decades only slightly. In the base case, nominal wages will increase by 3.6 and 4.7 percent, respectively (average annual growth between 2001 and 2025), for unskilled and skilled workers in high-income countries. With an increase in migration, the growth rate is unchanged for unskilled workers and drops to 4.6 percent for skilled workers. Even in the worst-case scenario for native workers, where foreign-born workers are assumed to be perfect substitutes for natives, the dynamic trends are almost exactly the same as in the baseline scenario.

The effects of the modeled shock are obviously larger for existing migrants. With labor differentiation, their long-term wage growth trend drops to 3.1 percent for unskilled workers and 3.9 percent for skilled workers from their baseline trend of 3.6 and 4.9 percent—

still positive but significantly lower. In the more optimistic scenario for existing migrants, where native workers bear a larger part of the burden, the trend growth in wages is virtually identical to the baseline, declining to 3.4 and 4.8 percent, respectively, for unskilled and skilled workers.

The assumption of perfect substitutability of native and migrant labor has a small impact on the global income gain ($379 billion instead of $356 billion), but significant distributional effects. First, in high-income countries perfect substitution implies a more pronounced pro-capital bias, as native labor suffers a larger loss. However, the negative impact on existing migrant households is much smaller: less than 1 percent, compared with the 6 percent suffered with labor differentiation. This has a positive impact for developing countries, because their loss in remittances from existing migrants drops dramatically. Second, with perfect substitution the new migrants benefit from a larger wage differential and thus a higher income gain. And again, for developing countries, this translates into higher remittances. Overall, the change in real net remittances is $129 billion under perfect substitutability, as opposed to $88 billion. The bottom-line is that the real income of new migrants increases by 250 percent, as opposed to 200 percent, and the gains for natives in developing countries rise to 1.2 percent, instead of 0.9 percent.

Several other parameters affect the relative impact of increased migration on wages and returns to capital. For example, as shown in box 2.5, the relative impact will depend on the substitution between capital and labor. The lesser the degree of substitution (or the less flexible the economy), the greater will be the negative impact on wages. Most econometric evidence suggests a capital–labor substitution elasticity of around 1, somewhat higher than that used in the model.[39] Another crucial assumption in the standard model is that skilled workers and capital are near complements. An alternative would be to assume that unskilled and skilled workers were both substitutes with capital. This would moderate the decline

Box 2.5 Increased migration and its impact on wages

The impact of increased migration on wages can be summarized by a few simple formulas. The key parameters are the share of foreign workers in the economy, the capital-labor elasticity of substitution, and the substitution between native and foreign workers. These relations are summarized in the table below.[a] The values refer to an economy where foreign labor is 5 percent of the labor force (s_f^l). The capital-labor substitution elasticity (s^v) is 0.9; and the substitution (s^l) between native and foreign workers is 4.[b] The point elasticity is given in the third column of the table. The estimated impact of a 50 percent increase in the stock of foreign workers is simply the point elasticity multiplied by 50. The actual impact comes from a calibrated numerical model. The two are relatively close, despite the size of the shock. This is because the results are largely driven by the low share of foreign workers in the economy; therefore most of the economy stays near its initial equilibrium. The aggregate wage falls by only 1 percent. This is allocated across the different workers depending on their substitutability. With an elasticity of 4 (used in the default scenario), migrant workers see a 10 percent decline in wages; domestic workers see only a 0.5 percent decline. If migrants

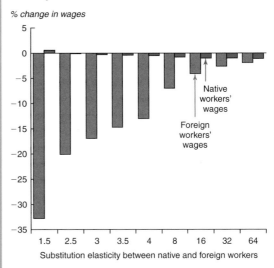

Wage impact from a 50 percent increase in foreign workers, under various substitution assumptions

% change in wages

Substitution elasticity between native and foreign workers

Source: World Bank staff calculation.

Summary of elasticities with respect to an increase in foreign workers

Expression	Description	Point elasticity	Estimated impact	Actual impact
$\varepsilon_{W,F} = -\dfrac{s_f^l s_k}{s^v}$	Aggregate wage	−0.0222	−1.1	−1.0
$\varepsilon_{FW,F} = -\dfrac{s_n^l}{s^l} - \dfrac{s_f^l s_k}{s^v}$	Wage of foreign workers	−0.2597	−13.0	−10.1
$\varepsilon_{NW,F} = \dfrac{s_f^l}{s^l} - \dfrac{s_f^l s_k}{s^v}$	Wage of native workers	−0.0097	−0.5	−0.5

and native workers are perfect substitutes, then wages of native workers would decline by 1 percent, that is, by the same amount as the aggregate wage.

The figure shows the impact on wages—of both foreign and native workers—using different assumptions about their substitutability. The shock is a 50 percent increase in the stock of foreign workers with the same assumptions used for the numerical example in the table. The impacts on wages converge only at very high levels of substitutability. In actual econometric work, it might be hard to es-

timate the substitution elasticity with great precision, particularly since the shocks are unlikely to be as considerable as those modeled here.

---

[a] These relations are for a small single-sector closed economy but line up relatively well with the impacts from the global model. Because it is closed and single-sector, the relations may not hold exactly because of other general equilibrium effects. See van der Mensbrugghe 2005b.

[b] The other parameters are the capital share (s_k), the share of foreign labor in output ($s_f = s_l . s_f^l$), and the share of native workers in the labor force (s_n^l).

of skilled wages and the rise in the returns to capital, essentially because there would be more (assumed) flexibility in the economy. When capital and skilled workers are complements, a sharp increase in skilled workers, without a concomitant increase in capital, raises the scarcity value of capital. If we make capital and skilled labor more substitutable, the decline in the wages of skilled workers will create more demand for them and dampen the negative impact on their wages.

Caveats—what the model leaves out

While the scenarios discussed here provide a wealth of insights, they do not address many important aspects of the impact of migration. Using side calculations, it is possible to get a sense of two such aspects.

The model does not account for changes in migrant characteristics over time

The model assumes that migrant characteristics do not change over time. This is useful in highlighting the immediate impact of migration, but less realistic over the medium term. As migrants remain in the destination country, they tend to take on the characteristics of native workers. For example, they learn or improve their fluency in the language, they better understand (and may tend to adopt) the social mores of the destination country, and they may become more educated. Employers are likely to view a migrant that has lived in the country for 20 years as being more similar to a native worker than a migrant who arrived yesterday. This issue has several implications for the calculation of the gains from migration. Migrants who have spent a longer time in the destination country will be less perfect substitutes for new migrants, mitigating the drop in their wages predicted by the model. Similarly, as the degree of labor differentiation declines, the impact on native wages will rise, thus reduc-ing native households' gains. On the other hand, increased productivity as migrants improve their education may generate larger gains to owners of capital and could benefit native workers through spillover effects such as training. Remittances may decline as migrants become more removed from the origin country.

The process of catch-up in productivity is not captured in our current model, but we have done some side calculations to see how the results could be affected. The catch-up rate and workers' length of stay are two factors that affect catch-up. How long does it take the average migrant to achieve the level of productivity of native workers? Borjas (2003b) provides mixed evidence on this point for migrants in the United States. First, he shows that the catch-up rate depends very much on when the migrants arrived, with earlier migrants doing better than later migrants. Second, he finds no absolute convergence, with migrants' wages remaining below those of native workers.

The second factor relates to workers' length of stay. The longer workers stay, the better placed they are to improve their skills and adapt to local work practices, including language skills (if necessary). At one extreme, all migrants may be assumed to be temporary workers staying for a short period to return home permanently. Or they may be assumed to be permanent workers arriving young and with high educational attainment or acquired skills.

Under the most optimistic scenario, where catch-up occurs within a year, our simple, calibrated model predicts gains in the output of high-income countries that are about 25 percent higher than in the case of no catch-up.[40] Under a more plausible scenario, where the process of catch-up takes 10 years and annual attrition[41] is around 10 percent, the output gain in high-income countries is about 12 percent higher than with no catch-up. It appears, therefore, that the catch-up phenomenon could boost the gains from migration substantially.

The model does not account for the potential of migration to spur higher investment

The model generates only a modest rise in the capital stock as a result of the increase in migration. Increased returns to capital, and thus interest rates, do increase savings. However, this effect is marginal, in keeping with empirical estimates of the responsiveness of savings to changes in interest rates. In reality, higher investment in response to the higher returns to capital may be financed by capital inflows, which do not change in the model. There is some evidence, however, that large immigration can attract capital flows. For example, Davis and Weinstein (2002) argue that skilled labor, unskilled labor, and capital are all attracted to the United States, owing to U.S. technological superiority. The mass migration from Europe to the new world before World War I encouraged large inflows of capital.

Higher investment would lessen the decline in wages suffered by skilled workers, dampen the rise in the return to capital, and increase the demand for unskilled workers in the high-income countries—but it could have the opposite effects in developing countries. To verify this intuition, we simulated the same migration shock and added to the shock a 0.4 percent decline in the level of investment in developing countries, with a concomitant transfer of these resources to high-income countries.[42] Those assumptions indeed have a positive impact for the high-income countries and dampen the capital-income gains and labor-income losses. Overall, the gain for native households in high-income countries improves by 4.5 percent (from $139 billion to $145 billion). But it comes at the expense of natives in developing countries, whose income gain drops from $143 billion to $125 billion, a drop of 12.5 percent. The global gains fall to $345 billion, a 3 percent fall. This suggests—in the absence of an increase in savings—that the potential reallocation of global savings toward high-income countries is negative at the global level and that capital is more productive in developing countries.

Other factors not covered by the model are more difficult to quantify

There are various costs associated with migration that the model does not take into account. One issue concerns adjustment costs, as changes in the technology of production and in the mix of goods imply transitional unemployment and changes in the pattern of investment. The magnitude of these costs depends in part on the structure of labor-market institutions (such as constraints on hiring and firing and minimum-wage legislation) and on the efficiency of capital markets. Countries with more flexible labor markets and sound banking, stock, and bond markets are likely to experience lower adjustment costs, underlining the importance of the investment climate for realizing the potential gains from migration. The size of adjustment costs will also depend on whether migration is concentrated or spread over time. This point also has policy implications. If a country anticipates needing migrants in the future or recognizes that migration pressures are bound to rise due to demographic changes, it would be better to loosen constraints on migration earlier and more gradually than to be confronted with a sharp rise later on. Migration also involves direct costs, including transportation and transitional expenses, as well as the noneconomic costs suffered by migrants separated from their families (for example, the impact on children raised without one or both parents—see chapter 3). In general these are either short-term costs that should not greatly change the calculation of benefits from permanent migration or problems that decline over time as migrants and families adjust to permanent changes or take steps to reunite.

Several other issues that may affect the gains from migration are impossible to quantify. First, our model does not distinguish between irregular and regular migrants. If migrants are irregular, they may be paid lower wages (see chapter 3), which would reduce their welfare gains (and remittances) relative to the model results, while it increases the gains of natives. However, irregular migrants also may impose costs on destination countries—among them the costs of enforcement (as governments seek to limit what some may view as undesirable changes in the country's culture and demographic characteristics); a possible burden on public spending, which may be higher for irregular migrants (see box 2.3); and the potential for other forms of illegality generated by the presence of a large, undocumented group of foreign workers.

Second, immigrants may improve the efficiency of employment from the perspective of firms by providing a source of labor that can easily be employed in new geographic locations, and hired or fired in response to changes in cyclical conditions. Piore (1986) describes how many migrants (at least initially) tend to view their stay as temporary, filling jobs with lower salaries and less stability than those of natives.[43] Large numbers of immigrants work in construction, which facilitates new developments in areas that require a mobile labor force. However, over time, migrants will become more permanent and demand jobs similar to those held by natives.

Third, our model does not reflect the social or economic implications of increasing diversity in the destination country. The social impact lies outside our present scope, but diversity has potential economic costs and benefits that should be considered. Some writers argue that increased diversity has an economic value. Glasser, Kolko, and Saiz (2001) emphasize the role of a rich variety of services and consumer goods in enhancing the attractiveness of cities. Florida (2002) relates an index of diversity to a concentration on high-technology industries. Ottaviano and Peri (2004) find that cultural diversity has a net positive effect on the productivity of U.S.-born citizens. By contrast, Schiff (1998) uses a theoretical model to underline how a society's shared values can reduce the cost of transacting business, owing to higher trust and easier enforceability of sanctions. Thus immigration, which increases diversity, may lower productivity by raising transaction costs. Finally, Alesina and Ferrara (2004) find that increases in ethnic

diversity are associated with lower growth rates, holding all else equal. However, diversity may be more beneficial to growth at higher income levels.[44] Clearly much will depend on the kinds of diversity involved: immigrants who rely on national affinities to cement loyalty to violent gangs presumably have a very different impact on growth and welfare than immigrants who open ethnic restaurants.

Fourth, the model may not fully capture the beneficial effect of immigration on increasing the supply of labor in the service sector. Although reductions in the prices of services are captured, the resulting expansion in the supply of native labor (as more parents can afford child care and workers have more time to devote to their jobs) is not.

Fifth, the model does not reflect the possibility that skilled migration may lower growth in origin countries, for example, because of positive externalities from the presence of skilled workers or increases in the price of services that require technical skills (see chapter 3).

Finally, the model assumes constant returns to scale, while immigration may be more beneficial if significant sectors enjoy increasing returns to scale. Increasing returns may be derived, for example, from fixed production costs, network effects (the unit price of providing telephone service falls as the customer base grows), reduced transport and communications costs (as the local market expands), or increased productivity due to interactions among highly skilled workers. In their role as consumers and workers, immigrants may facilitate an expansion of the market, thereby raising productivity by increasing returns. On the other hand, large inflows of immigrants may induce congestion, straining public transportation systems, for example, or bidding up the price of land. Such effects are particular to the sector and geographic area involved, so it is difficult to draw broad conclusions. However, skilled immigrants have made significant contributions to high-technology sectors that are subject to increasing returns to scale.

These qualifications to the scenario results illustrate how model exercises must abstract from reality to provide quantitative measures of the impact of migration. Some of the issues that the model does not consider would likely be small in the medium term (adjustment costs, transportation costs) or would tend to increase the economic benefits of migration (improved productivity of migrants over time, greater labor-market flexibility and supply of labor). Other issues would increase benefits to destination countries, while potentially harming origin countries (higher investment, economies of scale). Still others may have both economic and social effects, without lending themselves to determinations of their direction and size (diversity, irregular migration).

Notes

1. In keeping with the overall thrust of this report, we focus here on South-North migration, although it is important to recognize that a large portion of migrants from developing countries move to other developing countries.

2. Some readers may also find the chapter too technical, as it necessarily deals with detailed specification issues—for example, the degree of differentiation between native and migrant workers, the fiscal impact of migrants, and how to take into account the change in prices between developed and developing countries when evaluating gains to migrants.

3. Data on the stocks of migrants are generally taken from census reports in countries of destination and thus include both regular and irregular migrants. However, irregular migrants tend to be less likely to report their immigrant status, so the estimate of total migrants is probably low.

4. The breakup of the Soviet Union and emergence of 15 new independent countries in 1991 created new populations of "international" migrants without migration having taken place.

5. The exceptions were Belgium, France, Ireland, Portugal, and the United Kingdom.

6. In their regression equation explaining immigration to the United States, Hatton and Williamson (2002) calculate that IRCA doubled the Mexican immigration rate from 1989 to 1991.

7. Germany, Ireland, and the Czech Republic are in the process of establishing new immigration regimes, with a major focus on economic migration. The EU is also discussing the Green Paper on an EU Approach to Managing Economic Migration (EU 2005).

8. These numbers will be moderated to the extent that labor-force participation rates in the 65+ cohort are positive, if small. Moreover, labor-force participation rates for the elderly are likely to increase as pensions and benefits stagnate or decline with fiscal pressures and as life expectancy rates continue to increase. We may also witness an increase in labor-force participation rates among people of working age.

9. These global gains are comparable to the recent findings by Walmsley and Winters (2003), when adjusted for the size of the economy in 2001 relative to the projected size of 2025.

10. The model's specification is described in van der Mensbrugghe (2005a).

11. "Migrants" refers to migrants from developing countries unless otherwise stated.

12. The phase-in period is somewhat arbitrary. Because of its 10-year implementation, it minimizes adjustment costs to some extent. The five-year period between 2020 and 2025 enables an assessment of long-run steady-state impacts.

13. This is by design. An alternative would be to increase the stock of migrants in proportion to their current structure—by host region and skill level. In this case, the largest proportional increase would be for unskilled workers in the United States.

14. A switch of 14 million workers from developing to high-income countries has only a small impact (a decline of 0.4 percent) on aggregate employment in developing countries, albeit with potentially greater consequences among the relatively more scarce skilled workers.

15. Many factors determine the level of remittances. For example, new migrants may leave many dependents in their home countries, which would tend to raise remittances. On the other hand, at least in the short-term, moving and start-up costs could lower remittances.

16. For simplicity, migrants from other high-income countries are added to the true natives.

17. Again, for simplicity, all migrants in developing countries—both from rich and developing countries—are lumped together for the purposes of the aggregate analysis.

18. The impact on households other than the "new" migrants is not affected by cost-of-living adjustments. Since these households do not move, they face the same system of prices, and thus their change in real income simply depends on the standard real income measure.

19. This assumes a perhaps implausible Leontief utility function but the purpose is simply to illustrate the point that corrections need to be made for differences in the cost of living.

20. Were the true prices available, one could do a standard equivalent variation calculation that would take into consideration the change in prices.

21. In the high-income countries, new migrants' total real consumption is $562 billion, compared with $80 billion in the baseline, hence the real increase of $481 billion. When the $562 billion is adjusted for the difference in the cost of living, real consumption, as perceived from the point of view of the new migrant, is only $244 billion, taking the change in real income down to $162 billion. The cost-of-living adjustment averages 2.3, lower than the 3.1 GDP-weighted average PPP of developing countries. This occurs because middle-income countries (with a relatively low PPP adjustment) have a higher weight in migration than in developing countries' GDP.

22. High-income countries, on the other hand, see a substantial rise in exports, $211 billion (2.2 percent), and a more modest $113 billion rise in net imports (1.2 percent), with imports from developing countries declining by $23 billion. This implies that although a large part of the increase in high-income exports can be attributed to the increase in remittances, a significant portion is also coming through intraregional trade among high-income countries driven in part by changing comparative advantage.

23. A standard "Dutch disease" effect of foreign inflows.

24. Studies of the impact of trade reform in developing and industrial countries tend to show that wages in developing countries rise relatively more—particularly for unskilled workers—than in industrial countries, but those changes are relatively minor compared to the initial gap in wages. For example, unreported results from Anderson, Martin, and van der Mensbrugghe (2005) show that full merchandise trade reform would increase unskilled real wages in developing countries by 3.7 percent (unweighted average), but by only 0.7 percent in industrial countries. This could induce a small reduction in the incentive to migrate, but it would not substantially alter the significant wage multiple of 4 to 5 (taking into account cost-of-living differentials).

25. The cost-of-living adjustment for the new migrants treats their consumption of public goods and services the same as their private consumption—that is, it is adjusted by the same PPP factor.

26. The assumption is that the new migrant households come with the dependency ratio of their home country.

27. There will be compositional impacts in translating gains from 2025 to 2001, since developing countries are growing on average more rapidly than high-income countries.

28. Results presented at the eighth annual conference on Global Economic Analysis held in Lübeck, Germany. See http://www.gtap.agecon.purdue.edu/events/conferences/2005/program_day3.htm.

29. The full merchandise trade reform scenario is with a standard model and ignores any beneficial impact through higher trade-induced productivity or scale economy effects. Note that the gains from reform of services trade could be multiples of merchandise trade reform. See Anderson, Martin, and van der Mensbrugghe (2005).

30. In the case of high-income countries, 'similar' workers would be migrant workers from other high-income countries. Other migrant workers are bundled together in a so-called 'foreign-born' aggregate.

31. One would expect the elasticity to increase as the proportion of migrants in the population increases (box 2.5).

32. See, for example, Bchir and others (2002).

33. Box 2.5 shows how wages—native and foreign—are related to an increase in the stock of migrants. Two parameters are crucial—the substitution between native and foreign workers and the share of foreign workers in the labor force.

34. The general equilibrium elasticity is only 0.27 for unskilled workers; for roughly a 40 percent increase in supply, wages decline by around 10 percent.

35. Migrants from other high-income countries (also assumed to have no nonwage income) see only a small change in their real incomes, as their wages are closely linked to the wages of native workers.

36. Observed wage differentials can arise from a combination of two effects—differences in productivity and differentiated labor demand. If labor is perfectly substitutable, then the equilibrating condition is the equality of efficiency wages, that is, productivity-adjusted nominal wages. If labor is differentiated, efficiency wages are no longer necessarily equalized, and the equilibrium wage will be determined by supply and demand conditions for the differentiated labor.

37. The empirical evidence on "catch-up" is limited. In the case of migrants to the United States, Borjas (2003b) shows that migrants who arrived in the 1960s almost caught up with natives within a 10–15 year period. Those who arrived in the 1970s made less progress in closing the gap with natives. However, the wages of migrants arriving in the 1980s actually fell further behind those of natives after a 10-year period. The scenarios described in this chapter assume no change in the relative productivity of migrants. Such an assumption would require a more elaborate specification of migrants to capture their changing composition over time, similar to modeling capital vintages. By

ignoring the catch-up process, our results may underestimate the longer-term gains from migration.

38. The changes in wages by region of origin are identical for all workers in each high-income region, but due to aggregation effects, this will not necessarily be true when averaging across regions.

39. The model has a vintage structure with a lower substitution elasticity for "old" or installed capital and a higher substitution elasticity for "new" capital. The actual substitution will be a weighted average of the old and the new vintages, with a higher average for countries with relatively high rates of investment.

40. This follows directly from the assumption that the productivity level of migrants is initially 75 percent that of natives.

41. The attrition rate will be a combination of factors—return migration, retirement, and death. The first factor is probably most important the first year, whereas the other two factors will depend on the age of the migrant.

42. The value of 0.4 percent was chosen because it corresponds to the change in the number of workers in developing countries—though it should be noted that the change in workers represents a change in the stock level, whereas the change in investment is a change in flows.

43. He notes that this trend may be changing, as technology and globalization encourages smaller-scale production and more permanent immigration.

44. This may occur because "the productivity benefits of skill complementarities are realized only when the production process is sufficiently diversified," or because high-income economies are able to develop institutions that help them cope better with the potential for conflict inherent in ethnic diversity (Alesina and Ferrara 2004).

References

Alesina, Alberto, and Eliana La Ferrara. 2004. "Ethnic Diversity and Economic Performance." Centro Studi Luca D'Agliano Development Studies Working Papers 193. Milan and Turin. December.

Anderson, Kym, Will Martin, and Dominique van der Mensbrugghe. 2005. "Market and Welfare Implications of Doha Reform Scenarios." In *Agricultural Trade Reform and the Doha Development Agenda*, ed. Kym Anderson and Will Martin. New York: Palgrave Macmillan.

Angrist, Joshua, and Adriana Kugler. 2002. "Protective or Counter-Productive? European Labour Market Institutions and the Effect of Immigrants on EU Natives." Centre for Economic Policy Research Discussion Paper 3196. London.

Auerbach, Alan J., and Philip Oreopoulos. 1999. "Analyzing the Fiscal Impact of U.S. Immigration." *American Economic Review Papers and Proceedings* 89(2): 176–80.

Bchir, Mohamed Hedi, Yvan Decreux, Jean-Louis Guérin, and Sébastien Jean. 2002. "MIRAGE, a Computable General Equilibrium Model for Trade Policy Analysis." CEPII Working Paper 2002-17. Paris. December.

Bonin, Holger, Bernd Raffelhuschen, and Jan Walliser. 2000. "Can Immigration Alleviate the Demographic Burden?" *Finanz Archiv* 57(1): 1–21.

Borjas, George J. 1994. "The Economics of Immigration", *Journal of Economic Literature* 32 December (1994): 1667–1717.

———. 2003a. "The Labor Demand Curve IS Downward Sloping: Reexamining the Impact of Immigration on the Labor Market." *Quarterly Journal of Economics*. November.

———. 2003b. "The Economic Integration of Immigrants in the United States: Lessons for Policy." WIDER Discussion Paper DP2003/78. World Institute for Development Economics Research, United Nations University, Helskinki. December.

Borjas, George, Richard B. Freeman, and Lawrence Katz. 1997. "How Much Do Immigration and Trade Affect Labor Market Outcomes?" *Brookings Papers on Economic Activity* 1: 1–90.

Butcher, Kristin F. and David Card. 1991. "Immigration and Wages—Evidence from the 1980s." *American Economic Review* 81(2): 292–6.

Card, David. 1989. "The Impact of the Mariel Boat Lift on the Miami Labor Market." National Bureau of Economic Research Working Paper 3069. Cambridge, MA.

———. 2001. "Immigrant Inflows, Native Outflows, and the Local Labor Market Impacts of Higher Immigration." *Journal of Labor Economics* 19: 22–64.

Carrington, W., and P. de Lima. 1996. "The Impact of 1970s Repatriates from Africa on the Portuguese Labor Market." *Industrial and Labor Relations Review* 49(2): 330–47.

Collado, M. Dolores, Inigo Iturbe-Ormaetxe, and Guadalupe Valera. 2004. "Quantifying the Impact of Immigration on the Spanish Welfare State." *International Tax and Public Finance* 11: 335–53.

Coppel, Jonathan, Jean-Christophe Dumont, and Ignazio Visco. 2001. "Trends in Immigration and Economic Consequences." Economics Department Working Paper 284. Organisation for Economic Co-operation and Development, Paris.

Davis, Donald R., and David E. Weinstein. 2002. "Technological Superiority and the Losses from Migration." National Bureau of Economic Research Working Paper 8971. Cambridge, MA.

DeNew, John P., and Klaus F. Zimmermann. 1994. Native Wage Impacts of Foreign Labor. *Journal of Population Economics* 7: 177–92.

Dustmann, Christian, and Albrecht Glitz. 2005. "Immigration, Jobs and Wages: Theory, Evidence and Opinion." Centre for Research and Analysis of Migration, Department of Economics, University College London.

Dustmann, Christian, Francesca Fabbri, Ian Preston, and Jonathan Wadsworth. 2003. "The Local Labour Market Effects of Immigration in the UK." Home Office Online Report 06/03. London.

EU (European Union). 2005. "Green Paper on an EU Approach to Managing Economic Migration." COM(2004)811 final, Commission of the European Communities, Brussels. November.

Fehr, Hans, Sabine Jokisch, and Laurence Kotlikoff. 2004. "The Role of Immigration in Dealing with the Developed World's Demographic Transition." National Bureau of Economic Research Working Paper 10512. Cambridge, MA.

Florida, Richard. 2002. "Bohemia and Economic Geography." *Journal of Economic Geography* 2: 55–71.

Glasser, Edward L., Jed Kolko, and Albert Saiz. 2001. "Consumer City." *Journal of Economic Geography* 1: 27–50.

Gott, Ceri, and Karl Johnston. 2002. "The Migrant Population in the UK: Fiscal Effects." RDS Occasional Paper 77. Home Office, London.

Gross, Dominique. 1999. "Three Million Foreigners, Three Million Unemployed: Immigration and the French Labor Market." IMF Staff Working Paper 99/124. International Monetary Fund, Washington, DC.

Gustafsson, B., and T. Osterberg. 2001. "Immigrants and the Public Sector Budget: Accounting Exercises for Sweden." *Journal of Population Economics* 14(4): 689–708.

Gustmann, Alan L., and Thomas L. Steinmeier. 1998. "Social Security Benefits of Immigrants and U.S. Born." National Bureau of Economic Research Working Paper 6478. Cambridge, MA.

Hamilton, Bob, and John Whalley. 1984. "Efficiency and Distributional Implications of Global Restrictions on Labour Mobility." *Journal of Development Economics* 14: 61–75.

Hunt, Jennifer. 1992. "The Impact of the 1962 Repatriates from Algeria on the French Labor Market." *Industrial and Labor Relations Review* 45: 556–72. April.

IOM (International Organization for Migration). 2005. *World Migration 2005.* Geneva.

Jaeger, David A. 1996. "Local Labor Markets, Admission Categories, and Immigrant Location Choice." Unpublished paper. Hunter College, New York. June.

LaLonde, Robert J., and Robert H. Topel. 1997. "Economic Impact of International Migration and the Economic Performance of Migrants." In *Handbook of Population and Family Economics,* ed. Mark Rosenzweig and Oded Stark. Amsterdam: North-Holland.

Lee, Ronald, and Timothy Miller. 2000. "Immigration, Social Security, and Broader Fiscal Impacts." *American Economic Review Papers and Proceedings* 90(2): 350–54.

Longhi, Simonetta, Peter Nijkamp, and Jacques Poot. 2004. "A Meta-Analytic Assessment of the Effect of Immigration on Wages." Population Studies Centre Discussion Papers 47. University of Waikato, Hamilton, New Zealand. December.

Massey, Douglas. 2000. "Higher Education and Social Mobility in the United States, 1940–1998." Paper delivered at Association of American Universities Centennial Meeting, April 17, Washington, DC.

Mora, Jorge, and J. Edward Taylor. 2005. "Determinants of Migration, Destination and Sector Choice: Disentangling Individual, Household and Community Effects." In *International Migration, Remittances, and Development,* ed. Caglar Ozden and Maurice Schiff, Washington, DC: World Bank.

Moses, Jonathon W., and Bjørn Letnes. 2004. "The Economic Costs to International Labor Restrictions: Revisiting the Empirical Discussion." *World Development* 32(10): 1609–26.

Nana, Ganesh, and Julian Williams. 1999. "Fiscal Impacts of Migrants to New Zealand." Report to the New Zealand Immigration Service, Auckland.

Ottaviano, Gianmarco, and Giovanni Peri. 2004. "The Economic Value of Cultural Diversity." National Bureau of Economic Research Working Paper 10904. Cambridge, MA.

OECD (Organisation for Economic Co-operation and Development). 1997. *Trends in International Migration.* Paris.

———. 2005. *Trends in International Migration.* Paris.

Parsons, Christopher R., Ronald Skeldon, Terrie L. Walmsley, and L. Alan Winters. 2005. "Quantifying the International Bilateral Movements of Migrants." Paper presented at the Eighth Annual Conference on Global Economic Analysis, June 9–11, Lübeck, Germany.

Passel, Jeffrey S. 2005. "Estimates of the Size and Characteristics of the Undocumented Population." Pew Hispanic Center, Washington, DC.

Piore, Michael J. 1986. "Perspectives on Labor Market Flexibility." *Industrial Relations* 25: 146–66. Spring.

Pischke, Jorn-Steffen, and Johannes Velling. 1994. "Wage and Employment Effects of Immigration to Germany: An Analysis Based on Local Labor Markets." Centre for Economic Policy Research Discussion Paper 935. London. March.

Poot, Jacques, and Bill Cochrane. 2004. "Measuring the Economic Impact of Immigration: A Scoping Paper." Immigration Research Programme, New Zealand Immigration Service, Auckland. December.

Rowthorn, Robert. 2004. "The Economic Impact of Immigration." Civitas Online Report. Civitas: The Institute for the Study of Civil Society, London.

Schiff, Maurice. 1998. "Trade, Migration and Welfare: The Impact of Social Capital." In H. Singer, N. Hatti, and R. Tandon (eds.) *Globalization, Technology, and Trade in the 21st Century.* Vol. 19, New World Order, Delhi: B. R. Publishing.

Smith, James P., and Barry Edmonston. 1997. *The New Americans: Economic, Demographic and Fiscal Effects of Immigration.* Washington, DC: National Academy Press.

Sriskandarajah, Dhananjayan, Laurence Cooley, and Howard Reed. 2005. "Paying Their Way: The Fiscal Contribution of Immigrants in the UK." Institute for Public Policy Research, London.

Storesletten, Kjetil. 2000. "Sustaining Fiscal Policy through Immigration." *Journal of Political Economy* 108(21).

Timmer, Hans, and Dominique van der Mensbrugghe. 2005. "Migration, PPP and the Money Metric of Welfare Gains." Development Economics Department, World Bank, Washington, DC.

U.S. Binational Study on Migration. 1997. *Binational Study: Migration Between Mexico and the United States.* www.utexas.edu/lbj/uscir/binational.html.

U.S. Labor Survey. 2005. Bureau of Labor Statistics. http://bls.gov/cps/home.htm.

van der Mensbrugghe, Dominique. 2005a. "LINKAGE Technical Reference Document: Version 6.0." Unpublished paper. World Bank, Washington, DC.

———. 2005b. "Derivation of Output and Wage Elasticities Relative to an Increase in Migrants." Development Economics Department, World Bank, Washington, DC.

Walmsley, Terrie L., S. Amer Ahmed, and Christopher R. Parsons. 2005. "The GMig2 Data Base: A Data Base of Bilateral Labor Migration, Wages and Remittances." GTAP Research Memorandum No. 6. Center for Global Trade Analysis, Purdue University. September.

Walmsley, Terrie Louise, and L. Alan Winters. 2003. "Relaxing the Restrictions on the Temporary Movements of Natural Persons: A Simulation Analysis." Centre for Economic Policy Research Discussion Paper Series 3719. London. January.

Wickramasekera, Piyasiri. 2002. "Asian Labor Migration: Issues and Challenges in an Era of Globalization." International Labor Office, International Migration Program. Geneva.

Winter-Ebmer, Rudolf, and Josef Zweimuller. 1999. "Do Immigrants Displace Young Native Workers: The Austrian Experience." *Journal of Population Economics* 12: 327–40.

3

The Policy Challenges of Migration: The Origin Countries' Perspective

In evaluating the impact of remittances, the main subject of this report, it is important to take into account the implications of the initial decision to emigrate. This chapter will analyze the implications for migrants and origin countries of migration for economic gain from developing to high-income countries.[1] Focusing on this form of migration can highlight some key policy dilemmas that governments face in improving the developmental impact of migration.

Migration is an extremely diverse phenomenon. Its economic impact on each origin country, and the impact of policy, will depend on many circumstances—among them the skills and former employment of migrants, the history of migration (the existence and location of a large diaspora), the sectors affected, patterns of trade and production, the investment climate, and the size and geographical location of the country. For example, migration policies appropriate for a large developing country with substantial low-skilled emigration and effective institutions will differ from the policies for a small island economy with substantial high-skilled emigration and weak institutions.

Migration is as complex as it is diverse, so predicting the impact of policy changes will be problematic until more research is done and better data obtained. In particular, the gender implications of migration are poorly understood and require more research. Migration also has important social and political implications, that may be as important as the economic analysis provided here. For all of these reasons, the analysis and policy recommendations in this chapter must remain heavily qualified. Our purpose is to signal to policymakers in developing countries, and to the development community in general, the elements that should be considered in formulating migration policy.

International migration often generates great benefits for migrants and their families, although at some risk. Migration can greatly increase incomes of both migrants and their families and has helped countless households escape poverty. While most workers gain greatly from migration, the decision to migrate is sometimes made with inadequate information and at high risk and cost, particularly if the migration is irregular. By providing information on migration opportunities and risks, governments could help avoid unfortunate, costly migration decisions. Governments should also consider means to prevent and prosecute trafficking and other abuse of migrants, and to strengthen migration-related partnerships between origin and destination countries.

Increasing the emigration of low-skilled workers would significantly reduce poverty in developing countries. In addition to enabling emigrants to escape poverty and to reducing poverty in the country of origin through remittances (discussed in chapter 5), low-skilled emigration can increase wages and

57

reduce unemployment and underemployment of poor workers in the country of origin. Many of the poorest lack the financial resources or the skills required for successful emigration to high-income countries, but available data indicate that a significant number of them do emigrate, although at lower rates than the non-poor. Reducing the restrictions on low-skill emigration, while remaining sensitive to concerns in destination countries over social tensions, job opportunities for low-skilled natives and the potential burden on public expenditures, may best be achieved through managed migration programs designed jointly by origin and destination countries. Such programs should provide for temporary, low-skilled migration—with incentives for return.

Emigration of high-skilled workers may reduce living standards of those left behind and impair growth, but can also be beneficial. Like low-skilled migration, high-skilled migration can greatly benefit migrants and their families and can help relieve labor market pressures. In addition, a well-educated diaspora can improve access to capital, technology, information, foreign exchange, and business contacts for firms in the country of origin. At the same time, high-skilled emigration may reduce growth in the origin country because (a) other workers lose the opportunity for training and mutually beneficial exchanges of ideas; (b) opportunities to achieve economies of scale in skill-intensive activities may be reduced; (c) society loses its return on high-skilled workers trained at public expense; (d) the price of technical services (where the potential for substitution of low-skill workers is limited) may rise. Highly educated citizens may also help to improve governance, improve the quality of debate on public issues, encourage the education of children, and strengthen the administrative capacity of the state—all of which may be reduced through emigration of the highly skilled.

Because of the lack of data and the myriad of individual country circumstances that can

influence the impact, it is impossible to reliably estimate the net benefit, or cost, to origin countries of high-skilled emigration. We can only offer some rough observations that reflect the wide variation in high-skilled emigration rates among countries:

- Very high rates of high-skilled emigration affect a small share of developing countries' population, and many countries with high rates of high-skilled emigration have poor investment climates that likely limit the productive employment of high-skilled workers. On the other hand, the lack of high-skilled workers may contribute to the poor investment climate and limit the supply response to economic reform.
- Some countries also find it difficult to productively employ all high-skilled workers because of small economic scale or misguided educational policies that result in a large supply of college graduates for whom no suitable jobs exist.
- High-skilled emigration has had a severe impact on public services with positive externalities. The loss of skills through high-skilled emigration has particularly impaired health services in several developing countries.

Origin countries harmed by high-skilled emigration face difficulties in managing the problem. Service requirements for access to publicly financed education can be evaded and are likely to discourage return, and proposals for the taxation of emigrants to the benefit of the origin country have made little progress. Improved working conditions in public employment and investments in the infrastructure for research and development may be effective in retaining key workers. Working conditions can also be improved by strengthening governance, which may require political will rather than money. Origin countries can also encourage educated emigrants to return by identifying job opportunities, cooperating with destination countries that have programs to promote return, permitting dual nationality, and helping to facilitate the portability of social insurance benefits.

The migration decision and its impact on migrants and their families

Making the costly and sometimes risky decision to move to another country generally involves the expectation of large increases (or lower variability) in income, described by economists as the net present value of lifetime earnings.[2] The migrant's expected income gain from emigration also reflects his or her employment prospects at home and the likelihood of employment overseas.

Better economic prospects drive migration

Migrants from developing to high-income countries generally enjoy large increases in earnings.[3] A dataset compiled by the International Labour Organization (ILO) shows that workers in high-income countries earn a median wage that is almost five times the level of that of workers in low-income countries,

adjusted for differences in purchasing power (Freeman and Oostendorp 2000) (figure 3.1). These data may overstate the wages that migrants expect, because their earnings, at least initially, tend to be lower than those of natives (Lucas 2004a). Moreover, many poor workers who lack local language skills and have minimal education may find limited employment prospects in high-income country job markets. On the other hand, these data may understate the benefit of migration from the perspective of the household. In measuring differences in welfare between migrants and those who do not migrate, migrants' earnings in high-income countries are reduced to reflect the higher cost of living in high-income countries—or purchasing power parity (PPP). To the extent that migrants send earnings back home in the form of remittances, however, this adjustment is not relevant, so household gains may exceed the PPP-adjusted rise in earnings.[4] Furthermore, the data on income differences may influence expectations of future earnings for migrants and their children, and would undoubtedly generate much larger migration, in the absence of controls. Evidence of substantial migration pressure includes long queues of applicants for immigration to high-income countries, the rise in irregular immigration, the increase in asylum seekers (Hatton and Williamson 2002), and the high fees paid to smugglers who help migrants cross borders illegally (Cornelius 2001).

The expectation of higher earnings is not the only economic incentive for migration. Households may decide to send some members abroad to diversify the family's source of income and thus reduce risk, as shocks affecting the level of wages and the probability of employment in the destination country may not be correlated with the shocks affecting domestic workers (Daveri and Faini 1999).[5]

Migration involves considerable costs

Despite clear gains for many, migration involves costs and risks that, together with restrictions on migration, help explain why most people prefer to stay at home. Migration can entail

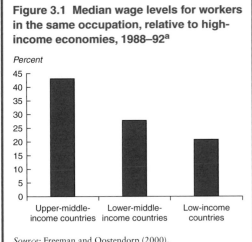

Figure 3.1 Median wage levels for workers in the same occupation, relative to high-income economies, 1988–92[a]

Percent

Source: Freeman and Oostendorp (2000).

Note: Chart reports the median wage in each country/skill group relative to the highest wage for that skill group, with the ratio in high-income economies as the numeraire. Thus the median wage in low-income countries (averaged across skill groups) is 20 percent of the median wage in high-income economies.

a. Adjusted for purchasing power parity.

substantial up-front costs—transportation, fees charged by recruitment agencies, fees to obtain a visa and work permit, maintenance while searching for work, forgone earnings (if the migrant was or could be employed at home), the reduction in value of location-specific skills (for example, knowing one's native language), and the pain of being separated from family and familiar surroundings. Obviously these costs will vary enormously among migrants.

Lack of data makes it difficult to directly test the relationship between costs and the decision to migrate. However, distance can be used as a proxy for costs, representing not only transport costs, but also migrants' limited familiarity with countries of destination. Adams and Page (2003) find that distance is a significant determinant of the direction of migration from developing countries to the United States, European members of the Organisation for Economic Co-operation and Development (OECD), and the Arab Gulf. Long, Tucker, and Urton (1988) found that distance was an important constraint on internal migration in the United States and the United Kingdom; what holds for internal migration (without political barriers or language differences, and with limited cultural differences) probably holds even more strongly for international migration. Household surveys also provide indirect evidence that distance has an important impact on migration: while some of the poorest do migrate internationally, they are more likely to remain at home or to migrate internally (see below).

Among the largest quantifiable costs to migrants are fees paid to private recruitment agencies, whose role in the international labor market has increased substantially, in part because of the rise of temporary labor migration programs.[6] A major conduit of job opportunities for migrant workers, private recruitment agencies often are instrumental in seeking out new markets for job opportunities abroad. They also provide services such as language training and assistance with settlement (see Xiang 2003 in the case of China). However, they also can be a source of abuse (ILO

Table 3.1 Fees charged by recruitment agencies

Country	US$	Year
Migration to the Middle East		
Bangladesh	1,727	1995
India	900	1995
Pakistan	768	1995
Sri Lanka	689	1995
Sri Lanka	893	1986
Migration to Japan		
Thailand	>8,000	1996
Migration to Malaysia		
Thailand	666–1,000	1991

Sources: Abella 2004; Lucas 2004a; Eelens and Speckmann 1990; Spaan 1994.

2003b). Because many migrants lack information on foreign job markets, and some agencies may have considerable market power, recruitment agencies have captured a substantial share of the rents generated by limits on immigration (Lucas 2004a). Available data (mostly from past years) indicate that recruitment charges range from $689 (in 1995) for Sri Lankan immigrants to the Middle East to $8,000 (in 1996) for Thais seeking work in Japan (table 3.1).

Recruitment agencies' potential for earning rents raises the issue of whether governments should regulate their fees. As constraints on migration generate significant excess profits, efforts to regulate recruitment fees would appear to have merit. However, limitations on the terms of mutually agreed contracts can be difficult to enforce, and excessive regulation can drive recruiters underground or lead them to switch to other countries. A few governments have attempted to regulate fees paid to recruiters, and require registration and minimum capital requirements or financial guarantees to limit abuses (ILO 2003a). In general, successful regulation of recruitment agencies involves a large pool of potential migrants (to reduce the likelihood of recruitment agencies switching to alternative sources), effective government institutions, and regulations that focus on the most egregious abuses (instead of just reducing the market rate). Even the Philippines, considered to have a model program, experiences difficulties in enforcing fee limits, while most recruiters, including the Union of Filipino Overseas Contract Workers, argue that stringent regulation of recruiters impairs the competitive position of Philippine migrants relative to workers from other countries (Martin 2005). Destination countries are probably in a stronger position to regulate recruitment agencies effectively.

Decisions to migrate are often made with inadequate information

The distance and differences in language and culture between countries of origin and destination imply that migration is particularly affected by inadequate information. Migrants may have a distorted notion of the possibilities of employment and the likely wage in countries of destination, as well as insufficient information on the costs and potential risks of the trip. Smugglers, recruitment agencies, and others with a financial stake in encouraging migration may present a biased picture of the migration experience, and poor information increases the potential for migrants to suffer from fraud and abuse.[7]

Some origin-country governments have attempted to protect their emigrant workers by regulating the terms of labor contracts. For example, Indonesia, the Philippines, and Sri Lanka have drafted model contracts for various occupations and host countries that detail working terms and conditions to be specified in advance (Abella 1997). Such efforts can be useful in articulating standards and informing migrants of their rights. However, enforcement of such contracts in destination countries can be problematic (IOM 2003). The Philippines, India, and Bangladesh review contracts prior to migrants' departure, and Bangladesh verifies the genuineness of overseas work visas. Some countries have entered into bilateral agreements that require destination countries to issue visas only if the contract is approved by the origin country. Restrictive policies of this kind run the risk of encouraging irregular migration if workers cannot secure approval of contracts in advance. Some countries use fi-

nancial incentives, such as special exemptions from travel taxes for those who clear contracts with government agencies, to facilitate government review of contracts. Some countries with large numbers of emigrants offer a comprehensive set of services, including predeparture training, information on labor markets in destination countries, legal services,[8] reintegration support, and welfare funds financed from fees paid to origin-country governments by departing workers.[9]

A diaspora can reduce the costs facing migrants

The stock of emigrants in countries of destination can reduce the costs facing new migrants from the same origin country. The major countries of origin with significant diasporas in high-income countries (figure 3.2) are for the United States: China, Cuba, El Salvador, India, Mexico, Philippines, and Vietnam; and in other countries: Turkey (for Germany); Serbia and Montenegro, Morocco, and Algeria (for France); and China (for Japan and Canada). As migrant networks spread, private institutions and voluntary associations emerge to provide a range of services, including counseling, social services, and legal advice; lodging, credit and job search assistance; and the means to reduce the cost of undocumented migration, including smuggling and transport, counterfeit documents, and arranged marriages (Massey and others 1993). The migrant diaspora can also reduce the likelihood of, and fears concerning, abuse (see Gunatilleke 1998 for the example of Sri Lanka).

Evidence of how the diaspora encourages migration can be seen in the grouping of immigrants from the same country or local region in countries of destination. Bartel (1989) and Jaeger (2000) find that U.S. immigrants tend to move near former immigrants of the same ethnicity. Munshi (2003) finds that an individual is more likely to be employed and to hold a higher paying nonagricultural job when a large number of migrants from his home community are in the United States.[10] Studies of the Asia Pacific region have shown that

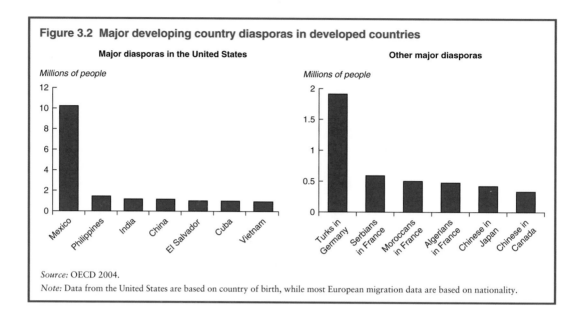

Figure 3.2 Major developing country diasporas in developed countries

Major diasporas in the United States

Millions of people

Other major diasporas

Millions of people

Source: OECD 2004.

Note: Data from the United States are based on country of birth, while most European migration data are based on nationality.

networks raise migration rates once a few initial migrants are established in destination countries (Massey and others 1998).

Irregular migration is often subject to substantial costs and risks

Irregular migration appears to have increased significantly in major countries of destination, although the estimates are unreliable. The estimates are based typically on the differences between census reports and other immigrant registries, arrests at the border or internally, and regularization programs (Jandl 2004).[11] Irregular migration may have doubled in the United States between 1990 and 2000, and may now account for some nine million people (Passel, Capps, and Fix 2004)—about 25 percent of the total stock of migrants. The scale of irregular migration in Europe may also be high. Just under 700,000 irregular migrants applied for regularization under the recent amnesty drive in Spain. Mid-range estimates provided by Jandl (2003) indicate that irregular migrants range from less than 10 percent of the total reported stock of migrants in France to 60 percent in Greece (figure 3.3).

Most irregular migrants are low-skilled because (a) immigration laws in high-income

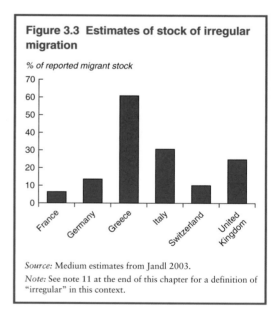

Figure 3.3 Estimates of stock of irregular migration

% of reported migrant stock

Source: Medium estimates from Jandl 2003.

Note: See note 11 at the end of this chapter for a definition of "irregular" in this context.

countries provide high-skilled workers with greater opportunities for legal entry and residence, and (b) it is more difficult for high-skilled workers to practice their professions without adequate documentation, such as educational credentials (Chiswick 2000). Also, skilled migrants often have more to lose at home and may be less inclined to run the risks involved in irregular migration. Irregular migrants also tend to be temporary, rather than permanent, immigrants (Carter 1999).[12]

Irregular migration imposes substantial costs on migrants, compared with permanent migration. It can be more expensive: the average price in 1991 for smuggling an illegal migrant from China to the United States was estimated at $30,000 and from $3,750 to $12,000 for migrants smuggled to Lithuania (Salt and Stein 1997). Irregular migrants can also be paid low wages, have poor working conditions, and be subject to violations of the protections afforded under industrial-country labor laws (Vayrynen 2003). Employers may be able to pay irregular migrants less than legal migrants and natives because only certain employers will hire irregular migrants, or because the migrants are reluctant to move away from support networks. Lower pay and higher costs of migration also make irregular migration less desirable for the origin country, because they cut into remittances. Remittances can be reduced by the relatively expensive money transfer operations used by irregular migrants who lack access to bank accounts (see chapter 6).

Irregular migrants can also be exposed to physical danger. Since 1994 an estimated 2,600 undocumented migrants have died crossing the United States–Mexico border (Meek 2003). Entrapment into prostitution is a danger for women and children (Wickramasekera 2002). Trafficking in persons is estimated globally to involve some 600,000 to 800,000 men, women, and children each year (U.S. Department of State 2004). Different national policies toward migration control make it difficult to combat trafficking and smuggling, although the international protocols against these activities provide a common instrument to criminalize them.[13] Several governments, notably in Southeast Asia, have instituted restrictions on the emigration of women, fearing their exploitation. Unskilled and semi-skilled women are allowed to emigrate from Bangladesh only when accompanied by a male partner (Siddiqui 2003). Such outright bans, in addition to being limitations

on what is generally viewed as a basic right to emigrate, are likely to be counterproductive: they may compel many women to move as undocumented migrants, thus increasing their vulnerability (Misra and Rosenberg 2003). More comprehensive, cooperative policies by governments are likely to have a more positive effect, including the dissemination of information on the risks of migration, strengthened protection for women in destination countries, and stepped-up identification and prosecution of traffickers. Migration agreements between countries of origin, transit, and destination can help achieve such policy coherence (as in the bilateral agreements between some EU states and Morocco and Tunisia, for example).

There are costs for those left behind

Finally, migration may impose costs on family members left behind, particularly children. For example, Battistella and Conaco (1996) find that the children of migrant parents from Luzon, Philippines, performed worse in school and tended to be less socially adjusted (particularly if the mother had emigrated) than children with both parents at home. On the other hand, Bryant (2005) found that the improvement in the children's health and schooling (financed by remittances), coupled with strong involvement of the extended family, tended to mitigate the social costs of a parent's migration. In general, emigration does impose hardships on family members left behind, but it also improves household income and improves families' ability to make compensating adjustments that mitigate those hardships.[14]

The impact of international migration on countries of origin varies

The impact of migration on countries of origin varies greatly, depending on the size of emigrant flows, the kinds of migrants, and labor and product market conditions in the country. In describing these effects, it is useful to distinguish between skill levels, given the differences in the labor markets for low- and high-skilled workers.

Low-skilled migration

Low-skilled migration can improve labor market conditions for other poor workers

The stock of low-skilled emigrants who moved from developing to industrial countries in 2000 averaged about 0.8 percent of developing countries' low-skilled, working-age residents—about the same as in 1990. The regions with countries close to the major destination countries had relatively high rates of low-skilled emigration (figure 3.4).[15]

The effects of South–North migration on working conditions for low-skilled workers in the developing world as a whole must be small. In individual countries, however, large-scale emigration can place increased pressure on wages or reduce unemployment of low-skilled workers at the margin. For example, real wages in Pakistan's construction sector and the Philippines' manufacturing sector closely trace the deployment of overseas workers (Majid 2000; Gazdar 2003).[16] Low-skill emigration also may reduce underemployment or raise labor-market participation without significant wage increases. Wage trends in Albania, Bangladesh, and Sri Lanka, for example, display no obvious signs of

improvement, despite massive emigration (Lucas 2004a). The wage response to emigration depends on the institutional setting in the labor market in the home country (such as the role of unions, public sector employment, and minimum wage laws); the extent of emigration relative to the domestic labor force; and the degree to which emigrants were productively employed before migrating.

The impact of international migration may differ considerably among regions within countries of origin, depending on the degree of geographic concentration of emigration and the links with other regions through internal migration. People in regions lying close to a common border with the destination country or with easier access to overseas markets (such as metropolitan centers or coastal areas) have a tendency to migrate (Long, Tucker, and Urton 1988; Malmberg 1997). These effects can be greatly magnified through the influence of migrant networks, once initiated from a specific location (Gunatilleke 1998; Shah 1998). Internal migration to areas of high departure can be quite important to the trickle-down benefits of international migration, and internal migration also can have an important poverty-reducing impact (box 3.1).

Migration of low-skilled workers is usually beneficial

Whether emigration results in reduced underemployment, increased labor-market participation, or higher wages, low-skilled workers in the home labor market gain, either directly or indirectly, from additional remittance spending. Emigration of low-skilled workers thus can act as a safety valve for the failure to create appropriate employment at home. There have been cases, however, usually in the context of South–South migration, where large outflows of temporary or irregular workers have resulted in massive return flows due to economic or political shocks in destination countries.[17] Also, reliance on large-scale emigration may retard efforts to address the issue of employment expansion over the long term, as a result of either the remittance-driven

Figure 3.4 Emigration rates for low-skilled workers

% of low-skilled workers in home region

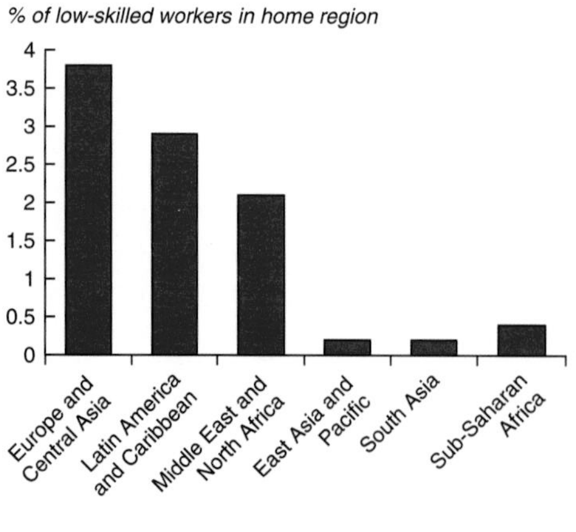

Source: Docquier and Marfouk 2004.

Box 3.1   Internal versus international migration

Although internal migration is much larger than international migration, they are in some respects similar phenomena. Both are largely driven by economic disparities among regions, although conflict and natural disasters (not discussed here) can also catalyze large movements of people. Both internal and international migration can be permanent or temporary, voluntary or forced. Both can subject migrants to substantial risks. Both can result in improved labor conditions in the regions of origin. Internal migration in Bangladesh, for example, makes more rural land available for tenancy (Afsar 2003). While the risks are often higher with international migration (particularly for irregular migrants), internal migration can also be plagued by trafficking of persons, particularly of women and children, as evident in parts of Sub-Saharan Africa (Black 2004) and in India and China (Lee 2005).

Internal and international migration also have their differences. Wage differentials are often lower within countries than between countries, reflecting smaller differences in economic conditions within countries than between countries.

Internal migration may have a larger role in reducing poverty than does international migration. While the expected wage gain is lower in internal migration, poor workers may have a better chance of finding work domestically than in economies with higher wages, where workers' lack of skills and language ability restrict job opportunities. Moreover, international migration tends to be more costly, so the poorest workers may not be able to afford it. While data are sparse, household surveys in a few countries indicate the important impact that internal migration has on poverty. In Sierra Leone, internal remittances helped reduce income inequality in poor areas in the 1980s (Black and others 2004). In the Asia Pacific region, international remittances accrue disproportionately to richer regions, while domestic transfers are directed mostly to poorer regions (UN-

ESCAP 2003). In Ghana, internal remittances are estimated to reduce the level of poverty by 14 percent, compared with only 5 percent for international remittances (Adams 2005).

Internal migration can have large costs on receiving areas. The proliferation of HIV/AIDs in Ghana has been linked to the movement of women from rural to urban areas, where unemployment and poverty often force them into the unprotected sex trade (Black 2004b). In some countries, internal migration to the cities has been so massive as to increase crowding and place inordinate burdens on public services, which lowers the quality of urban life.[a]

Internal migration often responds to substantial emigration abroad. In the Philippines, there are indications of large movements from rural areas of the Philippines into the Manila region from which most overseas workers are drawn, although this movement appears to have done little to help sustain wages in rural areas (Saith 1997). Bangladesh has seen rapid responses of intra-village migration to replace departing workers (Mahmud 1989). At the same time, as internal migrants gain skills, resources, information, and network contacts, they often emigrate internationally. For example, workers displaced by falling agricultural prices in southern Mexico often moved to northern towns to work in *maquiladoras,* later moving to the United States.

The links between internal and international migration are inadequately understood, in part because basic data are lacking. To gather more data, it has been recommended that a migration module in demographic and health surveys, censuses, household income and expenditure surveys, and labor force surveys be included (Afsar 2005).

---

[a]In China, for example, rapid urbanization has been accompanied by the emergence of urban enclaves of landless, unemployed migrants from rural areas (Pan 2004).

exchange-rate appreciation or the reduced pressure for policy reform. In general, however, the opportunity to send low-skilled workers abroad provides substantial benefits to origin countries because of the impact on labor markets and remittances.

Low-skilled migration has contributed to poverty alleviation

The reduced supply of low-skilled workers may help to alleviate poverty, if as a result of emigration, poor people receive higher wages or find new opportunities to work or receive remittances (see chapter 5). Low-skilled emigration also alleviates poverty to the extent that the people emigrating are poor.[18] It is unlikely, however, that a large proportion of migrants to industrial countries are poor according to the World Bank's definition of poverty as living on less than $2 a day—although certainly a very large share is poor compared to even the poorest in high-income countries. Most migrants from Mexico to the United States come from households located at the middle and upper-middle levels of the income distribution (Rivera 2005). Individuals with very low incomes are unlikely to be able to obtain the financial resources necessary for migration (see, for example, Mahmud 1989 for Bangladesh). Most of the world's poor people live in countries that are far away from industrial countries (Bangladesh, Brazil, China, India, Indonesia, and most of the countries of Sub-Saharan Africa), so transportation is expensive. Moreover, many poor people lack the rudimentary skills required to obtain a job in industrial countries, as well as the social networks that would facilitate migration and provide assistance once in the destination country.

Nevertheless, the limited data indicate that the very poor do move abroad to some extent. In Sri Lanka, returns from household surveys show that the share of households with a family member abroad is approximately equal across income groups.[19] Adams (2004) provides model-based estimates implying that about 5 percent of Guatemalan households with incomes of less than $2 a day received

remittances from abroad (used here as a proxy for having a household member who emigrated). Adams (2005) shows that less than 8 percent of Ghanaian households that received international remittances had estimated incomes (excluding remittances) that fell within the first to fourth deciles of households by per capita expenditures; 55 percent had expenditures in the top three deciles. Lucas (2004a) quotes studies of Kerala (India), Pakistan, the Philippines, and Thailand to support a conclusion that most emigrants were not from the lowest income levels, although the poorest did participate to some extent.

High-skilled emigration

There is a sharp increase in high-skilled migration

The emigration of high-skilled workers from developing countries has increased since the 1970s.[20] By 1990, the stock of high-skilled South–North migrants *in the United States alone* was more than eight times the total number of high-skilled migrants from developing to industrial countries over the 1961–72 period, not counting foreign students (Docquier and Rapoport 2004). The number of highly educated emigrants from developing countries residing in OECD countries doubled from 1990 to 2000, compared to an approximate 50 percent rise in the number of developing-country emigrants with only a primary education (Docquier and Marfouk 2004).

Rates of high-skill emigration vary enormously among developing countries, from less than 1 percent (Turkmenistan) to almost 90 percent (Suriname) and by region, from 15 percent for Sub-Saharan Africa to 5 percent for Europe and Central Asia (figure 3.5). It is important to keep in mind this degree of diversity, as high-skill emigration can have very different effects, depending on the size and economic conditions in origin countries.

The increase in high-skilled migration is partly due to the growing importance of selective immigration policies first introduced

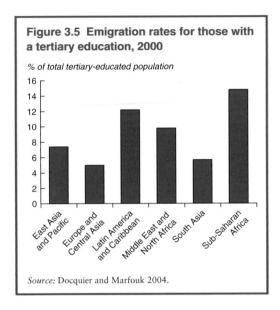

Figure 3.5 Emigration rates for those with a tertiary education, 2000

% of total tertiary-educated population

Source: Docquier and Marfouk 2004.

in Australia and Canada in the 1980s and later in other OECD countries.[21] Major recruiting countries have increased their intake of skilled migrants and relaxed their criteria relating to labor-market testing and job offers. Some countries (for example, Germany, Norway, and the United Kingdom) have introduced new programs; others (such as Austria, Republic of Korea, the Netherlands, and Sweden) offer fiscal incentives to attract talent to specific sectors (OECD 2005). These programs, and the migrants themselves, are responding to rising skill premiums in industrial countries that have tightened global competition for skilled workers.

In some instances, high-skilled emigration has a negative impact on living standards of those left behind and on growth

There are several reasons that migration of high-skilled workers may decrease living standards and growth. First, the total return to education may be greater than the private return, because highly educated workers may be more productive when interacting with similar workers, and they may help train other workers. One statistical measure of the beneficial impact of high-skilled immigrants is that in the United States, both international

graduate students and skilled immigrants were found to be positively correlated with patent applications (Chellaraj, Maskus, and Mattoo 2005). Highly educated citizens may also make contributions to public goods—for example, in improving governance and strengthening the administrative capacity of the state—which may be lost through high-skilled emigration (McMahon 1999).

Second, the productivity of firms may increase with size. If large firms require networks of professionals with specialized skills, then overall productivity will be higher with many professionals. For example, the value of telephone networks increases with the number of people connected. Expanding networks efficiently may require highly technical skills.

Third, emigration of high-skilled workers may impose a fiscal cost. In most developing countries education is heavily subsidized by the state, so that the permanent emigration of educated workers represents a loss of fiscal revenues.[22]

Finally, emigration of high-skilled workers will increase the price of services that require technical skills. It is difficult to provide comparable levels of service with low-skilled workers, and greater resources devoted to training may be lost through further emigration.

But high-skilled migration is often beneficial for origin countries

The costs of high-skilled emigration should be evaluated against the beneficial effects of migration, skilled and unskilled: increased remittances, higher wages (for migrants and workers who stay home), and benefits to destination countries (see chapter 2). Moreover, high-skilled emigration will have a limited impact if it is difficult for high-skilled workers to find productive employment in the country of origin. This may be the case for three reasons. First, the investment climate may be so poor, because of political instability or other reasons, that many high-skilled workers cannot pursue their professions. Even under such conditions, however, high-skilled emigration may be harmful if it deprives the government of competent administrators and limits the prospects for growth once the investment climate improves. Second, a significant proportion of high-skilled workers may not be trained in professions required by the economy, perhaps because of government subsidy policies. And third, some of the smallest developing countries lack the economic scale to productively employ a large number of specialized professionals.[23] These issues serve to underscore concerns over the appropriateness of state subsidization of university education in many countries.[24]

Some recent articles have claimed that high-skilled emigration, even of productively employed workers, may benefit development. The opportunity to emigrate increases the returns to education, leading more individuals to invest in education with a view to emigrating. However, only some of the educated people will actually emigrate. If the increase in human capital of those unable to emigrate exceeds the loss from those who do emigrate, then society's human capital rises following the opening of emigration opportunities (a phenomenon known as the "brain gain").[25] The effect will be largest in countries with large stocks of emigrants (so that the probability of emigration is high). These models have been questioned, however, because they assume that foreign firms are not able to discriminate among educated workers (otherwise they would take the best qualified, and so destroy incentives for education by marginal candidates), and because these models do not apply where family reunification programs, unrelated to the skills, predominate (Schiff 2005).

Findings on the impact of high-skilled emigration are mixed

It is difficult to generalize about the impact of skilled migration. The dispute over gains and losses has remained largely conjectural and has not been settled by the available empirical studies. On balance, it is not possible at present to provide an aggregate, reliable estimate of the true impact of high-skilled emigration. Some partial conclusions follow.

Table 3.2 Emigration rates of skilled workers, 2000
Percentage of workers with tertiary education living abroad

	Less than 10%	10% to 20%	20% to 30%	More than 30%
Number of countries	62	33	16	28
Share of developing country population (%)	75	19	3	3

Source: Docquier and Marfouk 2004.

The available data indicate that high rates of high-skill emigration affect only a small share of developing countries' population. A data set developed by Docquier and Marfouk (2004) indicates that the 77 countries with high-skilled emigration rates (to industrial countries) in excess of 10 percent account for only one-quarter of developing-country population (table 3.2).[26] Moreover, about half of these people live in countries with very poor investment climates (included in the bottom 25 percent of developing countries, as measured by the United Nations' Human Development Index), which may indicate that many high-skilled workers face limited opportunities to practice their professions. It is important to note that these data do not distinguish by profession (even though high emigration rates for literature professors and physicians would have different economic impacts) or by quality (the emigration of a Nobel laureate physicist would represent a greater loss than the emigration of an average university graduate).

Some countries encourage skilled migration. China, Cuba, India, the Philippines, Sri Lanka, and Vietnam all have programs to facilitate training for migration, suggesting that some policymakers see the benefits of skilled migration—among them remittances, relieving job market pressures, development of an extensive diaspora, and expectations that many migrants will eventually return with improved skills (as discussed below).

Direct, cross-country tests of the relationship between high-skilled emigration and growth have been mixed. The preponderance of evidence supports the view that education makes an important contribution to growth.[27] Beine, Docquier, and Rapoport (2001) detected a positive and significant impact on human capital formation from the opportunity for emigration, whereas Faini (2003) found that a higher probability of migration for workers with secondary education had no visible impact on secondary educational achievement in the home country.

High-skilled emigration has had enormous impact on some sectors, especially health

The sectoral distribution of high-skilled emigrants is important for assessing the implications for countries of origin. Meyer and Brown (1999) estimate that about 12 percent of developing-country nationals trained in science and technology live in the United States. If accurate, these estimates suggest that high-skilled emigration may be much more serious for production than shown by the data from Docquier and Marfouk (2004) given above, where total high-skilled emigration to industrial countries was estimated at about 8 percent of the stock of high-skilled developing-country nationals.

High-skilled emigration may have a particularly severe impact on the health sector, and the emigration of doctors and nurses may reduce the likelihood of some countries meeting the Millennium Development Goals for reducing child mortality, improving maternal health, and combating HIV/AIDS and tuberculosis. Chanda (2001) estimates that at least 12 percent of the doctors trained in India live in the United Kingdom, that Ethiopia lost half of its pathology graduates from 1984 to 1996, that Pakistan loses half of its medical school graduates every year; and that in Ghana only about one-third of medical school graduates remain in the country. Perhaps one-half of the graduates of South African medical schools emigrate to high-income countries (Pang, Lansang, and Haines 2002), and Jamaica had to train five doctors, and Grenada 22, to keep just one (Stalker 1994).[28] Of course, the incentive for migration is often conditioned not only by the opportunity for higher earnings abroad, but also by poor working conditions and public sector services in origin countries.

Origin countries face considerable difficulties in limiting high-skilled emigration

Even if high-skilled emigration were found to be detrimental to living standards and growth, countries of origin would face serious obstacles in reducing it. Some countries have required that graduates of publicly funded education work for a period of time in public sector jobs. But such requirements can be evaded, and their existence is likely to discourage return of migrants to the country of origin. Several proposals have been made for international schemes to tax high-skilled emigrants, with the funds earmarked for developing countries. Such schemes have made no progress, as they would be hard to enforce. Calculating the welfare loss from high-skilled emigration and thus setting an appropriate level of tax would be difficult. Moreover, the schemes would require the cooperation of migrants and countries of destination—something not likely to be achieved. Bhaghwati (1976) advocates that developing countries should subject their nationals working abroad to local taxes, as does the United States. However, many developing countries would find such a system of taxation difficult to administer.

Some governments encourage skilled workers to stay by improving working conditions, providing research facilities, and giving incentives for research (see the discussion of incentives for return, below). China has reported a nine-fold increase from 1995 to 2003 in foreign programs offered in cooperation with local institutions, which has resulted in lower numbers of students going abroad (Vincent-Lancrin 2004). Such programs may require substantial resources, and poorer countries will face difficulties in creating the conditions required to retain their most-skilled workers. In some cases improvements in governance, which may require political determination rather than large expenditures, may help to retain workers.

Cooperation from destination countries may help

Effective means of limiting high-skilled emigration, or increasing its benefits, will require the cooperation of countries of destination. One example has been the United Kingdom's code of practice for the international recruitment of health-care workers, which restricts the active solicitation of health care professionals from developing countries. However, implementation has been difficult because the code does not apply to private sector recruiters (House of Commons 2004). A recent proposal to require countries of destination to provide Caribbean countries with subsidies for training health professionals could increase the supply of health workers in both origin and destination countries (Commonwealth Secretariat 2005).[29] More broadly, contributions by destination countries to education in origin countries could both compensate origin-country governments for their training of emigrants and improve the qualifications of workers coming to destination countries. Another approach, which would improve the coherence of development policies, would be for destination countries to increase their investment in sectors in which they lack skills, rather than "raiding" those skills from poor countries.

Diasporas

A large diaspora can expand market access for origin countries

A potent benefit of high-skilled emigration is the creation of a large, well-educated diaspora, which improves access to capital, information, and contacts for firms in countries of origin. Immigrants play a role in facilitating trade by providing information and helping to enforce contracts (Rauch and Trindade 1999) and by acting as intermediaries that can match buyers with reliable local suppliers (Yusuf 2001). Johnson and Sedaca (2004) emphasize that diasporas can act as "first movers" who catalyze growth opportunities and make connections between markets that otherwise would not exist. Barré and others (2003) cite the importance of diasporas in generating possibilities for codevelopment between firms in the countries of origin and destination, and expanding technical cooperation. With the growth of outsourcing of manufacturing components and telecommunications and other services, diaspora networks may be of increasing importance. However, despite the broad agreement on the importance of diasporas and the many anecdotal comments on how they have assisted development, it is difficult to quantify these benefits.

The diaspora can be a significant source of foreign-exchange earnings (beyond remittances) for countries with sizeable emigration. Orozco (2003) documents diaspora-related increases in exports and tourism receipts for Central America. Gould (1994) and Head and Ries (1998) found that increased emigration to the United States and Canada raised exports from countries of origin.

There is some evidence that the diaspora plays an important role in the transfer of knowledge between destination and origin countries. Agrawal, Cockburn, and McHale (2003) find that patent applications are likely to be filed in both the country of residence and the country of origin. Meyer and Brown (1999) and Brown (2000) identify Internet-based expatriate networks of skilled professionals and students that facilitate the transfer of knowledge. However, the effectiveness of these networks is open to question: less than half of the 61 Internet-based networks examined in 2004 were updated regularly, and only 56 percent were updated within the past year.[30] Origin-country governments can help maintain ties to the diaspora by supporting professional networks, promoting dialogue with government, and funding educational, linguistic, and cultural programs.

The return of expatriates can benefit development

The return of expatriates to their home country is widely perceived as benefitting development (Ellerman 2003). Expatriates may be more effective than foreigners in transferring knowledge back home because of their understanding of local culture. However, returnees may also represent retirees, or the less-skilled of the skilled cohort of emigrants (Borjas and Bratsberg 1994; Lowell and Findlay 2001), or may have difficulties in readapting to the home country (Faini 2003), or their skills may have deteriorated while abroad (Ghosh 1996). Returnees may be those disappointed by the wages or working conditions or may have more difficulty in finding or retaining jobs.[31]

A range of programs have been established to encourage return of highly educated nationals living abroad, with mixed results. Among developing-country governments, for example, China, the Philippines, Taiwan (China), Thailand, and Tunisia have offered a wide range of incentives, including research funding, access to foreign exchange, expanded real estate investment options, and study opportunities.[32]

The domestic policy environment is critical to productive return. Cervantes and Guellec (2002) cite the favorable impact of returning expatriates in the Republic of Korea, attracted by strong research and development (R&D) environments and infrastructure investments. Industrial parks helped to lure entrepreneurs back to China. In Taiwan (China), the Hsinchu Industrial Park attracted more than 5,000 returning scientists in 2000 alone (Saxenian 2002). Conversely, a poor investment climate will inhibit return. In Armenia, barriers to foreign direct investment (FDI) and inadequate enforcement of contracts have prevented a more active involvement of the Armenian diaspora in local development (Gevorkyan and Grigorian 2003). Saxenian (2000) cites the reluctance of Indian entrepreneurs to return because of government regulations that increase the administrative cost of operating a business—although the Indian diaspora has contributed to the development of information technology in Bangalore.[33]

Both origin and destination countries can help facilitate return, on both a temporary and permanent basis, through changes in regulaion. Both can allow dual citizenship, an increasingly common practice (Aleinikoff and Klusmeyer 2002). Origin countries can eliminate rules that prevent emigrants from owning or investing in property back home. Permanent residents can be protected from losing their status if they leave for a relatively limited period of time, as this discourages productive temporary returns to the origin country. Destination countries can also allow returning migrants to benefit from the rights they acquire during their work abroad, such as pensions, health insurance, and disability programs (Holzmann, Koettl, and Chernetsky 2005).[34] Such arrangements, however, require effective institutions in the origin country to provide such services and are best achieved through negotiations between origin and destination countries.

Destination countries have provided various incentives for the return of migrants. For example, France has provided loans and technical assistance to migrants from Mali and Senegal to establish businesses in their home countries. However, few of the businesses appear to have been successful, either because of the inadequate investment climate in the recipient communities (Gubert 2005) or because participants had worked in low-level jobs in France and lacked entrepreneurial skills (Magoni 2004). Many of these programs are quite small.[35]

International organizations, too, have managed programs to promote return, although they tend to cover few emigrants. The IOM's Return of Qualified African Nationals program successfully attracted more than 2,000 highly skilled persons back to 41 African countries from 1974 to 1990, and the program was later expanded to the Migration for Development in Africa program (MIDA).[36] Similar programs have been run for Latin American countries, Afghanistan, and Bosnia and Herzegovina.[37] The United Nations Development Programme's TOKTEN project promotes temporary return (three-week to three-month development assignments), which is often easier to achieve.

Temporary migration and international agreements

The number of temporary workers admitted to high-income countries under skill-based programs rose substantially in the 1990s, doubling in the United Kingdom and almost quadrupling in the United States (figure 3.6). Foreign student programs are also proliferating, in part due to competitive marketing and entry policies by Australia, Canada, Germany, and the United Kingdom. Inflows of unskilled, seasonal workers also have increased since the early 1990s in most high-income countries that have such programs (UN 2004). Greater emphasis on temporary migration may reflect opposition to expanding permanent migration.

Temporary labor migration schemes vary greatly from country to country. Skilled migrants tend to have more opportunities under unilateral visa programs (such as the U.S. H-1B visa and the temporary skilled migration programs of Australia and Canada), while unskilled migrants often must rely on bilateral or regional agreements, such as the seasonal work programs between Germany and countries in central and eastern Europe.

Temporary migration may facilitate greater migration flows

While temporary migration programs can generate benefits similar to those of permanent migration (such as higher incomes for migrants, improved efficiency in destination countries, remittances for origin countries), in some respects those benefits differ between permanent and temporary migration. For the legal migrant, being admitted on a temporary basis may be less desirable than permanent residence, which provides for free movement between destination and origin countries. However, the existence of temporary migration programs (reflecting resistance to permanent migration) may facilitate larger legal flows.

From the point of view of the destination country, temporary migration offers the flexibility to target required skills and to adjust entry in response to changes in labor demand. Temporary migration can reduce fiscal pressures that may be associated with low-skilled immigration, in that temporary migrants tend not to bring their dependents (who may require public services). At the same time, programs can be made conditional on employment, thereby limiting social tensions from immigration. Provisions for temporary migration also can be viewed as offering an alternative to irregular migration.

The record of destination governments in ensuring that temporary migration programs are indeed temporary has been mixed. For example, over 22 years, most workers in the Mexico–U.S. guest workers program returned at the end of their seasonal jobs, although some found ways to obtain permanent status (Martin 2003). Similarly, from 1960 to 1973, three-quarters of the 18.5 million foreigners who came to work in Germany left. But 25 percent remained. Coupled with rules that allowed many to eventually bring their dependents, this resulted in significant permanent settlement. There is some evidence that the recent guest worker programs in Europe, particularly those involving subcontracting for short-term projects and some return incentives, have managed higher return rates (Lucas 2004a).

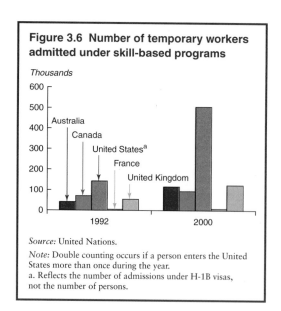

Figure 3.6 Number of temporary workers admitted under skill-based programs

Thousands

Australia
Canada
United States[a]
France
United Kingdom

Source: United Nations.

Note: Double counting occurs if a person enters the United States more than once during the year.
a. Reflects the number of admissions under H-1B visas, not the number of persons.

There are advantages and disadvantages to temporary migration

Reliance on repeated, temporary migration for workers also has some economic drawbacks. Hiring a temporary immigrant may mean a shorter duration of employment compared with hiring a permanent immigrant, and thus higher costs for training. Temporary migrants are also less likely than permanent ones to invest in skills specific to the destination country (such as language proficiency and licensing requirements), because the returns are enjoyed over a shorter period of time (Chiswick 2000). Nevertheless, for emigrants from developing countries, the wage differentials are so large that they may justify substantial investments in acquiring such skills, even for temporary stays.

For the origin country, remittances (and repatriation of assets) may be higher with temporary migration, because temporary migrants are less likely to bring their dependents and more likely to maintain close ties with the home country. Perhaps most importantly, temporary migration programs can provide an opening to increase legal, unskilled migration, which generates the greatest developmental impact for origin countries, as already noted. On the other hand, temporary migration may provide a less reliable means of exporting large labor surpluses, as cancellation of future access is easier for destination countries than expelling existing migrants. However, it is this flexibility (coupled with less long-run population pressure, fewer concerns over integration, and fewer pension commitments) that makes temporary migration desirable for destination countries, thus facilitating agreements for larger unskilled migration (Winters 2005).

Bilateral agreements can play an important role in low-skilled, temporary migration

Bilateral labor agreements have become a major vehicle for low-skilled, seasonal workers in agriculture, tourism, and construction, as evidenced by agreements between the United States and Mexico, Germany and central and eastern European states, and Saudi Arabia and Egypt and Libya. There are several hundred such agreements worldwide, including some 168 signed in the last 50 years in Latin America alone, half in the past 10 years (IOM 2005a).[38] Bilateral agreements could improve the benefits of temporary migration for origin countries through greater certainty of access and conditions. This may be particularly important in markets where increased competition from other suppliers might lead to a reduction in access (as occurred in Saudi Arabia and the Middle East in the 1990s). Bilateral agreements can help build the confidence in both origin and destination countries that a particular channel of migration will generate real benefits and minimize costs—for example, that migrants will be treated well and will return at the end of their contract.

Several factors impede the maximization of gains from bilateral agreements, however. Some origin countries may lack sufficiently reliable information on demand for their workers in destination countries, and in which sectors, to negotiate appropriate agreements. Destination countries may likewise have difficulty reliably estimating labor shortages in particular sectors. And origin countries may face resource constraints in implementing obligations with regard to prescreening of migrants or monitoring of their return, although these may be covered by the destination country (as in a nurses program between Romania and Italy). Origin countries may also lack bargaining power to conclude terms favorable to them or to conclude agreements at all. For example, of 18 bilateral agreements proposed by the Philippines with countries in Africa, Asia, Europe, and the Middle East, five countries refused to enter into agreements, and others have remained inactive (Go 2004).

Nevertheless, there is scattered evidence that countries like the Philippines have been able to use bilateral agreements to gain favorable employment conditions for their migrants—and in some cases to support their return and reintegration (Lucas 2004b).

Bilateral agreements can help ensure that origin-country credentials are accepted in destination countries, for example.[39] They can help ensure that temporary migration is indeed temporary, and that returning migrants are reintegrated, by supporting the transfer of technology and human resource development in the origin country, as under Spain's agreements with Colombia and Ecuador (IOM 2005a). Bilateral agreements can also ensure that the origin country cooperates in monitoring and managing migration, for example, by incorporating a readmission provision (as in the 1997 agreement between Italy and Albania).

They also can limit the effects of brain drain. For example, a pilot scheme between the Dutch and Polish ministries of health prepared Polish nurses for employment in the Dutch health care system for a maximum period of two years and to facilitate their subsequent return and reintegration into the Polish health care system.[40] Other proposals take a development-cooperation approach, under which destination countries fund the training (to their standards) of a given number of nurses in excess of origin country demand, with the surplus nurses granted temporary visas to work in destination countries for a specified period, with guaranteed return.

Except in the EU, regional and international agreements have had little impact on migration

At the regional level, there has been some progress on removing technical and administrative barriers to the cross-border exchange of skilled personnel for business purposes in Africa, Europe, Latin America, and parts of Asia. Also, several consultative processes on migration have emerged at the regional and global levels.[41] However, with the major exception of the EU, most regional arrangements have had little impact on the free movement of less-skilled foreign workers or on permanent migration (World Bank 2005).

International treaties have had only limited impact on migration. Mode 4 of the General Agreement on Trade in Services (GATS) has the potential to improve cooperation on labor services between countries of origin and destination, but so far it has not facilitated a significant rise in cross-border labor movements (box 3.2). The ILO has pioneered the development of international instruments for protecting the rights of migrant workers, and the UN General Assembly adopted the International Convention on the Protection of the Rights of All Migrant Workers and Members of Their Families, which clearly defines the rights of migrant workers, including irregular workers (Wickramasekera 2002). The convention entered into force in 2004. However, none of the major destination countries have ratified it yet, and its means of enforcement are limited.

International agreements governing migration contrast sharply with those for trade

A major impulse behind the General Agreement on Tariffs and Trade and its successor, the World Trade Organization, was that multilateral agreements that provide for nondiscrimination among countries would maximize the gains from trade. By contrast, there is little support for multilateral, nondiscriminatory approaches to migration, at least in destination countries. In part this is because the economic implications of nondiscrimination differ between trade and migration. In trade, nondiscrimination maximizes economic efficiency by allowing the lowest-cost supplier to compete, thus reducing prices and forcing high-cost producers to improve efficiency or exit the market. But labor markets in high-income countries are generally not permitted (through minimum-wage laws and social-insurance schemes) to adjust fully to the lowest-cost supplier. Thus the benefits of nondiscrimination are weaker in migration than in trade. U.S. consumers benefit if Indian shirts are cheaper than Mexican shirts, but U.S. employers benefit little if Indians are willing to work for less than Mexicans—the decline in wages is limited.

Box 3.2   Mode 4 and international migration

The WTO General Agreement on Trade in Services (GATS) does not cover labor migration per se, but rather the narrower concept of movement of people across borders as one of four modes of delivering services. Mode 4 covers the temporary movement of persons across borders for the purpose of supplying a service. "Temporary" movement is not defined, but permanent migration is explicitly excluded, as are workers in most nonservice sectors, such as agriculture or manufacturing.

Mode 4 service suppliers can be viewed in terms of both duration and purpose of stay: they enter a country for a specific purpose (to fulfill a service contract), for a limited and (generally) specified period of time, and are usually confined to one sector or one job (they do not enter the labor market and are not free to search for employment). Mode 4 is normally understood to include business visitors (persons who come for three months or less to negotiate a contract), intracorporate transferees (persons transferred within a company from one country to another), and suppliers of contractual services (individuals or employees of foreign companies with a contract to supply a service to a client in the receiving country). While Mode 4 includes persons at all skill levels, to date market-opening commitments by WTO members have been limited to the highly skilled.

Relatively few market-opening commitments on Mode 4 have been made by both developed and developing countries. Those that have been made tend to be subject to restrictions on number, type, and duration of stay of service suppliers. Countries' actual regimes for temporary entry of workers tend to be more liberal than their GATS commitments, however, and considerable movement on service issues is occurring in a range of sectors (such as health), notwithstanding the near-absence of relevant GATS commitments.

Five issues arise regarding GATS Mode 4 as an instrument to manage labor mobility. First, GATS commitments are fixed commitments of guaranteed treatment, while migration regimes seek to retain flexibility to make adjustments in line with labor-market conditions. Second, GATS commitments follow the most-favored-nation (MFN) principle—that is, treatment offered to one country must be extended to all WTO members—whereas migration regimes can offer special treatment to countries with which regulatory trust or other special relationships have been built (through visa waiver programs, for example). Third, GATS Mode 4 covers only a relatively limited subset of the workers moving around the globe. Agricultural workers, for example, are not generally viewed as falling under the GATS. Fourth, multilateral trade negotiations have a 50-year history, while migration has largely remained a national policy prerogative characterized by limited international dialogue. Finally, movement of people, especially the lower-skilled, raises a raft of issues related to social and cultural integration, exploitation, impact on local labor markets, and, more recently, security that trade agreements are ill-equipped to address.

Against this background, what role might the GATS play in managing labor mobility? The GATS is a narrow, but sharp, instrument that can deliver a powerful guarantee of access, but only for certain types of workers. Beyond this, however, GATS negotiations can be used to create a sense of urgency that may serve to bring migration authorities to the table to discuss ways to manage mobility. Bilateral or regional approaches could, for example, include low-skilled workers and develop creative, cooperative approaches to issues such as remittance transfer, brain drain, and loss of investment in education, prescreening of temporary workers, and return. These agreements could assist in building regulatory trust and improving management schemes in receiving and sending countries. Over time, by creating a template of basic requirements or criteria that could be applied to all countries on a nondiscriminatory basis, they could be used to extend access to a wider group of countries and so approach the MFN principle of GATS.

But the largest reason that nondiscriminatory approaches are limited is that people are not goods: migration has much broader implications for society than does trade. Destination countries tend to be concerned that immigrants from countries with very different cultures will not integrate easily into society, and high-income countries tend to limit low-income migrants for fear of overburdening public services (see chapter 2). Thus even those countries that have immigration regimes that do not discriminate by country tend to discriminate by level of skill.

A final important distinction between trade and migration is that trade is subject to relatively effective regulation, while many countries of destination face considerable difficulties (and internal disagreements) in regulating immigration. The lack of effective regulation and incomplete efforts to control immigration encourages many low-skilled migrants to run substantial risks that can lead to conditions akin to slavery, great physical danger, and even death. On the other hand, the same lack of control works to the advantage of migrants by offering opportunities that might not otherwise exist and by benefiting groups within destination countries. The evidence in this chapter suggests that cooperation between origin and destination countries, through agreements that provide for temporary, low-skilled migration, and through enforcement of laws protecting migrants from exploitation and abuse, can improve the impact of migration for countries and for migrants.

Notes

1. Of course, migration may arise out of a combination of economic, political, and social goals. Also, migration among developing countries is an increasingly important phenomenon, but given data limitations we focus here on migration from developing to industrial countries.

2. Empirical work largely confirms the view that income differentials are important determinants of migration. Borjas (1987), Karemera, Oguledo, and Davis (2000), and Hatton and Williamson (2002) found that migration to the United States was negatively related to source-country income per capita,

among other variables. Solimano (2002) found that real per capita income differentials between Argentina and source countries were the main determinant of net migration flows in the twentieth century.

3. See also chapter 2, which points out that migrants' earnings (per worker) increase eleven-fold, before adjusting for differences in purchasing power in high-income versus developing countries.

4. The basic idea is that the opportunity to earn money based on developed country prices but spend it (through remittances) based on developing country prices is a major benefit from migration. The same adjustment from the perspective of the migrant is discussed in the modeling exercise in chapter 2.

5. See the discussion of remittances and smoothing of household consumption in chapter 5.

6. By the late 1990s, public employment services already played an insignificant role in the recruitment of foreign workers, except where migration was covered by bilateral labor agreements (ILO 1997). For example, nine out of ten workers sent from Asia have used private recruiters (Abella 1997); and for Romania, most jobs in countries with which the government has not secured bilateral agreements are found by private intermediaries (Diminescu 2004).

7. Hugo (2004) describes how work contractors are the primary source of information for potential migrants from Indonesia, and relates this to the high levels of exploitation of Indonesian contract workers compared with workers from other countries.

8. Support services provided through Philippine labor attachés have provided critical legal counseling and protection (Moreno-Fontes Chammartin 2005).

9. The funds operated by the Philippines, Pakistan and Sri Lanka provide scholarships, legal aid in destination countries, insurance against death and disability, and loans for predeparture costs, housing, and self-employment. The administration and delivery can often be difficult, particularly on insurance (Tan 2004), and some emigrants may resent the mandatory nature of the schemes (Abella 1997).

10. Also regarding Mexico, Mora and Taylor (2005) find that the presence of a family member in the United States increases by 7 percent the probability that an individual will migrate, while McKenzie (2005) shows that larger migration networks increase the probability of other community members migrating.

11. An irregular migrant in this context is defined as any person entering, residing, and working in a country without proper documentation of their legal status in that country, or any person who has committed a crime or breach of immigration law in that country and therefore is not entitled to remain in that country.

12. However, Cornelius (2001) notes that the share of irregular migrants who settle permanently in the

United States has increased—a trend accelerated by tighter border enforcement adopted in the mid-1990s.

13. Protocol to Prevent, Suppress and Punish Trafficking in Persons, Especially Women and Children; and Protocol against the Smuggling of Migrants by Land, Sea and Air, 2000. These supplement the Convention against Transnational Crime, 2000.

14. Dedicated government offices such as the Philippines Overseas Workers Administration, unions such as the seamen's union in the Philippines, and nongovernmental organizations (NGOs) can help families and communities make adjustments when family members migrate.

15. These data are described in Docquier and Marfouk (2004), which relies on census data (plus extensive estimations), and thus undercounts irregular migrants, who are mostly low skilled. The data are taken largely from industrial countries, so that low-skilled migration to other developing countries, as well as high-income countries in the Middle East and Asia, is not reflected (which, for example, reduces the ratio of low-skilled emigrants from South Asia).

16. Similarly, mine labor recruiting in South Africa increased wages in the plantation sectors in both Malawi and Mozambique, which ultimately resulted in the curtailed permission to recruit in Malawi in the early 1970s (Lucas 1987).

17. For example, the compulsory repatriation of workers to Kerala following the Gulf conflict in 1990–91 threw Kerala into a fairly sharp recession (Lucas 2004b).

18. This is not invariably true, for example, if the departure of one household member leaves his or her dependents impoverished. In general, family income is likely to rise with emigration, but cases of real hardship caused by emigration do exist.

19. This calculation is based on income that includes remittances from the emigrant, so the number of Sri Lankan households with a family member abroad that were poor *prior to migration* is probably larger.

20. Much of the data on high-skilled migration refers to individuals who have some tertiary education, although other kinds of qualifications (electrician, plumber, ability to handle sophisticated machinery) are of economic interest.

21. See Lowell (2001) for a list of programs to attract high-skilled workers.

22. For example, forgone income tax revenues associated with Indian-born residents of the United States may be equal to one-third of current individual income tax receipts in India (Desai, Kapur, and McHale 2001), although this is a very low share of total government revenues.

23. Such countries benefit highly from remittances. Remittances to countries with populations of less than 1.5 million totaled about 6 percent of gross national income, compared with an average of 1.7 percent for all developing countries.

24. Available data do not distinguish émigrés educated at home from those educated abroad, an issue of growing importance as education is increasingly marketed to the developing world by high-income countries.

25. This theory is developed in Mountford (1997), Chau and Stark (1999), Stark (2003), and Drinkwater and others (2002).

26. These data do not include high-skilled emigrants to other developing countries, which may be an important issue for many developing countries.

27. Microeconomic evidence tends to find that education is associated with higher earnings (Mincer 1991). After some considerable debate, recent articles find that years of schooling have a positive impact on productivity growth (de la Fuente and Domenech 2002), and that the quality of education (as measured, for example, by pupil-student ratios or the dropout rate) may matter more than the quantity (Barro and Lee 2000).

28. Clemens (2005) presents an alternative view, arguing that health systems in Africa are not greatly weakened by emigration because the option to emigrate encourages entry into the medical field.

29. Institutions exist in countries of origin that train workers for external labor markets, for example some nursing schools in the Philippines and a medical school in Budapest that teaches in German. However, these schools do not receive funds from potential countries of destination (World Bank 2004).

30. Data are based on a survey carried out for a background paper, available on request.

31. Workers who stayed in Albania had higher-quality skills than returnees (De Coulon and Piracha 2002), and returnees from Sweden were found to be less successful economically than emigrants who stayed (Edin, LaLonde, and Åslund 2000). See also Hugo (2002) on re-emigration from Australia and Constant and Massey (2003) on Germany.

32. See Pang, Lansing, and Haines 2002 on Thailand, Lucas (2004a) on China, and the IOM office in Tunis on Tunisia.

33. The High-Level Committee on the Indian Diaspora (2001) notes the role of expatriates in attracting R&D investments from Intel, Oracle, Texas Instruments, Sun Microsystems, and IBM.

34. Recognizing benefits earned abroad may reduce costs to the destination-country government, as many such services are likely to be less expensive in developing countries. The cost implications have some uncertainty, as some migrants will choose to return even without portability of benefits.

35. For example, a program between Germany and Eritrea disbursed only 65 loans from 1993 to 1997, while a project in Italy's Veneto region trained only 30 Albanian immigrants in setting up companies or launching joint ventures with local companies in their country of origin.

36. The Return of Qualified Africans program was evaluated by the European Commission as contributing to development at micro levels (IOM 2005b).

37. The Return for Qualified Afghans has been criticized for offering low compensation packages and involving few individuals despite being expensive to run (Jazayery 2002).

38. Australia, Argentina, Canada, and the United States entered into bilateral labor agreements with countries of origin in the mid-twentieth century. The *bracero* program admitted some five million Mexican farm workers to the United States between 1942 and 1966. In Europe, Germany and France recruited guest workers from southern Europe, Turkey, and North Africa after the Second World War until the economic downturn of the 1970s.

39. An example is the agreement that provides for the acceptance of Vietnamese information technology credentials in Japan (Vietnam Trade 2005).

40. The pilot ended in January 2005, and the outcomes are being evaluated by the Dutch government.

41. Regional examples include the Regional Conference on Migration (Puebla Process) and Lima Process in the Americas; MIDSA and MIDWA in Africa; and the Manila, APC, and Bali Processes in Asia. Inter-regional processes include the "5 plus 5" (a migration dialogue established in 2002 between southern Europe—France, Italy, Malta, Portugal, Spain—and the Maghreb group—Algeria, Libya, Mauritania, Morocco, and Tunisia. Global consultation forums include the UN Global Commission on International Migration, the Berne Initiative, IOM's International Dialogue on Migration, and ILO's International Labor Conference.

References

Abella, M. 1997. *Sending Workers Abroad: A Manual for Low- and Middle-Income Countries.* Geneva: International Labour Office.

———. 2004. "The Role of Recruiters in Labor Migration." In *International Migration: Prospects and Policies in a Global Market*, ed. Douglas S. Massey and J. Edward Taylor. Oxford: Oxford University Press.

Adams, Richard. 2004. "Remittances and Poverty in Guatemala." Policy Research Working Paper 3418. World Bank, Washington, DC.

———. 2005. "Remittances and Poverty in Ghana." Mimeograph. World Bank, Washington, DC.

Adams, Richard, and John Page. 2003. "International Migration, Remittances, and Poverty in Developing Countries." Policy Research Working Paper 3179. World Bank, Washington, DC.

Afsar, Rita. 2003. "Internal Migration and the Development Nexus: The Case of Bangladesh." Bangladesh Institute of Development Studies, Dhaka.

———. 2005. "Internal Migration and Pro-Poor Policy." In *Migration, Development, and Poverty Reduction in Asia*, ed. Gervais Appave and Frank Laczko. Geneva: International Organization for Migration.

Agrawal, Ajay, Iain Cockburn, and John McHale. 2003. "Gone But Not Forgotten: Labor Flows, Knowledge Spillovers, and Enduring Social Capital." Working Paper 9950. National Bureau of Economic Research, Cambridge, MA.

Aleinikoff, T. A., and Klusmeyer, D. 2002. *Citizenship Policies for an Age of Migration.* Washington, DC: Carnegie Endowment for International Peace.

Barré, Rémi, Valéria Hernandez, Jean-Baptiste Meyer, and Dominique Vinck. 2003. *Diasporas scientifiques: Comment les pays en développement peuvent-ils tirer parti de leurs chercheurs et de leurs ingénieurs?* (Scientific diasporas: how can developing countries benefit from their expatriate scientists and engineers?) Paris: IRD Editions.

Barro, R., and J. W. Lee. 2000. "International Data on Educational Attainments—Updates and Implications." Working Paper 7911. National Bureau of Economic Research, Cambridge, MA.

Bartel, A. P. 1989. "Where Do the New U.S. Immigrants Live?" *Journal of Labor Economics* 7(4): 371–91.

Battistella, Graziano, and Ma. Cecilia G. Conaco. 1996. "Impact of Migration on the Children Left Behind." *Asian Migrant* 9(3): 86–91.

Beine, Michel, Frederic Docquier, and Hillel Rapoport. 2001. "Brain Drain and Economic Growth: Theory and Evidence." *Journal of Development Economics* 64: 275–89.

Bhagwati, Jagdish. 1976. "The Brain Drain." *International Social Science Journal* 28: 691–729.

Black, R., 2004. "Migration and Pro-Poor Policy in Africa." Working Paper C6. Sussex Centre for Migration Research, University of Sussex.

Black, Richard, Savinna Ammassari, Shannon Mouillesseaux, and Radha Rajkotia. 2004. "Migration and Pro Poor Policy in West Africa." Working Paper C8. Sussex Centre for Migration Research, University of Sussex.

Borjas, George. J. 1987. "Self-Selection and Earnings of Immigrants." *American Economic Review* 77(4): 531–53.

Borjas, George J., and Bernt Bratsberg. 1994. "Who Leaves? The Outmigration of the Foreign Born." National Bureau of Economic Research Working Paper 4913. Cambridge, MA.

Brown, Mercy. 2000. "Using the Intellectual Diaspora to Reverse the Brain Drain: Some Useful Examples." Paper presented at the Regional Conference on Brain Drain and Capacity Building in Africa. Addis Ababa, February 22–24.

Bryant, John. 2005. "Children of International Migrants in Indonesia, Thailand, and the Philippines: A Review of Evidence and Policies." Working Paper 2005-05. UNICEF Innocenti Research Center, Florence.

Carter, Thomas J. 1999. "Illegal Immigration in an Efficiency Wage Model." *Journal of International Economics* 49: 385–401.

Cervantes, M., and D. Guellec. 2002. "The Brain Drain: Old Myths, New Realities." *Observer*, May 7. www.oecdobsever.org/.

Chanda, Rupa. 2001. "Trade in Health Services." Paper prepared for the Working Group on Health and International Economy of the Commission on Macroeconomics and Health, World Health Organization, Geneva.

Chau, Nancy H., and Oded Stark. 1999. "Migration under Asymmetric Information and Human Capital Formation." *Review of International Economics* 7(3): 455–83.

Chellaraj, Gnanaraj, Keith Maskus, and Aaditya Mattoo. 2005. "The Contribution of Skilled Immigration and International Graduate Students to U.S. Innovation." In *International Migration, Remittances, and Development,* ed. Caglar Ozden and Maurice Schiff. Washington, DC: World Bank.

Chiswick, Barry R. 1988. "Illegal Immigration and Immigration Control." *Journal of Economic Perspectives* 2(3): 101–15.

———. 2000. "The Economics of Illegal Migration for the Host Economy." Paper presented at the National Association for Business Economics Annual Meeting. September.

Clemens, Michael. 2005. "Do No Harm—Is the Emigration of Health Professionals Bad for Africa?" Prepared for the G-20 Workshop on Demographic Challenges and Migration. Sydney, Australia, August.

Commonwealth Secretariat. 2005. "A Managed Migration Program for Teachers and Nurses." London.

Constant, Amelie, and Douglas S. Massey. 2003. "Self-Selection, Earnings, and Out-Migration: A Longitudinal Study of Immigrants to Germany." *Population Economics* 16: 631–53. November.

Cornelius, Wayne A. 2001. "Death at the Border: The Efficacy and 'Unintended' Consequences of U.S. Immigration Control Policy, 1993–2000." Working Paper 27, Center for Comparative Immigration Studies, University of California–San Diego.

Daveri, Francesco, and Riccardo Faini. 1999. "Where Do Migrants Go?" *Oxford Economic Papers* 51: 595–622. oep.oxfordjournals.org/cgi/content/abstract/51/4/595.

De Coulon, Augustin, and Matloob Piracha. 2002. "Self-Selection and the Performance of Return Migrants: The Case of Albania." Discussion Paper 0211. Department of Economics, University of Kent, Canterbury.

De la Fuente, A., and R. Domenech. 2002. "Human Capital in Growth Regressions: How Much Difference Does Data Quality Make? An Update and Further Results." Unpublished paper. Universidad Autonoma, Barcelona.

Desai, Mihir A., Devesh Kapur, and John McHale. 2001. "The Fiscal Impact of the Brain Drain: Indian Emigration to the U.S." Prepared for the Third Annual NBER-NCAER conference, December 17–18. Harvard University and National Bureau for Economic Research, Cambridge, MA.

Diminescu, Dana. 2004. "Assessment and Evaluation of Bilateral Labour Agreements Signed by Romania." In *Migration for Employment: Bilateral Agreements at a Crossroads*. Paris: Organisation for Economic Co-operation and Development.

Docquier, Frederic, and Abdeslam Marfouk. 2004. "Measuring the International Mobility of Skilled Workers (1990–2000)." Policy Research Working Paper 3381. Development Research Group, World Bank, Washington, DC.

Docquier, Frederic, and Hillel Rapoport. 2004. "Skilled Migration: The Perspective of Developing Countries." Policy Research Working Paper 3382. Development Research Group, World Bank, Washington, DC.

Drinkwater, Stephen, Paul Levine, Emanuela Lotti, and Joseph Pearlman. 2002. "The Economic Impact of Migration: A Survey." Paper prepared for Second Workshop of the Fifth Framework Programme Project, "European Enlargement: The Impact of East-West Migration on Growth and Employment," December 6–7, Vienna.

Edin, Per-Anders, Robert J. LaLonde, and Olof Åslund. 2000. "Emigration of Immigrants and Measures of Immigrant Assimilation: Evidence from Sweden." *Swedish Economic Policy Review* 7: 163–204. Fall.

Eelens, Frank, and J. D. Speckmann. 1990. "Recruitment of Labor Migrants for the Middle East: The Sri Lankan Case." *International Migration Review* 24(2): 297–322.

Ellerman, David. 2003. "Policy Research on Migration and Development." World Bank Policy Research Working Paper 3117. Washington, DC.

Faini, Riccardo. 2005. "Does the Brain Drain Boost Growth?" Research Program on International Migration and Development. DECRG. Mimeo. World Bank. Washington, DC.

Freeman, Richard B., and Remco H. Oostendorp. 2000. "Wages Around the World: Pay across Occupations and Countries." Working Paper 8058. National Bureau of Economic Research, Cambridge, MA.

Gazdar, Haris. 2003, "A Review of Migration Issues in Pakistan." Paper presented at the Regional Conference on Migration, Development and Pro-Poor Choices in Asia, June 22–24, Dhaka.

Gevorkyan, Alexandr V., and David A. Grigorian. 2003. "Armenia and Its Diaspora: Is There Scope for a Stronger Economic Link?" *Armenian Forum* 3(2): 1–35.

Ghosh, Bimal. 1996. "Economic Migration and the Sending Countries." In *The Economics of Labor Migration*, ed. Julien van den Broek. Cheltenham, UK: Edward Elgar.

Go, S. 2004. "Fighting for the Rights of Migrant Workers: The Case of the Philippines." In *Migration for Employment: Bilateral Agreeements at a Crossroads*. Paris. Organisation of Economic Co-operation and Development.

Gould, David. 1994. "Immigrant Links to the Home Country: Empirical Implications for U.S. Bilateral Trade Flows." *Review of Economics and Statistics* 76: 302–16. May.

Gubert, Flore. 2005. "Migrant Remittances and Their Impact on the Economic Development of Sending Countries: The Case of Africa." Paper presented at OECD International Conference on Migration, Remittances, and the Economic Development of Sending Countries, February 23–25, Marrakech.

Gunatilleke, Godfrey. 1998, "The Role of Social Networks and Community Structures in International Migration from Sri Lanka." In *Emigration Dynamics in Developing Countries II: South Asia*, ed. Reginald Appleyard. Aldershot, England: Ashgate.

Hatton, Timothy J., and Jeffrey G. Williamson. 2002. "What Fundamentals Drive World Migration?" Discussion Paper 3559. Centre for Economic Policy Research, London.

Head, K., and J. Ries. 1998. "Immigration and Trade Creation: Econometric Evidence from Canada." *Canadian Journal of Economics* 31(1).

High-Level Committee on the Indian Diaspora. 2001. "The Indian Diaspora." Ministry of External Affairs, Government of India. December. indiandiaspora.nic.in/contents.htm.

Holzmann, Robert, Johannes Koettl, Taras Chernetsky. 2005. "Portability Regimes of Pension and Health Care Benefits for International Migrants: An Analysis of Issues and Good Practices." Social Protection Discussion Paper Series 0519. World Bank, Washington, DC.

House of Commons. 2004. "Migration and Development: How to Make Migration Work for Poverty Reduction." Sixth Report of Session 2003–04, HC 79-1. London. July.

Hugo, Graeme J. 2002, "Migration Policies Designed to Facilitate the Recruitment of Skilled Workers in Australia." In *International Mobility of the Highly Skilled*. Paris: Organisation for Economic Co-operation and Development.

———. 2004. "Information, Exploitation, and Empowerment: The Case of Indonesian Contract Workers." Unpublished paper. University of Adelaide.

ILO (International Labour Office). 1997. "Protecting the Most Vulnerable of Today's Workers." International Migration Branch. Geneva.

———. 2003a. "Booklet 2: Decision-Making and Preparing for Employment Abroad." In *Preventing Discrimination, Exploitation and Abuse of Women Migrant Workers: An Information Guide*. Geneva: International Labour Office.

———. 2003b. "Booklet 4: Working and Living Abroad." In *Preventing Discrimination, Exploitation and Abuse of Women Migrant Workers: An Information Guide*. Geneva: International Labour Office.

IOM (International Organization for Migration). 2003. Labour Migration in Asia. Geneva.

———. 2005a. *Migration, Development, and Poverty Reduction in Asia*. Geneva.

———. 2005b. *World Migration 2005*. Geneva.

Jandl, Michael. 2003. "Estimates on the Numbers of Illegal and Smuggled Immigrants in Europe." Presentation at the Eighth International Metropolis Conference of the Inernational Centre for Migration Policy Development, September 17, Vienna.

———. 2004. "The Estimation of Illegal Migration in Europe." *Studi Emigrazione/Migration Studies* 61(153): 141–55. March.

Jaeger, David A. 2000. "Local Labor Markets, Admission Categories, and Immigrant Location

Choice." Unpublished paper. Hunter College, New York.

Jazayery, Leila. 2002. "The Migration-Development Nexus: Afghanistan Case Study." *International Migration* 40(5): 231–52.

Johnson, Brett, and Santiago Sedaca. 2004. "Diasporas, Émigrés, and Development: Economic Linkages and Programmatic Responses." Study conducted for the Trade Enhancement Service Sector (TESS) Project under contract with the U.S. Agency for International Development, Carana Corporation, Washington, DC. January.

Karemera, David, Victor I. Oguledo, and Bobby Davis. 2000. "A Gravity Model Analysis of International Migration to North America." *Applied Economics* 32(13): 1745–55.

Kanbur, Ravi, and Hillel Rapoport. 2005. "Migration Selectivity and the Evolution of Spatial Inequality." *Journal of Economic Geography* 5: 1–15.

Lee, J. 2005. "Human Trafficking in East Asia: Current Trends, Data Collection, and Knowledge Gap." In *Data and Research on Human Trafficking: A Global Survey.* Geneva. IOM.

Long, Larry, C. Jack Tucker, and William L. Urton. 1988. "Migration Distances: An International Comparison." *Demography* 25: 633–60. November.

Lowell, B. Lindsay. 2001. "Policy Responses to the International Mobility of Skilled Labour." International Labour Office, International Migration Branch, Geneva.

Lowell, B. Lindsay, and Allan Findlay. 2001. "Migration of Highly Skilled Persons from Developing Countries: Impact and Policy Responses. Synthesis Report." International Labour Office, International Migration Branch, Geneva.

Lucas, Robert E.B. 1987. "Emigration to South Africa's Mines." *American Economic Review* 77: 313–30. June.

———. 2004a. International Migration Regimes and Economic Development. Report from the seminar of the Executive Group on Development Issues on International Migration Regimes and Economic Development, May 13, Stockholm. www.egdi.gov.se/seminars6.htm.

———. 2004b. "International Migration to the High Income Countries: Some Consequences for the Sending Countries." Unpublished paper. Boston University. Economics Department.

Magoni, Raphaele. 2004. "France." In *International Migration and Relations with Third Countries: European and U.S. Approaches*, eds. Jan Niessen and Yongmi Schibel. Brussels: Migration Policy Group.

Mahmud, Wahiduddin. 1989. "The Impact of Overseas Labour Migration on the Bangladesh Economy: A Macro-Economic Perspective." In *To the Gulf and Back: Studies on the Economic Impact of Asian Labour Migration*, ed. Rashid Amjad. New Delhi: ILO-ARTEP.

Majid, Nomaan. 2000, "Pakistan: Employment, Output and Productivity." Issues in Development Discussion Paper 33. International Labour Office, Geneva.

Malmberg, Gunnar. 1997, "Time and Space in International Migration." In *International Migration, Immobility and Development: Multidisciplinary Perspectives*, ed. Tomas Hammar, Grete Brochmann, Kristof Tamas, and Thomas Faist. Oxford: Berg.

Martin, Philip. 2003. "Managing Labor Migration: Temporary Worker Programs for the Twenty-First Century." International Institute for Labour Studies, Geneva.

———. 2005. "Merchants of Labor: Agents of Evolving Migration Infrastructure." Discussion Paper 158/2005. International Institute for Labour Studies, Geneva.

Massey, Douglas S., Joaquin Arango, Graeme Hugo, Ali Kouaouci, Adela Pellegrino, and J. Edward Taylor. 1993. "Theories of International Migration: A Review and Appraisal." *Population and Development Review* 19(3): 431–66.

———. 1998. *Worlds in Motion: Understanding International Migration at the End of the Millennium.* Oxford: Clarendon.

McKenzie, David J. 2005. "Beyond Remittances: The Effects of Migration on Mexican Households." In *International Migration, Remittances, and Development*, ed. Caglar Ozden and Maurice Schiff. New York: Palgrave Macmillan.

McMahon, Walter M. 1999. *Education and Development: Measuring the Social Benefits.* Oxford: Oxford University Press.

Meek, Miki. 2003. "Life and Death on the Southwest Border." *National Geographic.* November.

Meyer, Jean-Baptiste, and Mercy Brown. 1999. "Scientific Diasporas: A New Approach to the Brain Drain." Paper prepared for the UNESCO-ICSU World Conference on Science, June 26–July 1, Budapest.

Mincer, Jacob. 1991. "Human Capital, Technology, and the Wage Structure: What Do Time Series Show?" Working Paper 3581. National Bureau of Economic Research, Cambridge, MA.

Misra, Neha, and Ruth Rosenberg. 2003. "Migrant Workers." In *Trafficking of Women and Children in Indonesia*, ed. Ruth Rosenberg. Jakarta: International Catholic Migration Commission

(ICMC) and American Center for International Labor Solidarity (Solidarity Center).

Mora, Jorge, and J. Edward Taylor. 2005. "Determinants of Migration, Destination and Sector Choice: Disentangling Individual, Household, and Community Effects." In *International Migration, Remittances, and Development,* ed. Caglar Ozden and Maurice Schiff. New York: Palgrave Macmillan.

Moreno-Fontes Chammartin, G. 2005. "Domestic Workers: Little Protection for the Underpaid." Migration Information Source. April. www.migrationinformation.org/.

Mountford, Andrew. 1997. "Can a Brain Drain Be Good for Growth in the Source Economy?" *Journal of Development Economics* 53(2): 287–303.

Munshi, Kaivan. 2003. "Networks in the Modern Economy: Mexican Migrants in the United States Labor Market." *Quarterly Journal of Economics* 118(2):

OECD (Organisation for Economic Co-operation and Development). 2004. *Trends in International Migration.* Paris.

———. 2005. *Trends in International Migration.* Paris.

Orozco, Manuel. 2003. "Worker Remittances, Transnationalism, and Development." Inter-American Dialogue, Washington, DC.

Pan, W. 2004. "Yikao nongmin gaosu tuijing chengshihua" (Making farmers accelerate urbanization). *Zhanlue Yu Guanli* (Strategy and Management) 6(2).

Pang, Tikki, Mary Ann Lansang, and Andy Haines. 2002. "Brain Drain and Health Professionals." *British Medical Journal* 324(7336): 499–500. March 2.

Passel, J. S., R. Capps, and M. E. Fix. 2004. Undocumented Immigrants: Facts and Figures. Urban Institute, Washington, DC. www.urban.org/url.cfm?ID=1000587.

Rauch, James E., and Victor Trindade. 1999. "Ethnic Chinese Networks in International Trade." NBER Working Paper 7189, National Bureau of Economic Research, Cambridge, MA. June.

Rivera, Jose Jorge Mora. 2005. "The Impact of Migration and Remittances on Distribution and Sources of Income: The Mexican Rural Case." Paper prepared for the meeting of the United Nations Expert Group on International Migration and Development, July 6–8, New York.

Saith, Ashwani. 1997. "Emigration Pressures and Structural Change: Case of the Philippines." International Migration Papers 19. International Labour Office, Geneva.

Salt, John, and Jeremy Stein. 1997. "Migration as a Business: The Case of Trafficking." *International Migration* 35(4).

Saxenian, AnnaLee. 2000. "Brain Drain or Brain Circulation? The Silicon Valley–Asia Connection." Lecture in the Modern Asia Series, Harvard University Asia Center, September 29.

———. 2002. *Local and Global Networks of Immigrant Professionals in Silicon Valley.* San Francisco: Public Policy Institute of California.

Schiff, Maurice. 2005. "Brain Gain: Its Size and Impact on Welfare and Growth Have Been Greatly Exaggerated." In Caglar Ozden and Maurice Schiff (eds.) *International Migration, Remittances and the Brain Drain.* New York: Palgrave Macmillan.

Shah, Nasra M. 1998, "The Role of Social Networks among South Asian Male Migrants in Kuwait." In *Emigration Dynamics in Developing Countries II: South Asia,* ed. Reginald Appleyard. Aldershot, England: Ashgate.

Siddiqui, T. 2003. "Migration as a Livelihood Strategy of the Poor: The Bangladesh Case." Paper presented at the Regional Conference on Migration, Development, and Pro-Poor Policy Choices in Asia, June 22–24, Dhaka, Bangladesh.

Solimano, Andres. 2002. "International Migration, Globalization and Development: Main Issues." Unpublished paper. UN Economic Commission for Latin America and the Caribbean, Santiago, Chile.

Spaan, Ernst. 1994. "Taikongs and Calos: The Role of Middlemen and Brokers in Javanese International Migration." *International Migration Review* 28(1): 93–113.

Stalker. 1994. "The Work of Strangers: A Survey of International Labour Migration." International Labour Office, Geneva.

Stark, Oded. 2003. "Rethinking the Brain Drain." *World Development.* 32(1): 15–22.

Tan, E. 2004. "Welfare Funds for Migrant Workers: A Comparative Study of Pakistan, Philippines, and Sri Lanka." International Organization for Migration, Geneva.

UNESCAP (UN Economic and Social Commission for Asia and the Pacific). 2003. "Migration Patterns and Policies in the Asian and Pacific Region." Asian Population Studies Series 160. United Nations, New York.

UN (United Nations). 2004. *World Economic and Social Survey.* New York.

U.S. Department of State. 2004. *Trafficking in Persons Report.* Washington, DC.

Vayrynen, Raimo. 2003. "Illegal Immigration, Human Trafficking, and Organized Crime." Discussion Paper 2003/72. World Institute for Development

Economics Research, United Nations University, Helsinki.

Vietnam Trade. 2005. "Japan Accepts Credentials of Vietnam's IT Engineers." *Vietnam Trade*. January 20. www.info.vn/index.php?news=1&id=9&nid=5783&lang=en&start\=20&archive=.

Vincent-Lancrin, S. 2004. "Building Capacity through Cross-Border Tertiary Education." Paper prepared for the conference of the UNESCO/OECD Australia Forum on Trade in Educational Services, "Bridging the Divide: Building Capacity for Post-Secondary Education through Cross-Border Provision," October 11–12, Sydney. www.oecd.org/dataoecd/43/25/33784331.pdf.

Wickramasekera, Piyasiri. 2002. "Asian Labour Migration: Issues and Challenges in an Era of Globalization." International Labour Office, International Migration Program, Geneva.

Winters, Alan. 2005. "Demographic Transition and the Temporary Mobility of Labor." Paper prepared for the G-20 Workshop on Demographic Challenges and Migration, August, Sydney.

World Bank. 2005. *Global Economic Prospects*. Washington, DC.

Xiang, B. 2003. "Emigration from China: A Sending Country Perspective." International Organization for Migration, Geneva.

Yusuf, Shahid. 2001. "Globalization and the Challenge for Developing Countries." Background paper for *World Development Report 1999/2000*. World Bank, Washington, DC.

4

Trends, Determinants, and Macroeconomic Effects of Remittances

Chapter 3 reviewed the trends, opportunities, and policy challenges associated with international migration. It also introduced the economic importance of the funds that international migrants send back to their country of origin. In recent years, those funds have emerged as a major source of external financing in developing countries. Although there is no universal agreement yet on how to measure international migrants' remittances to developing countries, a comprehensive measure of certain officially recorded flows—workers' remittances, compensation of employees, and migrant transfers—produced an estimate of $167 billion for 2005, up from $160 billion in 2004. Given measurement uncertainties, notably the unknown extent of unrecorded flows through formal and informal channels, the true size of remittance flows may be much higher—perhaps 50 percent or more. Because of their volume and their potential to reduce poverty, remittances are attracting growing attention from policymakers at the highest levels in both developed and developing countries.[1]

This chapter and chapters 5 and 6 consider remittances from several angles. The organizing framework is driven by three items on the international policy agenda: (1) understanding the true size and trends in remittance flows to developing countries, as well as their macroeconomic impact; (2) evaluating the impact of remittances on the households that receive

them; and (3) designing policies to reduce the transaction costs of remittances, strengthen the formal financial infrastructure supporting remittances, and leverage remittances to improve access to financial services in recipient economies.

Officially recorded remittance estimates may significantly underestimate the real magnitude of remittances. Model-based estimates and household surveys suggest that informal flows could add at least 50 percent to the official estimate, with significant regional and country variation. The true size of remittance flows could be even larger, in view of substantial underrecording of flows through formal channels.

Despite the prominence given to remittances from developed countries, South–South remittance flows make up 30–45 percent of total remittances received by developing countries, reflecting the fact that over half of migrants from developing countries migrate to other developing countries. Remittance flows to poor countries originate largely in the middle-income developing countries.

Recorded remittance flows have surged in recent years, driven by a combination of factors—among them better data collection, reflecting greater awareness of the development potential of remittances, as well as concerns about money laundering and terrorist financing; lower costs and wider networks in the industry that supports remittance; and growth in the number of migrants and their incomes. Government policies to improve banking access and the technology of money transfers have also helped increase the flow of remittances and promote their transfer through formal channels.

Efforts to encourage remittances, however, sometimes generate unwanted effects. Tax incentives may attract remittance inflows, for example, but they also create opportunities for tax evasion. Likewise, matching-fund programs for migrant associations may channel collective remittances to development projects, but in so doing they may divert funds from other local funding priorities.

For some recipient countries, remittances are large enough to have broader macroeconomic implications. By generating a steady stream of foreign-exchange earnings, they can improve a country's creditworthiness for external borrowing, and through innovative financing mechanisms (such as securitization), they can expand access to capital and lower borrowing costs. While large and sustained remittance inflows can contribute to currency appreciation and so affect the production of cost-sensitive tradables (such as labor-intensive manufactures), this outcome may be less severe than it is in the case of natural-resource earnings (since remittances are distributed more widely and may avoid exacerbating the strains on institutional capacity that are often associated with natural-resource booms). Furthermore, the "Dutch disease" effects of remittances are of relatively minor concern insofar as remittances grow gradually over long periods. Remittances have a large positive effect on national income in many developing countries, and there is compelling evidence that they contribute significantly to poverty reduction (see chapter 5). Although the evidence on the effect of remittances on long-term growth remains inconclusive, in economies where the financial system is underdeveloped, remittances appear to alleviate credit constraints and may stimulate economic growth.

The plan of this chapter is as follows. In the next section, trends in remittance flows to developing countries are presented along with a range of estimates for their true size—that is, with informal flows included. We identify the major sending and receiving countries, including those in the South. In the following section, we examine the factors affecting remittance flows, including the prospects for future remittance growth, and policies and regulations in source and destination countries that affect the cost of remittances. In the final section, we consider the macroeconomic effects of remittances, including the effects on stability, country creditworthiness, international capital-market access, the real exchange rate, and competitiveness.

Remittance data and trends

The quality and coverage of data on remittances leave much to be desired. First, there is no consensus on the boundaries of the phenomenon under study. Should only workers' remittances be counted, or should we include compensation of employees and migrant transfers? (See annex 4A.1 for more details on these nomenclatural disputes.) Second, in several countries, many types of *formal* remittance flows go unrecorded, due to weaknesses in data collection (related to both definitions and coverage).[2] Reporting of "small" remittance transactions made through formal channels is not mandatory in most countries,[3] and remittances sent through post offices, exchange bureaus, and other agents of money transfer operators (MTOs) are often not reflected in official statistics (de Luna Martinez 2005). Third, flows through *informal* channels (such as unregulated money transfer firms or family and friends who carry remittances) are rarely captured. Finally, remittances are often misclassified as export revenue, tourism receipts, nonresident deposits, or even foreign direct investment (FDI). Improving the quality of remittance statistics is the focus of ongoing cooperative international efforts (see box 4.1).

Box 4.1 International working group on improving data on remittances

At its meeting in Sea Island in April 2004, the G-8 called upon the international financial institutions (IFIs) to lead a global effort to improve remittance statistics. In January 2005, the World Bank and International Monetary Fund (IMF) held an international meeting of data users and compilers who agreed that balance-of-payments statistics were the appropriate framework for collecting, reporting, and improving official statistics on remittances; that balance-of-payments concepts and definitions relating to remittances should be reviewed; and that improved guidance for collecting and compiling remittance statistics, including through the use of household surveys, was needed. Participants at the international meeting also agreed that improvements to relevant statistical concepts and definitions should be discussed in a Technical Sub-Group on the Movement of Persons (TSG), chaired by the UN Statistics Division with membership from central banks and national and international statistical agencies.

The TSG recommended that the "workers' remittances" item in the balance of payments be replaced by "personal transfers." The new term would cover all current transfers in cash or in kind made or received by resident households to or from other nonresident households. It went on to recommend that a new aggregate, "personal remittances," be reported in the standard balance-of-payments presentation as a memorandum item. It was proposed that personal remittances comprise current and capital transfers in cash or in kind, made or received, by resident households to or from nonresident households, and "net" compensation of employees from persons working abroad for short periods of time (less than one year).

The TSG also recommended that institutional remittances—those involving government, corporations, and nonprofit institutions serving households—should also be reported as a new memorandum item in the standard presentation of balance-of-payments statistics. That item would lead to a further memorandum item, "total remittances," the sum of personal and institutional remittances.

Because the concepts of personal transfers and remittances are based on the concept of residence rather than migration status, the TSG recommended that the concept of "migrant" be replaced by the concept of "residence" in the balance-of payments-framework. Reporting of bilateral remittance flows is not currently required in the balance of payments, but the recommendation of the TSG is that flows to and from major partner countries be identified.

The TSG is expected to produce a final report in spring 2006.[a]

---

[a] A concurrent effort to improve remittance statistics is under way at the Center for Latin America Monetary Studies (CEMLA) with support from the Multilateral Investment Fund of the Inter-American Development Bank and technical advice from an international advisory council that includes the IMF and World Bank.

Officially recorded remittance flows are surging

In this report (as in past editions of the World Bank's annual *Global Development Finance* and the IMF's 2005 *World Economic Outlook*), migrant remittances are calculated as the sum of workers' remittances, compensation of employees, and migrant transfers (see annex 4A.1). Thus defined, remittances received by developing countries, estimated using officially recorded data, rose to $167 billion in 2005, up 73 percent from 2001 (table 4.1). More than half of that increase occurred in China, India, and Mexico. Low-income countries, led by India, registered an increase of $18 billion during this period (box 4.2). Of 34 developing countries that received remittances in excess of $1 billion in 2004, 26 countries registered more than 30 percent growth during 2001–4: Algeria

Table 4.1 Workers' remittances to developing countries, 1990–2005
$ billions

	1990	1995	2000	2001	2002	2003	2004e	2005e	*Change (%)* *2005–2001*
Developing countries	**31.2**	**57.8**	**85.6**	**96.5**	**113.4**	**142.1**	**160.4**	**166.9**	*73*
Lower middle income	13.9	30.0	42.6	47.4	57.3	72.5	83.5	88.0	*86*
Upper middle income	9.1	14.5	20.0	22.3	23.0	27.8	33.0	33.8	*52*
Low income	8.1	13.3	22.8	26.8	33.1	41.8	43.9	45	*68*
Latin America and the Caribbean	5.8	13.4	20.1	24.4	28.1	34.8	40.7	42.4	*74*
South Asia	5.6	10.0	17.2	19.2	24.2	31.1	31.4	32.0	*67*
East Asia and the Pacific	3.3	9.7	16.7	20.1	27.2	35.8	40.9	43.1	*114*
Middle East and North Africa	11.4	13.4	13.2	15.1	15.6	18.6	20.3	21.3	*41*
Europe and Central Asia	3.2	8.1	13.4	13.0	13.3	15.1	19.4	19.9	*53*
Sub-Saharan Africa	1.9	3.2	4.9	4.7	5.2	6.8	7.7	8.1	*72*
World (developing & industrial)	**68.6**	**101.6**	**131.5**	**147.1**	**166.2**	**200.2**	**225.8**	**232.3**	*58*
Outward remittances from developing countries	6.1	12.5	12.1	14.3	18.7	20.2	24.1	–	–
Outward remittances from Saudi Arabia	11.2	16.6	15.4	15.1	15.9	14.8	13.6	–	–

Source: World Bank staff estimates based on IMF BoP Yearbook 2004 and country sources.
Note: Remittances are defined as the sum of workers' remittances, compensation of employees, and migrant transfers (see annex 4A.1). e = estimate.
– Data not available.

and Guatemala reported more than a tripling of remittance inflows; Brazil, China, Honduras, Nigeria, Pakistan, and Serbia and Montenegro reported growth in the range of 101–170 percent. (Also, five high-income countries—Austria, Australia, Belgium, Germany, and Spain—reported 45–79 percent growth in remittance inflows during 2001–4.)

The growing importance of remittances as a source of foreign exchange is reflected in the fact that remittance growth has outpaced private capital flows and official development assistance (ODA) over the last decade (table 4.2). Recorded remittance receipts were equivalent to about 6.7 percent of developing countries' imports and 7.5 percent of domestic investment. They also were larger than official flows and private equity (non-FDI) flows in 2004. Remittances were larger than public and private capital inflows in 36 developing countries in 2004 and larger than total merchandise exports in Albania, Bosnia and

Table 4.2 Recorded remittances have grown faster than private capital flows and ODA
$ billions

	1995	2004
Workers' remittances	58	160
Foreign direct investment	107	166
Private debt and portfolio equity	170	136
Official development assistance	59	79

Source: World Bank (2005).

Herzegovina, Cape Verde, Gaza, Haiti, Jamaica, Kiribati, Lebanon, Nepal, Samoa, Serbia and Montenegro, and Tonga. In another 28 countries, they were larger than the earnings from the most important commodity export; for example, in Mexico, remittances are larger than FDI; in Sri Lanka, they are larger than tea exports; and in Morocco, they are larger than tourism receipts.

Box 4.2   The recent surge in remittance flows to India

India has reported a spectacular increase in remittance inflows—from $13 billion in 2001 to more than $20 billion in 2003 (see figure). Several factors account for this remarkable increase. First, the number of migrants has grown sharply. During the oil boom in the 1970s and 1980s, thousands of low-skilled Indian workers migrated to the Persian Gulf countries. In the 1990s, migration to Australia, Canada, and the United States, increased significantly, particularly among information technology (IT) workers on temporary work permits.[a]

Second, the swelling of migrants' ranks coincided with (a) better incentives to send and invest money in India's growing economy and (b) an easing of the regulations and controls, more flexible exchange rates, and gradual opening of the capital account. The elimination of the black-market premium on the rupee and convenient remittance services provided by Indian and international banks have no doubt shifted some remittance flows from informal *hawala* channels to formal channels.

Third, nonresident Indians have also responded to several attractive deposit schemes and bonds offered by the government of India. These offer attractive interest rates and an appreciating rupee. While nonresident deposits are conceptually different from remittances (they are a liability item in the capital account), evidence suggests that a large part of such deposits is converted to local currency. For example, for the Resurgent India Bond that matured in 2003, most of the redemption value stayed in India to meet various local currency needs of the nonresident depositors and their families. Nevertheless, remittances in the form of foreign-currency deposits can be speculative and may reverse in the event of deterioration in the investment sentiment.

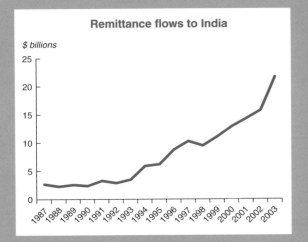

Remittance flows to India

$ billions

[a]In particular, migration to United States doubled during the 1990s. Remittances from United States as a share of total remittances to India grew from 37 percent in 1997 to 51 percent in 2003.

Figure 4.1 identifies the top 20 remittance recipients in 2004. Among developing countries, China, India, Mexico, and the Philippines were among the top recipients. Several industrial countries appear in this list as well.

When remittances are calculated in per capita terms or as a share of GDP, a different picture emerges. The top 20 recipients in shares of GDP are all developing countries; all receive more than 10 percent of GDP as remittance flows (figure 4.1). Small countries (Bosnia and Herzegovina, Haiti, Lesotho, Moldova, and Tonga) are among the most dependent on remittances.

High-income countries are the dominant source of global remittance flows (figure 4.2). The United States was the largest source country with nearly $39 billion in outward remittances in 2004. However, outward remittances from developing countries amounted to $24 billion in the same year.[4] When expressed in terms of GDP shares, outward remittances play the largest role in the upper-middle-income developing countries (0.7 percent of GDP in these countries compared to 0.2–0.4 percent in other developing countries and in high-income countries; figure 4.2).

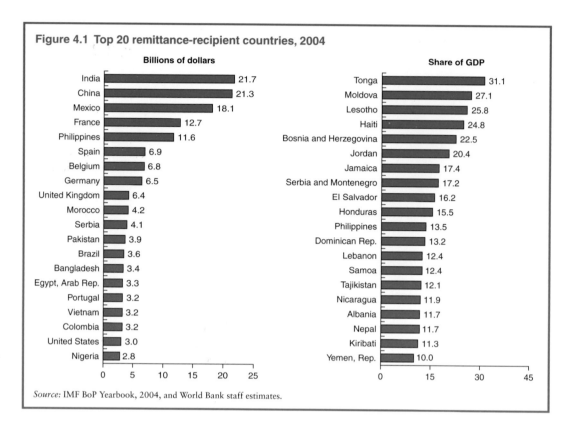

Figure 4.1 Top 20 remittance-recipient countries, 2004

Source: IMF BoP Yearbook, 2004, and World Bank staff estimates.

South–South remittance flows are considerable

Official data show that several developing countries (China, Malaysia, and the Russian Federation) are among the top 20 sources of remittances. Anecdotally, outward remittances from India and South Africa are also believed to be large, although this is not reflected in the official data (Genesis Analytics 2005). The World Bank (2005a) points out a strong association between remittance receipts and the length of the border shared with more prosperous neighbors. Harrison and others (2004) also report that most remittance flows occur within the same region.

These factors all point to the conclusion that South–South remittance flows are substantial. But placing more precision on these flows is hard to do. First, relatively little is known about bilateral migration flows—that is, about how many migrants (or what share) in each receiving country come from each sending country. Comprehensive global data are not available,[5] but estimates are that in poor countries of East Asia, South Asia, and Sub-Saharan Africa, more than two-thirds of emigrants migrate to a country in the same region. In South Asia and Sub-Saharan Africa, most migrate to another developing country.

Second, even less is known about how bilateral remittance patterns differ. We do not know, for example, how much, in total, is sent from one country to another, or how remittance propensities differ across sending and receiving countries. But by making plausible assumptions about these flows (in particular, that bilateral remittances are a function of the stock of migrants in the sending country), it is possible to estimate bilateral remittance flows and to calculate what proportion comes through South–South links.[6] Using this method, we estimate that nearly 30 percent of total remittance flows to developing countries originate in other developing countries. This

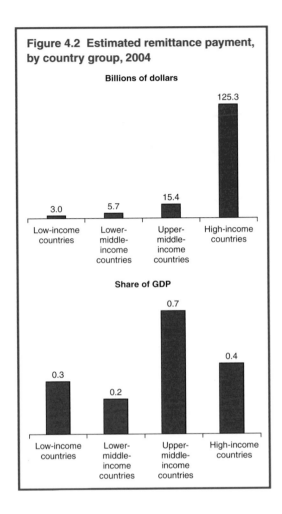

Figure 4.2 Estimated remittance payment, by country group, 2004

Billions of dollars

Share of GDP

Eastern Europe, Turkey, and North Africa; and the Persian Gulf to South and Southeast Asia.

Informal remittances are large

Remittances transferred through informal operators or hand carried by travelers are unlikely to be captured in official statistics, although they may represent a substantial addition to remittances sent through official channels. While it is extremely difficult to estimate the flows through informal channels, they appear to be large. First, the fact that recorded remittances to several countries through formal channels doubled, tripled, or quadrupled between 2001 and 2003 suggests that a significant part of the increase is likely to reflect a shift from informal to formal channels in response to the tightened regulatory scrutiny that has occurred since September 11, 2001.

Second, evidence from household surveys suggests widespread use of informal remittance channels (table 4.3).[8] Household surveys also help identify factors affecting the use of remittance channels. In the presence of a well-developed formal sector, regular remitters and large remitters are unlikely to use the informal sector. Trust in the financial system is an important prerequisite for a growing bank presence in the (formal) remittance market.

High remittance costs and the presence of dual exchange rates are two key factors affecting the choice of informal remittance

estimate is consistent with the fact that nearly half of the migrant stock from the South migrate to another country in the South.[7]

One of the challenges of understanding remittance flows is that their characteristics, costs, and channels can vary widely from one bilateral corridor to another (and also widely from different locations within each country). Understanding how remittance corridors differ in the kinds of migrants they serve and their means of transferring money is useful for providers of remittance services as well as policymakers (Hernandez-Coss 2004; Terry 2005; and chapter 6 of this volume). Some of the major remittance corridors are those that connect Canada and the United States to Latin America and Asia; the European Union to

Table 4.3 Choice of remittance channel in selected countries

% remittances

	Formal	Informal
Dominican Republic	96	4
Guatemala	95	5
El Salvador	85	15
Armenia	62	38
Moldova	53	47
Bangladesh	46	54
Uganda	20	80

Source: World Bank staff estimates based on household surveys. See also Freund and Spatafora 2005.

channels.[9] If there were no cost advantages to using informal channels, there would be little incentive to use them, and remittances could arguably shift entirely to formal channels. Thus if the costs of formal transfers were reduced to the range reported in the informal sector (2–5 percent), and if official and parallel exchange rates were unified, the resultant increase in recorded remittance flows could be interpreted as an estimate of the size of informal flows.

Table 4.4 reports the results of an exercise to estimate the size of the informal remittance sector (see annex 4A.2 for a fuller explanation). Cross-country regression analysis shows that reported remittances are lower, and informal flows higher, in corridors where remittance costs are higher and where there are significant black-market premiums over the official exchange rate. Using the estimated coefficients from these regressions, the predicted increase in officially recorded remittances is calculated in response to a 2–5 percent decline in remittance costs and elimination of the exchange-rate premium. These calculations suggest that the informal remittance sector is at least 50 percent of the official sector.[10] They also show significant regional variation. Informal remittances appear to be larger in Sub-Saharan Africa, the Middle East and North Africa, and Europe and Central Asia than in other regions.[11] While the magnitude of the regional estimates varies across methods, the relative ranking of regional effects is more robust.

Factors affecting remittance flows

The surge in remittance flows over the past few years reflects a mix of factors, as noted. In some areas, there have been significant reductions in remittance costs—60 percent in the United States–Mexico corridor since 1999. On the measurement side, the sizeable depreciation of the dollar against most other major currencies (the euro in particular) since 2002 has increased the dollar value of nondollar remittances over time.[12] Improvements in data recording by central banks—in response to growing recognition of the importance of remittances by national authorities, and as a result of broader efforts to improve data quality—have generated sharp increases in remittance flows in some cases. In addition, heightened security and scrutiny by immigration and finance authorities in many high-income countries may have encouraged outward surges in remittances, as undocumented migrants responded to increased uncertainty and risk of deportation or other legal action by remitting a larger share of their savings or income. This factor has reportedly been important in Pakistan, which recorded a tripling of remittance receipts from 2001 to 2003.

The surge in remittances is likely to continue in the medium term

In addition to these special factors, powerful economic factors also influence the growth of remittances. Increases in the number of migrants will have the greatest and most direct impact, of course, along with compositional features, such as the mix between temporary and permanent workers (temporary workers

Table 4.4 Estimated increase in formal remittances if transaction costs were reduced to 2 to 5 percent and dual exchange rates were eliminated

Percent

Region	Cross-sectional estimates	Panel estimates
All developing countries	69	54
Sub-Saharan Africa	201	122
Eastern Europe and Central Asia	151	73
East Asia and the Pacific	56	..
South Asia	25	55
Middle East and North Africa	165	..
Latin America and the Caribbean	51	99

Source: Freund and Spatafora 2005.
Note: Results averaged over 1995–2003. See annex 4A.2 for a fuller explanation of the procedures used. In column 3, a reduced form equation is estimated on the basis of the explanatory variables used in the cost regression reported in table 4A.2.2.
.. Negligible.

are believed to remit a larger share of their income) and the skill mix (low-skilled workers tend to send a higher proportion of their lower incomes). Employment opportunities in the host country affect income, and therefore remittances, while changes in the cost of living may affect the size of the surplus that remitters are able to send.

The complex interplay of these factors makes assessing the future growth potential of remittance flows quite difficult. It is plausible that in the coming years, official remittance flows will continue to rise at the 7–8 percent annual rate seen during the 1990s. With both the supply and demand for migrants growing, migration flows—especially temporary migration—are likely to continue to be strong. Growing income levels in source countries and rising costs of living in receiving countries, together with the falling costs of remittances, would also imply larger remittances, especially through recorded channels.

It is unlikely, however, that the surge in remittance flows seen in some countries since 2001 will continue much longer. The shift in flows from informal to formal channels, to the extent that it occurred in response to tightened scrutiny, is likely to dwindle. (In Pakistan, for example, remittance flows have flattened since 2003.) In the more mature United States–Mexico corridor, where remittance costs have already fallen drastically (by 60 percent since 1999), the effect of further cost reduction will not be as large as it was five years ago.

Some analysts argue that in the more mature markets, "remittance decay" may set in, especially if temporary or undocumented workers are allowed permanent and legal residence. While it is true that the marginal propensity to remit tends to decline with the length of a migrant's stay in a host country, and ties with the home country weaken over time, there is no empirical evidence that the dollar amount of remittances actually declines in these circumstances.[13] On the contrary, the effect of rising incomes of the migrant sender may show up as an increase in remittances over time.

Government policies can affect remittance flows

Many sending and receiving governments are only now beginning to think about policies to increase remittance flows and promote transfers through formal channels. In the remittance-receiving countries, these policies include tax exemptions for remittance income; improved access to banking services by recipients; incentives to attract investments by the diaspora; access to foreign exchange or lower duties on imports; support for the projects of migrant associations; and help for migrants in accessing financial systems. In the remittance-source countries, they include policies affecting access to banks, access to foreign exchange, support to migrant groups, types of immigration regimes, and cooperation with receiving countries.[14]

Policies in remittance-receiving countries

Taxes on incoming remittances. Most remittance-receiving countries today do not impose taxes on incoming remittances. There may be some implicit tax on remittances, however, in the form of a general financial services tax[15] or on remittances in kind (for example, food, clothing, electronic items, or vehicles). When Vietnam removed its 5 percent tax on remittances in 1997, it found that the flow of remittances through formal channels increased. Such tax exemptions may well increase remittance inflows,[16] but they also raise the possibility of misuse for tax evasion.

Travel and customs privileges for returns and imported goods. Many remittance-receiving countries give preferential treatment to migrants sending home or bringing with them goods and equipment. For example, once a year Tunisians are entitled to import goods and/or services up to a customs value of TD1,000 without paying tax, and a private vehicle, home equipment, and furniture are tax free when they return; Guatemala permits a once-a-year tax-free remittance of any commodity valued up to $500. Pakistan, Turkey, Vietnam, and many other countries also offer such import privileges.[17]

Relaxation of exchange and capital controls. Unification of exchange rates and allowing more banks and financial institutions to undertake foreign exchange transactions have been among the most successful ways of attracting remittances to formal channels and expanding remittance services in many countries. Also, allowing residents to hold foreign currency deposits using remittances from abroad is believed to have resulted in a large increase in formal remittances in many countries in South Asia and Africa (Siddiqui 2004). India's liberalization of the exchange rate in 1991 has been linked to a decrease in the use of illegal transfer channels to the state of Kerala; and the Philippines found that by abolishing exchange controls it quadrupled its formal inward remittances in the same year (Buencamino and Gorbunov 2002). Allowing the market to decide exchange rates in 2002 also helped the Bangladesh Bank to curb the informal *hundi* business significantly (Siddiqui 2004). In 2004, an increase in foreign currency reserves in Zimbabwe was ascribed, in part, to the introduction of a new money transfer system (Homelink) set up by the government to facilitate formal transfers.

Allowing domestic banks to operate overseas. Governments have allowed more of their domestic financial institutions (including microfinance institutions in some countries) to open branches and provide services to their migrants working in other countries. These domestic banks bring trust and offer remittance services at competitive prices. For example, the Groupe Banques Populaires has picked up 66 percent of total remittances to Morocco by offering low fees, simple procedures, and other nonfinancial services to Moroccans abroad (Amin and Freund 2005). Two small Armenian banks specializing in remittance transfers, Anelik and Unibank, have come to dominate the formal transfer system for Armenians in parts of Europe; and Fonkoze in Haiti has expanded its U.S.–based clientele in partnership with the City National Bank of New Jersey. In Bangladesh the dramatic increase in formal remittances since 2001 is, in part, the result of the improved services of the banking sector (Siddiqui 2004).

ID cards for migrants. Providing identification cards to migrants (regardless of their legal migration status) to access banking facilities has also opened up more opportunities for formal remittance transfer. Mexican immigrants, for example, can obtain a photo-identification card in the form of a *matricula consular* from the Mexican consulates abroad. This card is widely accepted by commercial banks in the United States to open bank accounts (and in many states, for issuing driving licenses, see box 6.1). Other Latin American governments are discussing similar arrangements for their nationals in the United States. Most sending countries require legal documentation for any bank transaction. Some receiving countries issue ID cards to expedite domestic services for their emigrants, for example, the Tunisian *carte consulaire* for special customs clearance, reduced airfares, and foreign currency bank accounts in Tunisia.[18]

Support to hometown associations (HTAs) and matching grants. Providing funds to supplement or match collective remittances made by emigrant groups is another means to engage migrants in the development of home communities. With enhanced institutional capacities, HTAs could be valuable development partners for governments, the private sector, and communities, but importantly as a complement to, not a substitute for, strengthened financial and investment systems on the ground (Gubert 2005). A careful evaluation of support to HTAs through matching grant schemes and other means is yet to be undertaken (see box 4.3).

Loans/pension schemes and bonds targeted at the diasporas. These measures can expand opportunities for investment and provide incentives for the formal transfer of money from abroad (see also chapter 6). While investments in the form of nonresident deposits or diaspora bonds are not, strictly speaking, remittances (because they involve the purchase of assets, rather than transfers to households), they may indirectly encourage remittances. Many countries have successfully issued premium bonds to their diaspora (for Bangladesh, China, Eritrea, India, Israel, Lebanon, Pakistan and the Philippines, see Carling 2005). Even when investments in these bonds are in foreign currency terms, after maturity some portion is likely to remain

in the country. Such schemes were a major factor behind the doubling of remittance flows to India between 2002 and 2003 (box 4.2).

Active policies and institutional arrangements to support the diaspora. Countries like Mexico and the Philippines with more successful remittance programs tend to have well established institutional frameworks to train, support, and ensure the welfare of their expatriates abroad. There is also a broad range of outreach activities to assist migrant welfare

---

Box 4.3 Collective remittances through hometown associations and matching schemes

Many migrants are increasingly pooling their resources and investing collectively in development-related activities in home communities, either through hometown associations (HTAs) or other migrant group schemes.[a] HTAs are the most prominent, because of their proliferation among the Latin American and Caribbean diaspora in Canada and the United States since the late 1990s. Similar associations exist in France (some 1,000 *organizations de solidarite internationale issues de migrations* or OSIMs), the United Kingdom, and Africa.[b] The activities of HTAs are mixed and poorly documented, but they range from diaspora support in the host country to community investment projects in villages in the home country.

Collective remittances via HTAs currently account for only 1 percent of all remittances in Central America, but it is estimated that they could rise to 3–5 percent in ten years if their management and institutional capacity improves (IFAD 2005).

Most HTAs tend to be small scale and philanthropic in orientation, and they invest in projects of no more than $10,000. They have traditionally focused on infrastructure and social projects (schools, churches, recreational parks, medical outreach clinics, and household support) and on channeling post-disaster humanitarian aid (for example, in El Salvador). In Africa, there is evidence that the more sustainable projects tend to facilitate household

distribution of consumer goods (as in general stores or grain banks) or the purchase of farming equipment (Gubert 2005). In Latin America, it is observed that when at least 30 percent of households in a town receive remittances, HTAs can help improve the quality of life of households (IOM 2005). But the focus of HTAs is expanding to include more investment in economic infrastructure and income-generating projects managed by the community and local NGOs or banks (Orozco 2003).

Governments have, on occasion, offered matching grants for remittances from diaspora groups or HTAs to attract funding for specific community projects.[c] The best known of these matching schemes is Mexico's 3-for-1 program, started in 1997, under which the local, state, and federal governments all contribute $1 for every $1 of remittances sent to a community for a designated development project. By 2002, the 3-for-1 program had established projects totaling $43.5 million, two-thirds of which benefited labor-intensive agricultural economies in four high emigration states (IOM 2005). In the period 2002–4, more than 3,000 such projects benefited some 1 million inhabitants in 23 Mexican states.[d]

Evidence from Mexico suggests, however, that HTAs have not been very successful. But in some cases (for example, Zacatecas) where HTAs have exchanged or debated project ideas and investment

Box 4.3 *(continued)*

climate issues with the local and state governments, they are believed to have been successful.[e]

On the positive side, HTA involvement in projects is argued to ensure that programs are focused on community needs. Resources have gone primarily to rural areas, where they have increased the supply of essential services (health, education, roads, and electricity). Donations by HTAs are often as much as or more than the municipal budget for public works, particularly in towns with small populations (Orozco 2003). HTAs can promote higher standards of transparency and accountability among local authorities, and higher labor standards.

There are obviously limitations on the potential for HTAs to serve as conduits for broader development projects. They may not have the best information about the needs of the local community, or they may have different priorities. The capacity of HTAs to scale up or form partnerships is limited by the fact that their members are volunteers, and their fundraising ability finite. They can also become divided and weaken their own advocacy potential (Newland and Patrick 2004). When matching funds come from fiscally constrained governments, there is also the problem that they may be diverted from other—perhaps higher priority—development

projects, or from other regions with a greater need for assistance.

---

[a]HTAs are grassroots migrant organizations, usually formed around the interests and needs of a mutual hometown. The term has been coined in the United States, where many thousands of Latin American and Caribbean HTAs have sprung up in the past 15 years or so (Orozco and Welle 2004).

[b]Migrant associations exist in many countries, but are mostly concerned with the conditions of the diaspora and networking abroad. Some, like the Sierra Leonean Women's Forum in the United Kingdom, are concerned with immediate survival needs (food, clothing) back home (Black and others 2004).

[c]In addition to Mexico, the Salvadoran government partners with HTAs in rural development projects in El Salvador. In 2001, the federation of HTAs (COMUNIDADES) and the National Corporation of Municipalities created the Social Investment for Local Development Fund (FISDL) to provide matching project funding. In France, the Osims can also receive institutional and financial subsidies from the government for social and economic development projects back home (Magoni 2004).

[d]See "3 por 1. Proyectos Compartidos," prepared for the seminar "Migracion, remesas y el Programa 3 por 1 para Migrantes," Secretaria de Desarollo Social, Mexico and IADB, Washington DC, June 2005.

[e]See Gubert 2005, Iskander 2005, and Orozco 2004. The literature is not clear on what "success" means in these cases (beyond mere survival of the HTAs).

---

and promote remittances and investment in the home country, from pre-migration information and orientation (Philippines), IDs for customs and other purposes (Colombia, Tunisia), finance for study (Tunisia), support in legal and administrative disputes (Morocco), fairs and re-orientation visits for émigrés and their families (Colombia, Tunisia), shortened military service (and payment of fee in lieu, Turkey), hotline for migrant investors (Tunisia), and a diaspora trust fund (Nigeria). Some countries like Bangladesh, Egypt, Eritrea, Pakistan, Philippines, and Thailand (and Mexico and Turkey in the 1960s) have tried to impose mandatory remittance require-

ments on their émigrés, but with little success. Also, restrictive emigration policies have driven migrants into using clandestine remittance channels.[19]

Policies in remittance-source countries

Only a handful of remittance-sending countries have proactive remittance-supporting policies. Most are noninterventionist or have had little engagement to date, but this is changing with the growing appreciation of the significance of remittances for development in countries such as Australia, Canada, the United States, and most West European states (Ellerman 2003, Carling 2005). USAID has undertaken extensive research on remittances, as has the United Kingdom's Department for International Development (DFID) and the Norwegian International Peace Institute (PRIO). All propose ways forward for more proactive policies by sending countries—for example, to support migrant associations, facilitate low cost, reduce bureaucratic remittance transfer, greater competition in the remittance market, and inform decision making by migrants and affected communities.

Immigration policies. Policies that affect the size, type, and tenure of migration flows also affect remittance patterns. A larger migration stock would in general imply larger remittance flows to the country of origin. Given the migration stock, a larger share of temporary migrants is likely to lead to larger remittances. Also, as discussed above, the ties of migrants to their home country weaken with the passage of time, causing remittances to decline.

Given the personalized nature of remittances, governments are unlikely to have much success in using remittance policies to steer migration differently. Some countries, like Canada, France, and Germany, have tried to direct remittance flows to investments in the home country to encourage return migration, but these efforts have met with little success. There are also some examples of "forced" remittance transfer programs between sending and receiving countries, although these raise vexing legal issues and do not appear to be effective either in encouraging migrant return or mobilizing resources (box 4.4).

Box 4.4   Forced remittances

While it is generally assumed that migrant workers are free to choose how much, when, and to whom to send money, there have been cases when sending or receiving governments, banks in the home country, or employers have decided to retain a certain proportion of pay for remittances. The rationale for such "forced" remittances is to ensure that temporary migrant workers do not stay on, but return home after the end of their contract. Sometimes, the objective of such measures is to steer the use of remittances to investment in the country of origin.

For example, from 1942 to 1964 the "Bracero program" regulated migration of 4.6 million farm workers between Mexico and the United States. From 1942–9, a tenth of the wages earned by these *braceros* was deducted from their pay by the U.S. employers and paid into accounts held by the Bank of Mexico at two commercial banks in San Francisco. From there it was transferred to the Bank of Mexico and then on to the Banco de Credito Agricola. Alternatively, the employers gave the worker a check for the deducted amount at the end of the contract to be cashed back home in Mexico. A 1946 report by the Mexican government claimed that

$8 million in forced savings had been paid out to ex-*braceros* and only $6 million was unaccounted for; but the *LA Times* reported (on March 30, 2001) that a total of $34 million in forced savings was collected during 1942–6. The loss of the money was explained by successive bank consolidations and restructuring, and as a result, records of accounts had disappeared (Migration News, http://migration.ucdavis.edu/mn). The *braceros* were mostly poorly educated peasants, who did not even know about the deductions and who later were intimidated by the forms and correspondence needed to claim their money (*LA Times*). op.cit.). In March 2001, a class action suit was filed on behalf of former *braceros* at a San Francisco district court claiming $30 million–$50 million in savings not returned and additional punitive damages. This claim was rejected because of the statute of limitations (*San Francisco Chronicle,* August 29, 2002). In 2003, the Mexican government agreed to reimburse, within six months, an upfront sum of $150 per person and then monthly rates of pesos 200 for up to pesos 60,000, provided the ex-*braceros* could produce identification (the Bracero Net program).

Forced remittances may also be used by a government to encourage the use of remittances for

Box 4.4 *(continued)*

investment in the domestic economy. Under the Deferred Pay Scheme, mine workers from Lesotho have 30 percent (initially 60 percent, until 1990) of their pay deposited at a Lesotho bank and the balance into a savings account at TEBA (The Employment Bureau of Africa) Bank. The certificate confirming the identity of the account holder is handed out by the TEBA Bank at the end of the contract, before the mine worker goes home to collect the balance from the deferred pay scheme.

A similar arrangement is foreseen in the memorandum of understanding between the Governments of Thailand and Laos on employment cooperation. All Laotian guest workers are obliged to pay 15 percent of their earnings into a "deportation fund" set up by the host country, Thailand. Workers who wish to return home can claim their contribution in full with interest. The request must be filed three months before the return date, and the money is to be paid to the workers within 45 days after the last day of employment (articles 11 and 12).

A milder form of induced remittances has been introduced for temporary Mexican farm workers in the United States and Canada. Before their departure visas and work permits are issued, the temporary farm workers register with the Ministry of Labor in Mexico. After the papers are delivered, migrants open a savings account with the subsidiary or an associated institution of a North American bank in Mexico. Once they arrive in the United States or Canada, the temporary workers either make the remittance transaction themselves or arrange with

the farmer-employer to pay directly into their savings account via payroll deduction.

Forced savings of this type raise legal issues in that they violate an accepted principle of wage protection, that is, the idea that "wages shall be paid directly to the worker concerned" (article 5 ILO Convention 95 of 1949). The only exception provided for is that the "worker concerned has agreed to the contrary." It is not clear whether that has been the case with the *braceros* or with the other examples cited here. Convention 95 states that "employers shall be prohibited from limiting in any manner the freedom of the worker to dispose of his/her wages." Article 8.2 further spells out that "workers shall be informed of the conditions under which such deductions may be made." (Mexico ratified this convention in 1955. The United States has not ratified it.)

Forced remittances are also probably not the most effective measure to ensure that temporary migrant workers return home. If they return, it is likely not driven by their desire to reclaim their savings. When offered a choice, migrants avoid such systems. In South Africa a considerable number of mine workers from Lesotho did not participate in the deferred pay scheme, often in complicity with the mining companies (Sparreboom 1996, p. 13). If the Lesotho deferred pay scheme was voluntary, then the volume of savings would drop to a level of the voluntary schemes of workers from Botswana and Swaziland, namely 1 percent of the levels of the obligatory scheme (TEBA 1995).

Banking and financial markets. Greater relaxation and competition in money transfer markets leads to reduced prices and more money reaching the beneficiaries. This process is facilitated further by improving access of remittance service providers to national payment and settlement systems. This seems to have worked well within framed agreements such as the United States–Mexican Partnership for Prosperity program of 2001, involving the *matricula consular* to improve banking access

of Mexican immigrants in the United States and low-cost electronic transfers through the Federal Reserve Bank's automated clearinghouse system for Mexico (see chapter 6). Spain has initiated agreements between Spanish and Latin American financial institutions to reduce transfer fees and foster the entry of new agents into the financial market, particularly in rural areas. In the past, Germany worked closely with Turkey to encourage remittances into formal channels

(UN 2005). In some remittance-source countries, outward remittance flows are affected by exchange controls. For example, South Africa's policy of limiting foreign exchange dealings only to banks has prompted (unbanked) remitters to use informal channels—only 5 percent of remittances to other Southern African Development Community (SADC) countries are being sent via formal channels, according to Genesis Analytics (2005).[20]

ID arrangements for migrants. The U.S. facilitation of banking for both regular and irregular migrants from Mexico through the *matricula consular* mechanism has been highly successful in drawing more migrants into safer and cheaper remittance modes. The Federal Deposit Insurance Corporation (FDIC) through its New Alliance Task Force initiative, in collaboration with the Mexican consulates and commercial banks, has been successful in improving banking access as well as the financial literacy of immigrants.[21]

Support to HTAs or migrant associations. HTAs and similar entities receive some support from host governments in the United States, France, and parts of Africa in recognition of their development assistance potential. While HTAs could potentially play a useful role in community infrastructure and other collectively funded projects, their ability to effectively channel large amounts of aid remains untested.[22]

Macroeconomic effects of remittances

Until recently most of the discussion and research on remittances was focused on the (microeconomic) end use by the recipient households, including the effects on poverty (see chapter 5). But as outlined earlier in this chapter, the large size of remittances relative to other external flows and to the GDP in many countries suggests that the macroeconomic effects of remittances may be of critical importance in many countries (recall that the top 19 remittance recipients receive more than 10 percent of their GDP in remittances).

High levels (or large increases) in remittance flows can be expected to have direct repercussions on foreign exchange rates, domestic interest rates, and the balance of payments, and indirect repercussions on macrovariables. Because of their relative stability and targeting (directly to households), they may bring some additional benefits. However, as the experience with and analysis of natural resource booms have shown, large inflows can also have some undesirable side effects (see also box 4.5). And to the extent that remittance flows may naturally just go to countries that are doing poorly or respond anticyclically (increase during downturns, due to a drought, for example), it may be hard to disentangle how remittances affect macro-performance. In this section, we consider some of the macroeconomic channels through which remittances affect recipient countries.

Remittances are stable and may be countercyclical

Remittances may move countercyclically relative to the economic cycle of the recipient country. Remittances may rise when the recipient economy suffers a downturn in activity or macroeconomic shocks due to financial crisis, natural disaster, or political conflict, because migrants may send more funds during hard times to help their families and friends. Remittances may thus smooth consumption and contribute to the stability of recipient economies by compensating for foreign exchange losses due to macroeconomic shocks.

Many authors have observed an increase in remittance inflows following a natural disaster (Clarke and Wallsten 2004) or an economic downturn (Kapur 2003). Yang (2004) showed that remittance receipts by Filipino households increased following the 1997 financial crisis. A 10 percent appreciation of a migrant's currency against the Philippine peso led to increases in household remittance receipts and a 0.6 percentage point decline in the poverty rate in migrant households. He also found evidence of positive spillover effects on households without migrant members due to

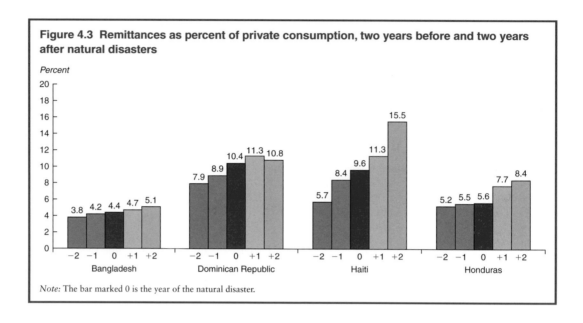

Figure 4.3 Remittances as percent of private consumption, two years before and two years after natural disasters

Percent

Note: The bar marked 0 is the year of the natural disaster.

increases in remittance-driven economic activity as well as by direct transfers from the migrant's origin household. Mishra (2005) finds that a 1 percent decrease in real GDP was associated with a 3 percent increase in remittances after a two-year lag in 13 Caribbean countries during 1980–2002. To the extent that remittances are used for investment purposes, however, they may behave procyclically just as other investment flows do. In Turkey and the Philippines, remittances were more volatile and procyclical in the 1990s than in the 1980s.[23]

Remittance flows (as a share of personal consumption) continued to rise after natural disasters in Bangladesh, Dominican Republic, Haiti, and Honduras (figure 4.3). In Albania, after an initial disruption in remittance inflows (as a share of personal consumption) in the year of conflict, remittance flows recovered quickly (figure 4.4). In Sierra Leone, remittances *increased* in the year of the conflict.[24] Remittances as a share of personal consumption rose in response to the financial crisis in Mexico in 1995 and in Indonesia and Thailand in 1997 (figure 4.5).

Yang (2005) found that the increase in remittances makes up for 13 percent of income losses in the current year and 28 percent

within four years of a hurricane. In contrast, increases in ODA and FDI make up for roughly 26 and 21 percent, respectively, within four years.

Remittances can improve country creditworthiness

Remittances can improve a country's creditworthiness and thereby enhance its access to international capital markets. The ratio of

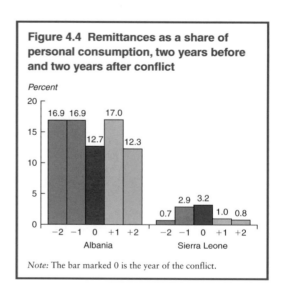

Figure 4.4 Remittances as a share of personal consumption, two years before and two years after conflict

Percent

Note: The bar marked 0 is the year of the conflict.

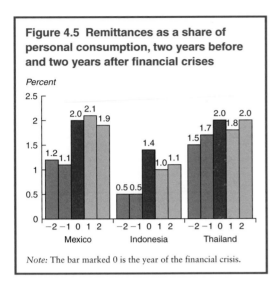

Figure 4.5 Remittances as a share of personal consumption, two years before and two years after financial crises

Percent

Note: The bar marked 0 is the year of the financial crisis.

credit ratings for Lebanon and Haiti by two notches; these would result in implied sovereign spread reductions ranging from 130 to 334 basis points (table 4.5).[26]

Remittance securitization can help countries raise external financing

Another way in which remittances affect international capital market access is through the use of structured finance techniques. Several banks in developing countries (for instance, Brazil) have been able to raise relatively cheap and long-term financing from international capital markets via securitization of future remittance flows.

Remittance securitization typically involves the borrowing entity (such as a bank) pledging its future remittance receivables to an offshore special purpose vehicle (SPV). The SPV issues the debt (figure 4.7). Designated correspondent banks are directed to channel remittance flows of the borrowing bank through an offshore collection account managed by a trustee. The collection agent makes principal and interest payments to the investors and sends excess collections to the borrowing bank. Since remittances do not enter the issuer's home country, the rating agencies

debt to exports of goods and services, a key indebtedness indicator, would increase significantly if remittances were excluded from the denominator (figure 4.6). Country credit ratings by major international rating agencies often fail to account for remittances.[25] Model-based calculations using debt-to-export ratios that include remittances in the denominator indicate that including remittances in creditworthiness assessments would improve

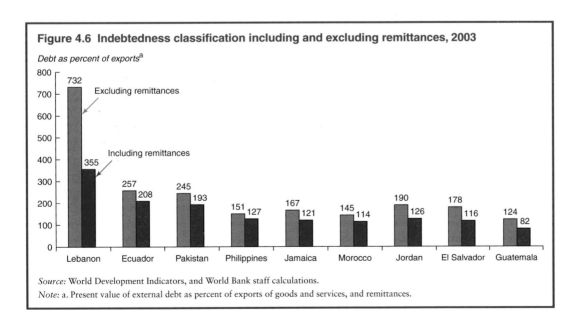

Figure 4.6 Indebtedness classification including and excluding remittances, 2003

Debt as percent of exports[a]

Source: World Development Indicators, and World Bank staff calculations.

Note: a. Present value of external debt as percent of exports of goods and services, and remittances.

Table 4.5 Impact of remittances on country credit rating and sovereign spread

	Remittances as % of GDP, 2004	Rating excluding remittances	Rating including remittances[a]	Spread saving (basis points)
Serbia and Montenegro	7	B+	BB−	150
Lebanon	14	B−	B+	130
Haiti[a]	28	CCC	B−	334
Nicaragua[a]	11	CCC+	B−	209
Uganda[a]	5	B−	B	161

Sources: Standard and Poors and World Bank staff calculations.
Note: a. Calculated using a model similar to Cantor and Packer (1995); see Ratha and De (2005).

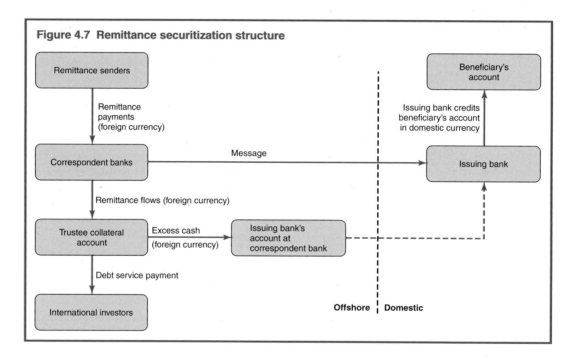

Figure 4.7 Remittance securitization structure

believe that the structure mitigates the usual sovereign transfer and convertibility risks. Such transactions also often resort to excess coverage to mitigate the risk of volatility and seasonality in remittances.

By mitigating currency convertibility risk, a key component of sovereign risk, the future flow securitization structure allows securities to be rated better than the sovereign credit rating. These securities are typically structured to obtain an investment grade rating. In the case of El Salvador, for example, the remittance-backed securities were rated investment grade, two to four notches above the sub-investment grade sovereign rating. Investment-grade rat-

ing makes these transactions attractive to a wider range of "buy-and-hold" investors (for example, insurance companies) that face limitations on buying sub-investment grade. As a result, the issuer can access international capital markets at a lower interest rate spread and longer maturity. Moreover, by establishing a credit history for the borrower, these deals enhance the ability and reduce the costs of accessing capital markets in the future.

The first major securitization deal involving international migrant remittances occurred in 1994 in Mexico. The volume of remittance securitization has grown rapidly since then (figure 4.8a). Using this instrument,

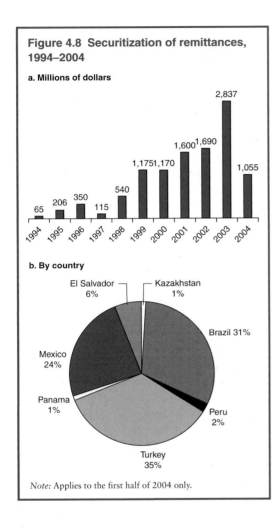

Figure 4.8 Securitization of remittances, 1994–2004

a. Millions of dollars

2,837

1,600 1,690

1,175 1,170

540

1,055

65 206 350 115

1994 1995 1996 1997 1998 1999 2000 2001 2002 2003 2004

b. By country

El Salvador 6%

Kazakhstan 1%

Brazil 31%

Mexico 24%

Panama 1%

Peru 2%

Turkey 35%

Note: Applies to the first half of 2004 only.

versified payment rights. These bonds resulted in a spread saving of more than 700 basis points compared to Brazil's sovereign spread.

As experience with this instrument broadens, and investors become more comfortable with its characteristics, it is possible that it could be used by a wider range of countries (including poor countries) and for a broader range of external flows (remittances, tourism receipts, and commodity earnings). It is not easy to estimate the potential size of such future-flow securitization. But preliminary calculations, assuming an over-collateralization ratio of 5:1 and using migrant remittance figures for 2003, show that developing countries could potentially issue nearly $9 billion and low-income countries could raise up to $3 billion annually from international capital markets.

Several policy hurdles need to be crossed before securitization deals can proceed. High fixed costs of legal, investment banking, and credit-rating services and long lead times can pose difficulties for developing countries with few large entities and high borrowing needs. A master trust arrangement can permit issuers to structure a large deal but to tap the market in several tranches. Pooling receivables of several branches (or even several borrowers) could also help increase the deal size to justify large fixed costs. While the absence of an appropriate legal infrastructure can also constrain issuance, this need not require an overhaul of the entire legal system. A more focused approach that concentrates on bankruptcy law may suffice, by making sure that pledged assets remain pledged in the event of default.

So far, only the top-rated (in local currency terms) financial institutions have issued future remittance-backed bonds in an effort to pierce the sovereign foreign currency rating ceiling (that is, to obtain a higher rating for these bonds than the sovereign foreign currency rating). The securitization transactions typically do not affect financial institutions' ability to deliver remittances to the ultimate beneficiaries. Loosely speaking, the financial institutions that undertake a securitization transaction are pledging their *rights* to foreign

Mexico, El Salvador, and Turkey raised about $2.3 billion during 1994–2000. As electronic transfers became more widespread, it was easier to track complex transactions, and remittances securitization gave way to securitization of diversified payment rights (DPRs), including migrant remittances, but also payments related to exports and FDI. During 2000–4, a total of $10.4 billion was raised through securitization of DPRs by Brazil ($5.3 billion), Turkey ($4.1 billion), El Salvador, Kazakhstan, Mexico, and Peru (figure 4.8b). Following a sharp increase in borrowing costs in 2002 (in part because of election-year uncertainties), Brazil has raised over $4 billion by issuing bonds backed by di-

currency, but not their obligations to deliver remittances (typically in local currency terms). Potential issuers should be reminded, however, of significant risks—currency devaluation and, in the case of flexible rate debt, unexpected increases in interest rates—that are associated with market-based foreign currency debt. Moreover, securitized debt is inflexible debt. Securitization of remittances (and other future flows) by public sector entities reduces the government's flexibility in managing its external payments and can conflict with the negative pledge provision included in multilateral agencies' loan and guarantee agreements, which prohibit the establishment of a priority for other debts over the multilateral debts.

Large remittance inflows can lead to exchange rate appreciation and lower export competitiveness

Large and sustained remittance inflows can cause an appreciation of the real exchange rate and make the production of cost-sensitive tradables, including cash crops and manufacturing less profitable. Although empirical evidence on the adverse effect of large inflows of foreign exchange in terms of trade and growth is limited,[27] it is plausible that this effect exists and is significant for some small economies where remittances are very high. Amuedo-Dorantes and Pozo (2004) found that a doubling of workers' remittances resulted in real exchange rate appreciation of about 22 percent in a panel of 13 LAC countries (see also Winters and Martins 2004). Rajan and Subramanian (2005), however, did not find any evidence that remittance flows slow down growth by affecting competitiveness.[28] Moreover, as remittances tend to be relatively stable and persistent over long periods, the "Dutch disease" effects of remittances are less of a concern than similar effects of natural resource windfalls and other cyclical flows, and the real exchange rate level achieved through sensible policies may be sustainable (IMF 2005). Governments in countries receiving large remittances can mitigate the effects of real exchange rate appreciation by allocating a larger portion of government expenditures on infrastructure and also practicing more liberal trade policies; both these measures would tend to increase exports and also contribute to improved labor productivity and competitiveness.

A related concern is whether reliance on unearned income in the form of remittances has adverse effects on the incentives to work, as well as on the quality of economic policies and governance, similar to the well-documented effects of windfall gains from natural resources such as oil. While oil exports are almost always found to have a strong negative impact on various governance indicators, such as control of corruption and rule of law, preliminary cross-country analysis suggests that remittance flows may not have such negative effects (box 4.5).[29]

The evidence on the effect of remittances on long-term growth is inconclusive

To the extent that they finance education and health and increase investment, remittances could have a positive effect on economic growth. Remittances may relieve credit constraints in the recipient community and spur entrepreneurial activity (Funkhouser 1992, Yang 2004, Woodruff and Zenteno 2004). Faini (2002) finds that the impact of remittances on growth is positive. He argues that remittances overcome capital market imperfections and allow migrant households to accumulate positive assets, as claimed by Stark and Lucas (1988) and Taylor (1994). Mishra (2005) found that a 1 percentage point increase in remittance inflows in 13 Caribbean countries increased private investment by 0.6 percentage point (all measured relative to GDP). To the extent that they increase consumption, remittances may increase per capita income *levels* and reduce poverty and income inequality, even if they do not directly impact growth (see chapter 5).

On the other hand, large outflow of workers, especially skilled workers, can reduce growth in labor-sending countries. Remittances may also indirectly affect labor supply,

Box 4.5 Unlike oil windfalls, remittance inflows do not weaken institutional capacity

The economic performance of most mineral exporters, in particular oil exporters, has been far less impressive than that of resource-poor countries (Gelb and others 1988; Auty 2001; Gelb, Eifert, and Tallroth 2002). To a large extent this outcome seems driven by mismanagement of the economy and weak institutions. Sala-i-Martin and Subramanian (2003) show empirically that concentration of resource flows has deleterious effects on the institutional framework and capacity of a country. Natural resource windfalls—oil rents, for example—often foster weak institutions because they allow the authorities to pursue arbitrary, costly, and inefficient policies (Ross 2001). States that control such resources may resist secular modernization pressures because they create alternative sources of power (Isham and others 2003). These rents also perpetuate economic inequality, which results in nepotism and a weak civil society. Resource rents are also believed to be associated with civil conflict (Collier and Hoeffler 2002).

In contrast, remittances are widely dispersed, the great bulk of them is allocated in small amounts, and for the most part, remittances avoid the government "middleman." Hence the expectation is that they can avoid the negative effects of natural resource windfalls on poverty, growth, and institutional capacity. This is similar to an argument by Birdsall and Subramanian (2004) that countries would be better off if they distributed the bulk of the returns from resource flows to the general population, who would use the funds more effectively than a highly centralized government, and also greatly reduce the incentives for corruption.

by encouraging some remittance-recipient households to choose more leisure than labor. Chami, Fullenkamp, and Jahjah (2005) argue that remittances may slow down growth by reducing work efforts by remittance recipients.[30]

One recent study of the impact of remittances on growth over an extended period (1970–2003) for 101 developing countries found no significant link between remittances and per capita output growth, or between remittances and other variables such as education or investment rates (IMF 2005). This study, however, attributed this inconclusive result to measurement difficulties arising from the fact that remittances may behave countercyclically with respect to growth.[31] Also, empirically it is difficult to measure the effects of remittances on human capital formation, which may occur over a very long period of time.

Remittances, like aid, may be more effective in a good policy environment. For instance, a good investment climate with well-developed financial systems and sound institutions is likely to imply that a higher share of remittances is invested in physical and human capital (IMF 2005). Indeed, Giuliano and Ruiz-Arranz (2005) show that in the economies where the financial system is underdeveloped, remittances alleviate credit constraints and work as a substitute for financial development, improving the allocation of capital and therefore accelerating economic growth. Recent research also shows that remittances may promote financial development (Aggarwal and others 2005), which in turn can enhance growth and reduce poverty (Beck and others 2004).

Annex 4A.1 World Bank data on remittances

Using the definition in chapter 7 of *Global Development Finance 2003*, migrant remittances are considered the sum of workers' remittances, compensation of employees, and migrants' transfers. Data for these variables

Table 4A.1.1 Countries with alternative estimates in 2004

$ millions

Algeria	2,460
China	21,283
Gambia	8
Iran	1,032
Kenya	464
Lebanon	2,700
Malaysia	987
Mauritious	215
Nigeria	2,751
Serbia and Montenegro	4,129
Vietnam	3,200
Total	$39,259

are taken mostly from the balance of payments (BoP) data file of the IMF (see also Ratha 2003). However, many countries do not report data on remittances in the IMF BoP statistics, even though it is known that emigration from those countries took place (see table 4A.1.1 for a list of these countries). In 2003 about 87 countries did not report any remittances' data. Further, there was no consistency in reporting the data. For example, only 28 countries report workers' remittances, compensation of employees, and migrants' transfers. Forty-five countries report both workers' remittances and compensation of employees; 11 countries report compensation of employees and migrants' transfers; and 3 countries report workers' remittances and migrants' transfers. There are 14 countries that report only workers' remittances and 19 countries that report only compensation of employees.

Reported data for developing countries show only $113.4 billion in total remittances for the year 2003 (workers' remittances $97.3 billion, compensation of employees $14.8 billion, and migrants' transfers $1.3 billion), and 83.8 billion in 2004 (workers' remittances $68.7 billion, compensation of employees $13.5 billion, and migrants' transfers $1.5 billion). By filling in gaps for some developing countries for which remittance data were missing, we arrived at an estimate of $142 billion in 2003, and $160 billion in

2004 (the latest year for which BoP data are currently available). The gap-filling methods followed, and the reasons for making the adjustments are documented below.

Workers' remittances, as defined in the IMF Balance of Payments manual, published in 1993 (fifth edition), are current private transfers from migrant workers who are considered *residents* of the host country to recipients in their country of origin. If the migrants live in the host country for a year or longer, they are considered residents, regardless of their immigration status. If the migrants have lived in the host country for less than a year, their entire income in the host country should be classified as compensation of employees. Workers' remittances are transfers, whereas compensation of employees is considered factor income. In the earlier, fourth edition of the BoP manual, compensation of employees was called labor income and was classified as nonfactor services (referred to just as services in the fifth edition).

Although the residence guideline in the manual is clear, this rule is often not followed for various reasons. Many countries compile data based on the citizenship of the migrant worker rather than on their residency status. Further, data are shown entirely as either compensation of employees or as worker remittances, although they should be split between the two categories if the guidelines were correctly followed; for example, Saudi Arabia and Israel record only compensation of employees. India shows very little compensation of employees, but large workers' remittances, although it is well known that India supplies a large number of temporary IT workers to the United States and European countries. On the other hand, the Philippines shows large compensation of employees and very few migrants' transfers. The distinction between these two categories appears to be entirely arbitrary, depending on country preference, convenience, and tax laws or data availability. This fact has been recognized at the World Bank since the 1980s, and worker remittances have been treated as part of labor income and added to exports of goods and services in calculating debt service ratios.

Though small in comparison to compensation of employees and workers' remittances, migrants' transfers have become another source of confusion. Migrants' transfers are the net worth of migrants that are transferred from one country to another at the time of migration (for a period of at least one year). Migrants' transfers are considered capital transfers in the BoP fifth edition manual, although they were considered current private transfers in the fourth edition. As the number of temporary workers increases, the importance of migrants' transfers may increase. Therefore, in order to get a complete picture of the resource flow, one has to consider these three items together.

There are four main reasons for gaps in remittance data: vintage, missing data, data recorded under other than the three categories mentioned above, and data collection practices.

Vintage

The Balance of Payments Yearbook publishes data with a one-year lag. That is, the yearbook published in December of the current year should have data up to December of the previous year. However, this is not true for a number of developing countries, for which the latest data available are two or even more than three years old. For about 28 countries in 2003, and 59 countries in 2004, data have been obtained from World Bank country desks or extrapolated on the basis of earlier trends.

In addition, two countries, Algeria and Nigeria, have not reported data to the IMF for a number of years. For Algeria the IMF data stop in 1991, and for Nigeria data, stop in 1999. However, data for these countries are available from the country and reported in the country databases of the World Bank and IMF.

Missing data

Several developing countries (for example, Lebanon) do not report to the IMF.[32] Data from the country desks are used for The Gambia, Iran, and Serbia and Montenegro; and data from central banks were used for Lebanon and Vietnam. Some high-income countries (notably Canada, Singapore, United Arab Emirates) also do not report remittance data.

Classification under other categories

Due to the difficulty in classifications, countries have often classified workers' remittances either as other current transfers or as transfers from other sectors. For example, in the case of Haiti, before 1989 and after 1997, data were recorded as workers' remittances, but during 1990–7, they were recorded as transfers from other sectors. Kenya and Malaysia data have similar difficulties. For these countries, data under "other sectors" from the IMF are treated as worker remittances. In China a large proportion of workers' remittances are classified as other private transfers in the IMF BoP file. Therefore, instead of the IMF's workers' remittances, we have used workers' remittances data from the country desk. It is not just the developing countries that follow this practice, many high-income OECD countries (for example, the United Kingdom) do the same.

There are also other problems in the data, such as the difficulty in separating travel expenditure from remittances, which have not been addressed here. The increased acceptance of credit and debit cards in developing countries further complicates the issue. In some countries, notably China, remittances may have been misclassified as FDI. The OECD definition of FDI (including the purchase of holiday or second homes by nonresidents) may be counted as FDI—a likely case in China. In the case of India and many other countries, remittances may have been classified as nonresident deposits, especially those in local currency terms.

Data collection practices

A survey of central banks, based on responses from 40 central banks, reveals widespread problems with remittance data collection methodology (de Luna Martinez 2005). Most of the central banks use remittance data reported by commercial banks, but leave out flows through money transfer operators and informal personal channels.

Even when data are available and properly classified, in many cases they are not based on actual exchange records. In a number of cases, the preferred methodology of estimating the workers' remittances is based on taking the number of emigrants, and multiplying by an average amount sent. The sources for these data are migration records, surveys of exchange and financial houses, and household surveys. However, these data are often weak or out of date. Also the methodology for preparing estimates is not the same in all countries, and it is not always described in the country notes in the publicly available balance-of-payments data. It is hoped that the increased awareness about the importance of remittances and the shortcomings in both the remittance and migrant workers' data will result in efforts to improve the data transmission.

Table 4A.1.1 shows the countries where we have used alternative estimates of workers' remittances' using either country desk or the central bank data.

Perhaps the most difficult aspect of remittance data is estimating informal flows. In annex 4A.2, we discuss different ways of estimating informal flows. One way to estimate the true size of remittances is to undertake surveys of remittance senders and recipients. Unless new, adequately randomized and representative surveys of recipients and senders are carried out, evidence from existing household surveys would only be indicative rather than comprehensive.

Annex 4A.2 A model-based estimation of informal remittance flows

Estimating the size of unrecorded flows is almost impossible. In what follows, we make an effort to arrive at some crude

estimates using a set of variables that are noted in the literature to affect the choice of the remittance channel. Empirically, this involves first estimating officially recorded remittances as a function of fee, exchange commission, and the presence of a dual exchange rate (and other variables shown in the equation below). Next, using the estimated coefficients on these variables, we predict what remittances would be if the values of these variables become closer to those prevailing in regions where informal flows are small. We then interpret the difference between these predicted remittances and the actual remittances as an estimate of informal flows.

For this purpose, we propose the following model of remittances:

$$REMIT = b_0 + b_1 Host + b_2 Home$$
$$+ b_3 Migrant + b_4 Fee200$$
$$+ b_5 Spread200 + b_6 Dual$$

where $REMIT$ is the log of remittances (or remittance per migrant or per capita); $Host$ is the log of the host-country per capita output (trade or migration weighted across hosts); $Home$ is the log of home-country per-capita output; $Migrant$ is the log of the stock of migrant workers in OECD countries; $Fee200$ is the fixed fee for sending \$200 from the United States to the source country; $Spread200$ is the exchange commission for sending \$200; and $Dual$ is a dummy variable for dual exchange rates. The last three variables are likely to have large impacts on the extent to which money is sent via formal channels. The data on remittances are available on a panel basis; data on transaction costs and on the number of migrant workers are only available for a cross-section. In table 4A.2.1 below, we report regression results for a cross-section of countries (using average figures for 1995–2003 for remittances and other time series variables). In table 4A.2.2, we show results of remittance cost functions estimated using cross-country data. These equations estimate panel data on remittance costs for use in panel data regressions reported in table 4A.2.3. Reduced form

Table 4A.2.1 Regression results: determinants of worker remittances

Explanatory variables	Dependent variable: Ln (Remittances) (1)	Dependent variable: Ln (Remittances) IV[a] (2)	Dependent variable: Ln (Remittances per emigrant) (3)	Dependent variable: Ln (Remittance per capita) (4)
Dual exchange rate	−0.42	−0.18	−0.31	−0.74**
	(−1.32)	(−0.46)	(−0.90)	(−2.04)
Service fee	−0.06**	−0.12*	−0.07**	−0.04
	(−2.32)	(−1.94)	(−2.47)	(−1.00)
Exchange-rate spread	−0.04		−0.02	−0.05
	(−0.50)		(−0.26)	(−0.52)
Stock of migrant workers	0.73**	0.64		0.22**
	(7.66)	(5.41)		(2.45)
Main host per capita income	−0.10	−0.05	−0.22*	0.11
	(−0.77)	(−0.31)	(−1.75)	(0.69)
Home per capita income	−0.15	−0.17	−0.06	0.72**
	(−1.03)	(−1.00)	(0.40)	(4.35)
Income	0.31**	0.31		
	(4.05)	(3.75)		
Number of observations	104	85	104	104
R^2	0.70	0.69	0.08	0.35

Source: Freund and Spatafora (2005).
Note: Robust t-statistics appear in parentheses.
a. Instruments include financial development and dollarization. Hansen's J-statistic is 2.49 (p-value 0.12), and the Shea partial R-squared of the instruments is 0.37.
**significant at the 5 percent level; *significant at the 10 percent level.

Table 4A.2.2 Regression results: determinants of transaction costs

Dependent variable: remittance cost

Explanatory variables	(1)	(2)	(3)	(4)	(5)
Bank concentration	0.05**	0.03	0.03		
	(2.29)	(1.10)	(1.35)		
Financial development	−0.05**	−0.05**	−0.05**	−0.06**	−0.05**
	(−2.41)	(−2.38)	(−2.42)	(−2.54)	(−2.53)
Financial risk	0.04	−0.04	0.03	−0.04	0.01
	(0.32)	(−0.26)	(0.24)	(−0.31)	(0.02)
Dollarization	−4.12**	−3.92**	−3.92**	−4.10**	−4.00**
	(−4.47)	(−3.87)	(−4.20)	(−4.14)	(−4.33)
Domestic output	−0.22	−0.56	−0.32	−0.75	−0.46
	(−0.46)	(−1.02)	(−0.66)	(−1.47)	(−0.98)
Remittances		−0.30		−0.42*	
		(−1.18)		(−1.85)	
Emigrant stock			−0.34		−0.59**
			(−1.18)		(−2.40)
R^2	0.52	0.56	0.53	0.52	0.52
Number of observations	76	69	76	70	78

Source: Freund and Spatafora (2005).
Note: The dependent variable is the percentage cost of remitting $200. Robust t-statistics appear in parentheses.
**significant at the 5 percent level; *significant at the 10 percent level.

Table 4A.2.3 Panel regression results: determinants of remittances

Explanatory variables	Ln (Remittances) (1)	Ln (Remittances) (2)	Ln (Remittances per capita) (3)	Ln (Remittances per capita) (4)
Dual exchange rates	−0.28**	−0.22**	−0.26**	−0.21**
	(−2.69)	(−2.18)	(−2.48)	(−2.03)
Fitted cost	−0.08*		−0.08*	
	(−1.70)		(−1.74)	
Bank concentration		−0.00		−0.00
		(−1.00)		(−1.03)
Financial development		0.03**		0.02**
		(5.13)		(4.30)
Financial risk		0.00		0.01
		(0.02)		(1.12)
Dollarization		0.62*		0.58
		(1.73)		(1.60)
Net errors and omissions	−0.02**	−0.02**	−0.02**	−0.02*
	(−2.07)	(−2.03)	(−2.12)	(−1.97)
Home per capita income	2.10*	3.64**	0.43**	0.63**
	(1.71)	(2.92)	(2.37)	(3.31)
Host per capita income	1.37	1.28	1.33	1.41
	(1.39)	(1.34)	(1.33)	(1.46)
Home income	−1.71	−3.13**		
	(−1.38)	(−2.46)		
Number of observations	295	295	295	295
R^2	0.27	0.35	0.21	0.29

Source: Freund and Spatafora (2005).

Note: All regressions include country and year fixed effects. Robust t-statistics appear in parentheses.

**significant at 5 percent level; *significant at 10 percent level.

equations for remittances using statistically significant variables in the cost regressions are also shown in table 4A.2.3.

Notes

1. In March 2004, the G-7 finance ministers indicated their intention to "continue to work on initiatives to reduce barriers that raise the cost of sending remittances and to integrate remittance services in the formal financial sector" and their commitment to "work with governments, the private sector, and multilateral development banks to broaden the access for families and entrepreneurs to financial services." At the Sea Island Summit in June 2004, the G-8 heads of state called for "better coherence and coordination of international organizations working to enhance remittance services and heighten the developmental impact of remittance receipts." They indicated that "G-8 countries will work with the World Bank, IMF, and other bodies to improve data on remittance flows and to develop standards for data collection in both sending and receiving countries."

2. One market study estimates that *global* remittances are about 2.5 times the size reported in the IMF balance of payments (Aite Group 2005). The recent upward revision of China's remittances to $21 billion in 2004, from an earlier estimate of $4.6 billion, lends some support to this notion, although there is no strong evidence that systematic misreporting is so large. The discrepancy for China is reportedly due to the fact that the Chinese figures include compensation only for state employees. Some authors believe that a portion of China's FDI attributed to overseas Chinese may actually be a misclassification of migrant remittances. Some also believe that the recent surge in remittances to China in part reflected speculative inflows in anticipation of a revaluation of the yuan.

3. For example, the reporting threshold (typically per person per day) is $10,000 in the United States, 12,500 euros in western European countries (on average), and 3 million yen in Japan.

4. Saudi Arabia, the second largest source of remittances at $13.6 billion (or 5.4 percent of GDP) in 2004, is now classified as a high-income country. Saudi Arabia's per capita income level has risen in response

to the current high oil prices. The authorities prefer that Saudia Arabia be treated as a developing country.

5. Efforts are under way through the GTAP consortium to compile and estimate a comprehensive set of bilateral migrant stocks, which are used here. See Walmsley, Ahmed, and Parsons 2005.

6. More precisely, bilateral remittance flows are calculated by allocating reported remittance inflows in each country according to weights constructed as follows:

$R(i,j)$ = [Remittance flows to country j] * [$M(j,i)$/[sum over i of the nominator]]

$R(i,j)$ = remittance flows from country i to country j and $M(j,i)$ = stock of migrants from country j in country i. Data on migrant stocks $M(.)$ are taken from the GTAP database (Walmsley, Ahmed, and Parsons 2005).

7. Including Saudi Arabia as a developing country would raise South–South remittances to 45 percent and South–South migration stock to 60 percent.

8. A World Bank survey of the African diaspora in Belgium conducted in spring 2005 revealed that 42 percent of remittances from Belgium to Senegal, and 55 percent to Congo and Nigeria, go through informal channels. Anecodotal evidence suggests that nearly 70 percent of remittances in the France–Mali corridor take place through informal channels. Hand-carriage is a popular yet informal channel of remittances in many countries. In the Philippines, 40 percent of total flows are estimated to be remittances brought home by migrants in person. Nearly 42 percent of outward remittances from South Africa are believed to move through informal channels (Genesis Analytics 2005).

9. In a calibration model, El Qorchi, Maimbo, and Wilson (2003) argue that the black-market premium is the key factor determining informal flows. Other factors affecting the choice of the channel are trust in the intermediary and anonymity and convenience factors, such as location, hours of operation, and language.

10. Results will underestimate the size of informal flows to the extent that they are affected by other factors, such as a lack of legal documentation of migrants and high tax rates. To the extent that there would still be some informal flows even at this lower remittance cost level, the estimates are actually lower bounds on the true size of informal remittances. However, it is possible that the increases estimated in table 4.4 represent new remittance flows, and not just the shift from the informal to the formal sector, in which case these estimates would overstate informality.

11. Page and Plaza (2005) use a similar methodology and find that the share of unrecorded remittances relative to the total remittances averages 48 percent worldwide (and 73 percent in Sub-Saharan Africa).

12. Between 2001 and 2004, the euro appreciated by 28 percent relative to the U.S. dollar. During this period, outward remittances from France and Germany actually declined by 5 percent in euro terms. Remittances from Italy and Spain increased nearly 40 percent in euro terms and 93 percent in U.S. dollar terms.

13. A survey of Congolese, Senegalese, and Nigerian diasporas in Belgium did not reveal any significant relationship between the propensity to remit and the number of years a migrant has lived in Belgium. On the contrary, several migrants who had been in Belgium for more than two decades continued to send significant amounts of remittances. Evidence from the Pacific Islands also do not support remittance decay (Connell and Brown 2005; Simati and Gibson 2001). Grieco (2003), however, reported evidence of remittance decay in the case of Micronesian migrants in Guam and Hawaii, caused by family reunification or death of the beneficiaries.

14. The information presented here derives from a survey of IOM country missions on the policies of their host countries, as well as studies by ADB, ECOSOC, USAID, DFID, and the World Bank.

15. For example, Colombia has a 0.4 percent tax on transactions through money exchange bureaux and banks, a temporary arrangement in effect until 2007. Belarus also taxes remittances from nonimmediate family members.

16. For example, in Tajikistan the removal of the state tax on cross-border bank transactions in 2003 reportedly helped raise remittances from $78 million in 2002 to $256 million in 2003 (Olimova and Bosc 2003).

17. For example, nonresident Pakistanis remitting over $10,000 through banking channels can import any personal item valued up to $1,200 duty-free per annum (World Bank 2005b).

18. Extension of voting franchise to migrants overseas and other policies of political inclusion may also catalyze remittances and other financial flows to the country of origin (Carey 2003; Yang 2003).

19. For example, Pakistan does not permit women under 35 to emigrate as domestic workers and Vietnam bans females from working overseas in the entertainment sector. Bangladesh recently abandoned similar restrictions recognizing that although such restrictions may protect migrants from exploitation, they may also encourage more irregular migration, rendering them even more vulnerable.

20. This is in part responsible for Western Union's withdrawal from the South African market (Genesis Analytics 2005).

21. Such activities complement government objectives to improve banking access in poor neighborhoods

(e.g., through the Community Reinvestment Act; see Frias 2004).

22. USAID also established an 18-month pilot program in 2004 with the PanAmerican Development Foundation to strengthen the capacity of U.S.-based HTAs. The UK government is also looking at the possibility of using HTAs as a conduit for development aid.

23. See also *Global Development Finance 2003*, chapter 7, and Sayan (2004). A separate study by Sayan (2005) finds that in a sample of 12 low-income and lower-middle-income countries during 1976–2003, real remittances responded to a fall in real GDP with a one-year lag. He also found evidence of countercyclicality due to consumption smoothing in India and Bangladesh and procyclicality due to a stronger investment motive in Jordan and Morocco.

24. Black (2004, p. 12) reports that remittances remained substantial during the civil war in Côte d'Ivoire.

25. This is likely to be the case in countries (such as the Philippines or Lebanon) where the headline worker remittance variable has underestimated or missing data.

26. Sovereign spread rises exponentially as credit ratings worsen along the rating scale. A one-notch improvement in credit ratings, therefore, results in higher spread saving for countries at the bottom of the rating scale.

27. See McMahon (1997) for a review of empirical studies on the so-called Dutch disease, a term coined by *The Economist* in 1977.

28. They argue that migrants may lose interest in remitting money and prefer to send goods instead, if the currency in the remittance recipient country is overvalued. Thus controlling overvaluation through prudent macroeconomic policies can help attract remittances.

29. Note that this result applies to cross-country comparison. It would be extremely difficult to empirically estimate the effect of remittances on institutional capacity over time in a given country, since institutional changes take place over a very long time. Also such an exercise would require controlling for reverse causality: remittances may respond to cyclical or abrupt changes in economic growth and governance. A priori, the effect of institutions on remittances can run either way: On the one hand, better institutional capacity may attract remittances meant for investment purposes. On the other hand, better institutional capacity (if they also mean better performance) may mean less emigration and dependence on remittances.

30. However, reduced work effort by some individuals may not reduce the aggregate work effort in a typical developing country with a large pool of unemployed.

31. It is difficult to disentangle the reverse-causality problem (that growth also affects remittances) while measuring the effect of remittances on growth. Some researchers argue that the empirical results showing a negative association between remittances and growth may largely reflect the fact that remittances tend to rise when growth is weak in the remittance-recipient country.

32. The list of countries that do not report remittance data also includes the following 29 countries: Afghanistan, Angola, Bahamas, Bahrain, Bhutan, Burundi, Canada, Central African Republic, Chad, Congo Democratic Republic, Equatorial Guinea, Iraq, Kuwait, Liberia, Singapore, Somalia, Taiwan (China), Turkmenistan, United Arab Emirates, Uzbekistan, Zambia, and Zimbabwe.

References

Aggarwal, Reena, Asli Demirguc-Kunt, and Maria Soledad Martinez Peria. 2005. "Do Remittances Promote Financial Development? Evidence from a Panel of Developing Countries." Unpublished paper, World Bank, Washington, DC.

Aite Group. 2005. "Consumer Money Transfers: Powering Global Remittances." Unpublished paper. January. www.aitegroup.com.

Alesina, Alberto, Arnaud Devleeschauwer, William Easterly, Sergio Kurlat, and Romain Wacziarg. 2003. Fractionalization. *Journal of Economic Growth* 8(2): 155–94.

Amin, Mohammad, and Caroline Freund. 2005. "Migration and Remittances in ESA Countries." Washington, DC: The World Bank.

Amuedo-Dorantes, Catalina, and Susan Pozo. 2004. "Workers' Remittances and the Real Exchange Rate: A Paradox of Gifts." *World Development* 32(8): 1407–17.

Annual Finance & Accounting International Conference—Managing Securitization for Lebanon and the MENA Region, December 3-4, 2004. Lebanese American University, School of Business, Beirut.

Auty, Richard. 2001. "Introduction and Overview." In *Resource Abundance and Economic Development*, ed. R. M. Auy. New York: Oxford University Press.

Beck, Thorsten, Asli Demirguc-Kunt, and Ross Levine. 2004. "Finance, Inequality and Poverty: Cross-Country Evidence." NBER Working Paper 10979. National Bureau of Economic Research, Cambridge, MA.

Birdsall, Nancy, and Arvind Subramanian. 2004. "Saving Iraq from Its Oil." *Foreign Affairs* (July/August): 77–89.

Black, Richard, Savina Ammassari, Shannon Mouillesseaux, and Radha Rajkotia. 2004. "Migration and Pro-Poor Policy in West Africa." Working Paper C8. Sussex Centre for Migration Research, University of Sussex. November.

Buencamino, Leonidas, and Sergei Gorbunov. 2002. "Informal Money Transfer Systems: Opportunities and Challenges for Development Finance." DESA Discussion Paper 26.

Cantor, Richard, and Frank Packer. 1995. "Sovereign Credit Ratings." *Current Issues in Economics and Finance* 1(3): 1–6. June.

Carey, John M. 2003. "Political Institutions in El Salvador: Proposals for Reform to Improve Elections, Transparency, and Accountability." Unpublished paper. Dartmouth College. www.dartmouth.edu/~jcarey/el percent20salvador.pdf.

Carling, Jorgen. 2005. "Migrant Remittances and Development Cooperation." PRIO Report 1/2005, Oslo.

Chami, Ralph, Connel Fullenkamp, and Samir Jahjah. 2005. "Are Immigrant Remittance Flows a Source of Capital for Development?" *IMF Staff Papers* 52(1).

Clarke, George, and Scott Wallsten. 2004. "Do Remittances Protect Households in Developing Countries against Shocks? Evidence from a Natural Disaster in Jamaica." Unpublished paper. World Bank, Washington, DC.

Collier, Paul, and Anke Hoeffler. 2002. "Greed and Grievance in Civil War." In *Annual Bank Conference on Development Economics*. Washington, DC: World Bank.

Collyer, Michael. 2004, "The Development Impact of Temporary International Labour Migration on Southern Mediterranean Sending Countries: Contrasting Examples of Morocco and Egypt," Working Paper T6. Development Research Centre on Migration, Globalisation and Poverty, University of Sussex, Brighton, UK.

Connell, John, and Richard P. C. Brown. 2005. "Remittances in the Pacific: An Overview." Asian Development Bank, Manila. March. www.adb.org/Documents/Reports/Remittances-Pacific/default.asp.

de Luna Martinez, Jose. 2005. "Workers' Remittances to Developing Countries: A Survey with Central Banks on Selected Public Policy Issues." Policy Research Working Paper 3638. World Bank.

El Qorchi, M., S. Maimbo, and J. Wilson. 2003. "Informal Funds Transfer Systems: An Analysis of the Informal Hawala System." IMF Occasional Paper 222. International Monetary Fund, Washington, DC.

Ellerman, David. 2003. "Policy Research on Migration and Development." World Bank Policy Research Working Paper 3117. Washington, DC.

Faini, Ricardo. 2002. "Migration, Remittances, and Growth." Unpublished paper. University of Brescia. www.wider.unu.edu/conference/conference-2002-3/ conference%20papers/faini.pdf.

Freund, Caroline, and Nikola Spatafora. 2005. "Remittances: Costs, Determinants, and Informality." Background paper prepared for this report. World Bank.

Frias, Michael. 2004. "Linking International Remittance Flows to Financial Services: Tapping the Latino Immigrant Market." *Supervisory Insights*. FDIC. Winter 2004.

Funkhouser, E. 1992. "Migration from Nicaragua: Some Recent Evidence." *World Development* 20(8): 1209–18.

Gelb, Alan, and others. 1988. *Oil Windfalls: Blessings or Curse?* New York: Oxford University Press.

Gelb, Alan, Benn Eifert, and Nils Borje Tallroth. 2002. "The Political Economy of Fiscal Policy and Economic Management in Oil Exporting Countries." World Bank Policy Research Working Paper 2899. Washington, DC.

Genesis Analytics. 2005. "Supporting Remittances in Southern Africa: Estimating Market Potential and Assessing Regulatory Obstacles." Johannesburg, South Africa.

Giuliano, Paola, and Marta Ruiz-Arranz. 2005. "Remittances, Financial Development, and Growth." IMF Working Paper. Washington, DC.

Grieco, Elizabeth. 2003. *The Remittance Behavior of Immigrant Households: Micronesians in Hawaii and Guam.* New York: LFB Scholarly Publishing.

Gubert, Flore. 2005. "Migrant Remittances and Their Impact on the Economic Development of Sending Countries: The Case of Africa." Paper presented at the OECD International Conference on Migration, Remittances, and the Economic Development of Sending Countries, February 23–25, Marrakech.

Harrison, Anne, assisted by Tolani Britton and Annika Swanson. 2004. "Working Abroad—The Benefits Flowing from Nationals Working in Other Countries." Paper prepared for the OECD Round Table on Sustainable Development, Paris. September. www.worldbank.org/data/Remittances/3aHarrison.pdf.

Hernandez-Coss, Raul E. 2004. "The U.S.-Mexico Remittance Corridor: Lessons on Shifting from

Informal to Formal Remittance Systems." Financial Sector, World Bank.

IFAD (International Fund for Agricultural Development). 2004. "Remittances and Rural Development." Discussion paper for the Governing Council, 27th session, Rome, February 18–19, 2004.

IMF (International Monetary Fund). 2005. *World Economic Outlook: Globalization and External Imbalances* (chapter 2). Washington, DC. April.

IOM. 2003b. World Migration 2003: Managing Migration—Challenges and Responses for People on the Move, Geneva.

IOM (International Organization for Migration). 2005. *World Migration Report.* Geneva.

Isham, Jonathan, Michael Woolcock, Lant Pritchett, and Gwen Busby. Forthcoming. "The Varieties of Resource Experience: Natural Resource Export Structures and the Political Economy of Economic Growth." In *World Bank Economic Review.*

Iskander, Natasha. 2005. "Social Learning as a Productive Project (Zacatecas and Guanajuato's Cautionary Tales)." Paper presented at OECD International Conference on Migration, Remittances, and the Economic Development of Sending Countries, February 23–25, Marrakech.

Kaufmann, Dani, Art Kraay, and M. Mastruzzi. 2005. "Governance Matters IV: Governance Indicators for 1996–2004." World Bank Institute. Draft, May 9, 2005.

Ketkar, Suhas and Dilip Ratha. 2001. "Securitization of Future Flow Receivables: A Useful Tool for Developing Countries." Finance and Development. International Monetary Fund. Washington, DC.

Ketkar, Suhas and Dilip Ratha. 2004. "Recent Advances in Future-Flow Securitization." Paper presented at the OECD International Conference on Migration, Remittances and the Economic Development of Sending Countries." February 23–25, Marrakech.

La Porta, Rafael, Florencio Lopez-de-Silanes, Andrei Shleifer, and Robert Vishny. 1999. "The Quality of Government," *Journal of Law, Economics, and Organization* 15(1): 222–79.

Lam, Ricky and Leonard Wantchekon. 2003. Political Dutch Disease. April 10. New York University. www.nyu.edu/gsas/dept/politics/faculty/wantchekon/research/lr-04-10.pdf.

Magoni, Raphaele. 2004. "France." In *International Migration and Relations with Third Countries: European and U.S. Approaches,* ed. Jan Niessen and Yongmi Schibel. Migration Policy Group.

McMahon, Gary. 1997. "The Natural Resource Curse: Myth or Reality?" Unpublished paper. World Bank Institute, Washington, DC.

Mishra, Prachi. 2005. "Macroeconomic Impact of Remittances in the Caribbean." Unpublished paper. International Monetary Fund, Washington, DC.

Newland, Kathleen, and Erin Patrick. 2004. "Beyond Remittances: The Role of Diaspora in Poverty Reduction in Their Countries of Origin." Migration Policy Institute, Washington, DC.

Olimova, Saodat, and Igor Bosc. 2003. Labour Migration from Tajikistan. Dushanbe: Mission of the International Organization for Migration. www.untj.org/library/?mode=details&id=73.

Orozco, Manuel. 2003. "Hometown Associations and Their Present and Future Partnerships: New Development Opportunities? Report commissioned by the U.S. Agency for International Development.

Orozco, Manuel, and Katherine Welle. 2004. "Hometown Associations and Development: A Look at Ownership, Sustainability, Correspondence, and Replicability." Inter-American Dialogue. Unpublished paper.

Page, John, and Sonia Plaza. 2005. "Migration, Remittances, and Development: A Review of Global Evidence." Paper presented at the Plenary Session of the African Economic Research Consortium, May 29, Nairobi.

Rajan, Raghuram, and Arvind Subramanian. 2005. "What Undermines Aid's Impact on Growth?" NBER Working Paper 11657. October.

Ratha, Dilip. 2003. "Workers' Remittances: An Important and Stable Source of External Development Finance." In *Global Development Finance 2003,* Chapter 7. World Bank. Updated in *Remittances and Development: Development Impact and Future Prospects,* ed. Samuel Maimbo and Dilip Ratha. Washington, DC: World Bank.

Ratha, Dilip. 2004. "Understanding the Importance of Remittance Flows." Migration Policy Institute. Migrationinformationsource.org.

Ratha, Dilip, and Prabal De. 2005. "Predicting Sovereign Rating: International Capital Market Access for Unrated Countries." Background paper for this report. World Bank.

Ravallion, Martin. 2003. "Measuring Aggregate Welfare in Developing Countries: How Well Do National Accounts and Surveys Agree?" *The Review of Economics and Statistics* 85(3): 645–52.

Reuter, Peter, and Edwin M. Truman. 2004. Chasing Dirty Money: The Fight against Money Laundering. Institute for International Economics. Washington.

Ross, Michael. 2001. "Does Oil Hinder Democracy?" *World Politics* 53(3): 325–61.

Sala-i-Martin, Xavier, and Arvind Subramanian. 2003. "Addressing the Natural Resource Curse: An Illustration from Nigeria." IMF Working Paper WP/03/139. International Monetary Fund, Washington, DC.

Sayan, Serdar. 2004. "Guest Workers' Remittances and Output Fluctuations in Host and Home Countries." *Emerging Markets Finance and Trade* 40(6): 68–81.

———. 2005. "Business Cycles and Workers' Remittances: How Do Migrant Workers Respond to Cyclical Movements of GDP at Home?" Unpublished paper. Bilkent University.

Siddiqui, Tasneem. 2004. "Efficiency of Migrant Workers' Remittances." Prepared for the Asian Development Bank.

Simati, A., and J. Gibson. 2001. "Do Remittances Decay? Evidence from Tuvaluan Migrants in New Zealand." *Pacific Economic Bulletin* 16(1): 55–63.

Sparreboom, P. 1996. "Migrant Worker Remittances in Lesotho: A Review of the Deferred Pay Scheme." Social Finance Programme Working Paper 16. International Labour Office, Geneva.

Stark, Oded, and Robert E.B. Lucas. 1988. "Migration, Remittances, and the Family." *Economic Development and Cultural Change* 36: 465–81.

Taylor, Edward. 1994. "International Migration and Economic Development: A Micro Economy-wide Analysis." In *Development Strategy, Employment and Migration*, ed. J. Edward Taylor. Paris: Organisation for Economic Co-operation and Development.

TEBA (The Employment Bureau of Africa). 2005. "A Presentation on the Existing and Potential Contribution to Rural Southern Africa." Marshall Town, Johannesburg.

Terry, Donald. 2005. "Sending Money Home: Remittances as a Tool in Latin America and the Caribbean." Development Bank, Manila, Joint Conference on Remittances, September 12–13, 2005.

UN (United Nations). 2005. Letter of February 23, 2005, to the Secretary General from the Permanent Representatives of Brazil, Chile, France, Germany, and Spain (A/59/719-E/2005/12) Technical Group on Innovative Financing Mechanisms. Economic and Social Council. New York.

Walmsley, Terrie, Syud Amer Ahmed, and Christopher Parsons. 2005. "The GMig2 Data Base: A Data Base of Bilateral Labor Migration, Wages and Remittances." GTAP Research Memorandum 6, Center for Global Trade Analysis, University of Sussex. www.gtap.agecon.purdue.edu/resources/download/2338.pdf.

Winters, L.A., and Pedro M.G. Martins. 2004. "When Comparative Advantage Is Not Enough: Business Costs in Small Remote Economies." *World Trade Review* 3(3): 1–37.

Woodruff, Christopher, and Rene Zenteno. (2004). "Remittances and Microenterprises in Mexico." IR/PS working paper. Graduate School of International Relations and Pacific Studies, University of California–San Diego.

World Bank. 2005a. *Global Development Finance 2005*. Washington, DC.

World Bank. 2005b. "Migrant Labor Remittances in the South Asia Region." Finance and Private Sector Development Unit/South Asia Region. Report No. 31577. February 2005.

Yang, Dean. 2003. "Salvadorans Overseas: The Foundation of a Pro-Poor Growth Strategy." Unpublished paper. Gerald R. Ford School of Public Policy, University of Michigan. www-personal.umich.edu/~deanyang/yang_cv.pdf.

———. 2004.

———. 2005. "Coping with Disaster: The Impact of Hurricanes on International Financial Flows, 1970–2001." Research Program on International Migration and Development. DECRG. World Bank.

Yang, Dean, and Claudia Martinez. 2005. "Remittances and Poverty in Migrants' Home Areas: Evidence from the Philippines." In *International Migration, Remittances, and the Brain Drain*, ed. Caglar Ozden and Maurice Schiff. New York: Palgrave Macmillan.

5

Remittances, Households, and Poverty

Chapter 4 presented evidence on the macroeconomic dimensions of remittance flows—their overall size, determinants of their composition (formal versus informal), the role of government policies in determining their magnitude and use, and their macroeconomic impacts—to developing countries. But as previously noted, these aggregate flows are comprised of millions of individual remittance transfers among private households, all undertaken by senders and receivers striving to improve household welfare. This chapter considers the impact of remittance flows at the micro-level, in particular on the welfare and opportunities of the recipient households and their members.

Evaluating household impact depends on data and analysis carried out at the household level, often through household surveys. Surveys are available for many countries and periods, and many of these have common or comparable structures, but substantial differences in coverage and circumstances complicate their interpretation. Such caveats notwithstanding, the evidence presented in this chapter suggests that remittances can:

- Reduce poverty, even where they appear to have little impact on measured inequality;
- Help smooth household consumption by responding positively to adverse shocks

(for example, crop failure, job loss, or a health crisis);
- Ease working capital constraints on farms and small-scale entrepreneurs;
- Lead to increased household expenditures in areas considered to be important for development, particularly education, entrepreneurship, and health.[1]

Our evaluation of the empirical analysis on remittances and development is structured as follows. In the next section, we consider the effects of remittances on poverty and inequality. We then explore how remittances can alleviate the difficulties that households face in smoothing consumption. The next section considers the indirect effects of remittances on household budgets in terms of induced labor supply effects, increased access to working capital, and multiplier effects. We then examine how households allocate remittances to various categories of spending, with a particular emphasis on evidence of remittance-funded investments in human capital, micro-enterprises, and property.

Before continuing, two broad observations on the scope and interpretation of the available analysis help to put the results in perspective. First, in evaluating the impact of remittances, it is important to consider the alternative (or counterfactual) situation that serves as a comparison. If a household member migrates and sends back remittances, one could evaluate the *net* change in the migrant's contribution—that is, adding the remittances and subtracting the income of the migrant had he or she stayed and worked at home.[2] That approach is the appropriate focus when the goal of migration is to generate remittances, or when we are interested in the overall effect of migration on remaining household members. The alternative is to ignore the lost domestic contribution—so that the counterfactual is now simply *no remittances*. This approach measures the narrow impact of remittances, which seems appropriate when migration is being treated as exogenously given, and our interest is simply in the remittance flows generated by the *existing* migration stock. The second approach merits close attention because the existing migrant stock is large, and also because not all remittances are received from migrant relatives abroad; third-party remittances are common.[3]

Second, in evaluating the benefits of remittances, we also need to weigh the welfare of the migrants themselves. To take a concrete example, imagine the migration decision facing a young husband and father in a country with a long-established migration history that borders on a much richer country. Economic opportunity (and possibly social pressure) may make remittance-motivated migration irresistible. However, separated from family and community support, this young man could end up living a quite miserable existence. Clearly, a simple tracking of cash provides an inadequate guide to the welfare implications of the move.

Remittances, poverty, and inequality

Remittances directly affect poverty by increasing the income of the recipient. They also indirectly affect poverty in the recipient country through their effects on growth, inflation, exchange rates, and access to capital. Measuring the impact of remittances is complex (in part because of the difficulties of accounting for the counterfactual loss of income from migration, as just mentioned). But a growing body of evidence from poverty simulation models, cross-country regressions, and analysis of household survey data shows that remittances, in fact, do reduce poverty—although the evidence of their effect on inequality is mixed.

Remittances reduce poverty

In what follows, we present evidence on the poverty effects of remittances, based on three sources: a poverty simulation model, a cross-country regression analysis, and household survey data from selected countries. The illustrative poverty simulation model asks a straightforward question: how would poverty rates change in our sample of developing countries if remittances were to disappear completely? Because this model is easy to implement for most countries, it can provide some sense of the effect of remittances across countries. However, the model is relatively crude and cannot account for the fact that while remittances affect poverty, the level of poverty also affects the volume of remittances. In comparison, cross-country regression analysis requires more data and is harder to implement, but it is better able to control for reverse causality between remittances and poverty. Household surveys are most likely to provide the data required for a rigorous analysis of the relationship between remittances and poverty. The surveys also allow one to analyze the counterfactual loss of income due to migration. It is difficult, however, to generalize across countries on the basis of household data, particularly because most available household surveys do not have usable data on remittances, especially international remittances.

To understand how remittance flows might affect measures of poverty, we start with an illustrative poverty simulation model and ask a straightforward (although unrealistic) question. The model relates the *change* in poverty to *income growth* and *inequality change*. It is estimated using cross-country data for

Box 5.1 Estimating a cross-country poverty change model

The basic idea behind a poverty change model is that a particular measure of poverty (say the fraction of the population with incomes below $1 per day) is a function of descriptive parameters of the income distribution, such as the mean and the Gini coefficient. Building on Ravallion (1997), we posit a conditional constant elasticity specification, in which there is a constant growth elasticity of poverty reduction that varies with the initial level of inequality. After reformulation, the basic relationship (see annex 5A.1) relates the *rate of poverty change* to a measure of inequality-adjusted *income growth* and an income-adjusted *change in inequality*.

To estimate the relationship, we use the dataset assembled by Adams and Page (2005), in which the observations relate to the period between comparable nationally representative household surveys. For each country, we have data from surveys for the initial and final values of poverty, inequality, and per capita income. Below is the estimated poverty change equation for the headcount measure of poverty.

Using survey income and consumption data as the income variable (last column), results from the model are robust, with statistically significant impacts from both income growth and inequality change on the headcount rate.

Estimated poverty change model		
Income variable	Income variable	Survey mean income or consumption
Dependent variable—proportionate change in the headcount rate	GDP per capita	
Intercept	0.39	0.33
	(2.21)	(2.42)
Inequality-adjusted growth	−4.93	−5.60
	(−2.57)	(−2.27)
Income-adjusted inequality change	0.60	1.11
	(1.57)	(2.82)
R^2	0.08	0.30
Number of observations	81	81

Source: World Bank staff estimates.
Note: Standard errors are robust to country-level clustering; *t* statistics are in parentheses. The model is estimated using first difference of variables. The poverty line for the headcount poverty calculation is $1.08 in purchasing-power-parity-adjusted 1993 dollars (equivalent to $1 in 1985 dollars). The per capita income measure is mean survey income or consumption (depending on availability from the survey).

81 countries. The methodology and results are presented in box 5.1 and in annex 5A.1. The premise behind the analysis is that the incremental income from remittances can be analyzed in the same way as incremental income from economic growth—so we can simulate the impact of eliminating remittances by modeling an income decline equal to the original remittance level. For the sake of simplicity, we assume that nothing else changes—that there are no offsetting increases in domestic sources of income or other adjustments to spending behavior or labor supply.[4]

Results from the simulation are summarized in table 5.1 (see also annex 5A.1). We report averaged results for different groups of countries—first, by distinguishing between higher-remittance recipients (greater than

Table 5.1 Simulated impact of eliminating remittances on poverty rate

Country group	No. of countries	Remittances/GDP (%)	Poverty headcount rate	Change in headcount rate, no Gini change
Low remittances	23	2.2	25.6	5.0
Low headcount rate	12	2.0	11.8	1.2
High headcount rate	11	2.5	40.6	9.1
High remittances	14	11.0	24.8	12.2
Low headcount rate	7	8.0	10.7	4.1
High headcount rate	7	14.1	38.9	20.3

Source: World Bank staff estimates.
Note: Low (high) remittances refer to the remittance share in GDP less (greater) than 4 percent. Low (high) headcount rate refers to a rate less (greater) than 20 percent. Allowing inequality to change ±2 Gini points has minimal effects on the change in the headcount rate. See annex 5A.1 for detailed results.

4 percent of GDP) and lower (less than 4 percent but greater than 1 percent), and second, by the extent of poverty (headcount above 20 percent or below 20 percent).

These results show that the impact of eliminating remittances depends on how large they are to begin with (higher initial levels mean steeper income declines), the initial extent of poverty, and the degree of inequality. For example, the average increase in the headcount ratio for higher-remittance countries (12.2 percentage points) is more than twice that of the lower-remittance countries (5 percentage points). Similarly, with each of these two groups, the impact is much greater for those countries with higher headcount ratios to start with. The estimated impact of inequality—an assumed 2 point worsening in the Gini coefficient—has only a small marginal impact on the estimated change in the poverty rate.

This simple analysis has significant limitations. First, the simulated effects depend on accurate country-level measures of remittances, which, as emphasized in chapter 4, are of variable reliability. Second, many of the country simulations are made outside the sample used for the regression analysis and are therefore subject to the standard out-of-sample prediction problems. Third, the analysis assumes that remittances are included in household income when calculating the measures of poverty and inequality from household surveys. In reality, there is variation across surveys in how remittances are accounted for in the household surveys.[5]

The results just described provide an indication of the role that remittances can play in reducing poverty, but because of the simplicity of the model and other limitations, the results are not conclusive. More rigorous analytic work has been undertaken to investigate the link between remittances and poverty based on careful analysis of cross-country data.

In a model that relates national poverty levels to mean income and the Gini measure of inequality for 71 developing countries, a 10 percent increase in per capita official international remittances leads to a 3.5 percent decline in the share of people living in poverty (Adams and Page 2005).[6] Other recent studies have broadly confirmed these findings, including IMF (2005) (see chapter 2), which uses a sample of 101 countries for the period 1970–2003.

Although the available evidence is still relatively limited, growing evidence from household survey data complements the findings of the model that international remittances have reduced the incidence and severity of poverty in several low-income countries. According to that evidence, remittances are believed to have reduced the poverty headcount ratio by 11 percentage points in Uganda, 6 percentage points in Bangladesh, and 5 percentage points in Ghana (Adams 2005b). Completely removing remittances for Lesotho would raise the headcount poverty ratio (with a poverty line equal to 60 percent of mean household expenditure) from 52 to 63 percent (Gustafsson and Makonnen 1993).

While remittances had only a limited role in reducing the number of poor people in Guatemala, they did significantly reduce the depth and severity of poverty (Adams 2004a).[7] International remittances accounted for 60 percent of income for households in the lowest income decile, but were not very large for households located near the poverty line (roughly the fifth income decile). As a result, international remittances had more impact on reducing the depth of poverty than on the poverty headcount; in other words, they were really helpful for the poorest of the poor.

Wodon and others (2002) conclude that in Guerrero and Oaxaca, two southern Mexican states with significant international emigration and remittance inflows, the share of the population living in poverty is lower by 2 percentage points due to remittance income. They argue that this poverty effect is similar in magnitude to that of many government programs in poverty reduction, education, health, and nutrition. Taylor, Mora, and Adams (2005), using data from a 2003 survey, find that international remittances account for 15 percent of per capita household income in rural Mexico. They conclude that an increase in international remittances would reduce both the poverty headcount and the poverty gap.

Yang and Martinez (2005) studied the impact of variations in the exchange rate on remittances sent by Filipino workers and the ultimate impact of remittances on poverty in the recipient regions. Using a large dataset from the Overseas Filipino Survey, they found that an appreciation of the Philippine peso led to an increase in remittance flows, which contributed to the reduction in poverty. Interestingly, increased remittances not only reduced poverty in the migrant families, they also had spillover effects on nonmigrant families. (We will have more to say on multiplier effects later in this chapter.)

The effect of remittances on inequality is unclear

In contrast to the link between remittances and poverty, no strong conclusion is found in household studies of the relationship between remittances and inequality: remittances sometimes go disproportionately to better-off households and so widen disparities, but in other cases they appear to target the less well off, causing disparities to shrink. Some studies suggest that the remittances from new migration may raise inequality in the short term, but the effect on inequality is small over the long term.[8] Calculations that impute incomes for the migrant had he stayed and worked at home generally show an increase in inequality from the combined effect of migration and remittances. For example, inequality was found to have increased in Bluefields, Nicaragua, when an imputation was made for the lost domestic income of migrants, but it fell when the domestic income of migrants was ignored (Barham and Boucher 1998).

Two recent studies, however, did not find an increase in inequality even after controlling for the counterfactual income loss from migration: Adams (2005a) found that in Ghana, the inclusion of international remittances in household expenditures led to only a slight increase in income inequality, but that the Gini coefficient remained relatively stable, between 0.38 and 0.40.[9] De and Ratha (2005) found that in Sri Lanka, the Gini coefficient drops from 0.46 to 0.40 as a result of remittance receipt.

Differences in findings on the impact of remittances on inequality also stem from varying geographic and historic circumstances, such as the distance from high-income destination countries and the prevalence of networks of earlier migrants. Both proximity to high-income countries and established networks will tend to reduce the cost of migration, making migration an option for poorer (and often credit-constrained) households.[10] For example, remittances to a Mexican village with a well-established history of international migration had an equalizing effect, whereas remittances to another Mexican village for which international migration was a relatively new phenomenon tended to make the distribution of income more unequal (Stark, Taylor, and Yitzhaki 1986). For a large number of Mexican communities, the overall impact of migration and remittances is estimated to reduce inequality for communities with relatively high levels of past migration (McKenzie and Rapoport 2004).[11]

One reason for the inconclusive empirical evidence on inequality effects is that the Gini coefficient does not adequately capture income mobility; it remains unchanged, for example, if one person moves up and another moves down the income ladder. Using household survey data from Sri Lanka, De and Ratha (2005) show that the poor income deciles also have significant overseas migration and that remittance recipients in the middle income deciles move up the income ladder (figure 5.1).[12]

Beyond the contradictory or inconclusive results, some scholars question whether the link between remittances and inequality is all that important. Inequality matters when it interferes with the functioning of the economy (for example, when credit constraints bind more households[13]) or the political system (for example, when growing inequality increases support for governments that pursue damaging populist policies[14]). Greater inequality may also be considered bad because of its impact on social welfare (see Sen 1973 for a discussion). But it should be kept in mind that in the context of remittances, inequality relates to income differences among groups that would all be viewed as relatively poor in an industrial-country context. The rich in developing countries probably receive little in the way of remittances; the rich who migrate tend to take their families with them.

Remittances and household consumption smoothing

Remittances may play a significant role in smoothing consumption. Poor households

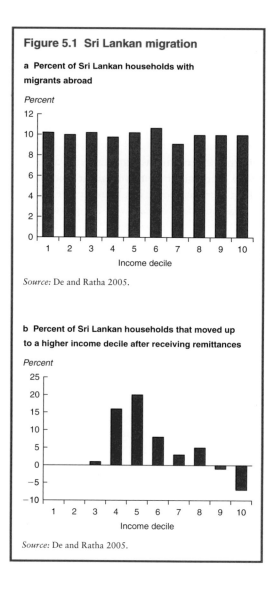

Figure 5.1 Sri Lankan migration

a Percent of Sri Lankan households with migrants abroad

Percent

Income decile

Source: De and Ratha 2005.

b Percent of Sri Lankan households that moved up to a higher income decile after receiving remittances

Percent

Income decile

Source: De and Ratha 2005.

that lack access to insurance and credit markets are vulnerable to severe declines in income from adverse shocks, and they may be forced to forgo income-generating—but risky—strategies (Morduch 1994). Informal community institutions generally play a limited role in mitigating risk (see, for example, Coate and Ravallion 1993 and Fafchamps 2004), especially in the face of adverse events such as a community-wide crop failure. One strategy to reduce risk is for households to send family members to other regions or countries, where they are not likely to face the same income shocks as those found in the domestic market.[15] Migration patterns and policies that encourage migrants to travel unaccompanied by family members encourage this form of risk sharing.

There is some evidence that remittances from internal migration provide insurance. Remittances to Botswana increased with the extent of drought in the migrant's home region, and the responsiveness of remittance levels to drought was greater for households with more drought-sensitive assets such as cattle (Lucas and Stark 1985).[16] The anticipation of insurance may allow the household to pursue a more risky asset accumulation strategy—although it is also possible that households with more to lose from drought (whatever the reason) are simply more likely to receive remittances. The likelihood that Thai internal migrants move to Bangkok is reduced the more closely income in Bangkok aligns with income in the province of origin (Paulson 2000).[17] The effect is particularly strong for remittances to rural households, which are likely to be poorer and have less access to formal insurance products to mitigate weather-related risks. The more volatile a household's income (and the more restricted its ability to self-insure), the greater the distance that households in rural India tend to send their daughters to marry (Rosenzweig and Stark 1989). Greater distance means that the covariance of income shocks with the home region will be smaller, facilitating consumption-smoothing transfers between these related households.

Studies of how remittances respond to adverse household shocks generally support the view that remittances provide some insurance. However, interpreting these correlations is complicated by the likelihood of reverse causality (remittances can influence household outcomes as well as be influenced by them) and omitted variable bias (certain hard-to-measure household characteristics may affect a household's susceptibility to risks as well as the likelihood of receiving remittances).

Consider, for example:

- Migrants responded to the cost of hurricane damage borne by Jamaican households, with each additional dollar of hurricane damage leading to $0.25 in additional remittances (Clarke and Wallsten 2004. The authors use panel data to control for the household-level risk aversion and vulnerability effects that potentially bias the estimates.[18])
- Remittances are estimated to have replaced 60 percent of income loss due to weather-related shocks in a sample of Filipino households (Yang and Choi 2005.[19] Rainfall is used as an instrument for income to avoid reverse causality; panel data are used to control for the tendency for risk-averse households to locate in places where incomes are more stable and to send migrants to manage risk.)
- In cross-country data, a dollar's worth of hurricane damage leads to roughly $0.13 in additional remittances in the year of the hurricane and $0.28 cents over five years (Yang 2005). (Yang uses meteorological data to instrument for reported disaster damage, because damage reports may be affected by the anticipation of financial flows.)

Remittances and indirect effects on household income

Remittances may indirectly affect household income through changes to the labor supply of those remaining behind; relaxation of working capital constraints that expand income from entrepreneurial or farming activities; and multiplier effects on household income. Unfortunately, the evidence on each of these channels is quite limited, so we are constrained here to identifying important areas for additional research.

Remittances may affect labor supply
Remittances may tend to reduce the supply of labor provided by remaining household members, who may take a portion of the

remittance gain as leisure. This *income effect* is generally not a concern, because it represents part of the welfare gain from remittances. By contrast, remittances may change the return to supplying labor, for example, if the migrant conditions the remittance on low household income.[20] Such a *substitution effect* will reduce the welfare gain from remittances by distorting household labor decisions.

However, it is difficult to separate income and substitution effects of remittances on the labor supply of those remaining behind. Looking at the overall effect, a rise in remittances reduced labor force participation in Managua, Nicaragua, but increased self-employment (Funkhouser 1992). Remittances were estimated to reduce the participation rates of remaining household heads in a number of Caribbean countries, although the direction of causality was hard to establish (Itzigsohn 1995). Yang (2004) points to more encouraging labor-supply effects than the standard model when he determined that remittances reduce the supply of child labor but increase that of adult labor.

Remittances provide working capital

There is some evidence that remittances provide working capital to households that lack access to credit markets. For example, migration to South Africa's mines initially reduced agricultural production in countries of origin, because labor was removed from the farm (Lucas 1987). However, over time production rose with migration, perhaps due to remittance-funded capital investment and a greater willingness to take risks with agricultural production, owing to the more diversified sources of family income. Remittances had a small negative effect on household income for Mexico in 1982, but a large positive effect for 1988 (Taylor 1992). One possible explanation is that over time the development of migrant networks allowed migration from poorer households that are more likely to be credit constrained (see the discussion of inequality, above). The effect of remittances on household income depends on both the liquidity of household assets (which determines their value as collateral) and on the availability of inputs that complement entrepreneurial activity (Taylor and Wyatt 1996). The role of remittances in relaxing household credit constraints in rural cropping income in China dominated the direct loss of productive labor from migration, so that internal migration increased per capita household income (excluding remittances) by 14 to 30 percent (de Brauw, Taylor, and Rozelle 2001). Mishra (2005) found that a 1 percentage point increase in remittance inflows in 13 Caribbean countries increased private investment by 0.6 percentage point (all measured relative to GDP).

Remittances may ease credit constraints because a stable stream of remittance income may make households more creditworthy in the eyes of formal sector financial institutions. Remittance receipts that increase when the household receives an adverse shock may be even more important in relaxing credit constraints, since they increase the lender's confidence that they will be repaid even if things turn out badly for the household. This creditworthiness effect deserves careful empirical investigation, given the increasing interest in channeling remittances through formal financial channels.

Remittances may have multiplier effects

Some studies have found that remittances have a multiplier effect, whereby the increase in domestic income is some multiple of the remittance income. For example, each dollar sent by Mexican migrants to the United States was estimated to boost Mexican GDP by $2.90 (Adelman and Taylor 1992). Such multipliers will occur if output is constrained by insufficient demand. However, in many developing countries sustained underemployment is likely to have supply-side causes, for example, government policies that increase the cost of hiring and firing workers, so that increased demand will ultimately result in higher inflation rather than increased output.[21]

Nevertheless, there may be greater scope for sustained multiplier effects at the regional level. The local spending of remittance income will generate further income for other local households, which in turn is likely to cause local inflation for nontraded goods and possibly a small increase in national inflation. A national government with a formal or informal inflation target is likely to respond to any increase in the national inflation rate by tightening monetary policy, thereby leading to an offsetting effect on national aggregate demand. The net effect would be multiplier effects at the local level but not at the national level. Indeed, the local gains come partly at the expense of the regions that do not receive the remittances but are forced to suffer the tighter monetary policy.

Remittances also may have multiplier effects in the context of increasing returns, typically as the expansion of one sector increases the optimal size of other sectors.[22] Although such income-expanding feedback loops could be present at the national level, they are again more likely to be relevant at the regional level, because expanding regions attract labor and capital from elsewhere in the economy. The bottom line is that remittance-induced multiplier effects cannot be ruled out—especially at the regional level—but our current empirical understanding of their importance is quite limited.

Remittances, savings, and investment

Does it matter how households allocate remittance income between consumption and saving? Allocations to the latter may boost household investment or national investment through allocation to financial assets. But from a welfare perspective, an extra dollar of investment is only better than an extra dollar of present consumption if the marginal social value of investment is greater than its marginal private value.[23] Although a number of factors can drive a wedge between social and private values (such as capital income taxes, monopoly powers, and credit constraints), one prominent reason raised in the development context is the possible existence of positive externalities from investment expenditure.[24] Thus the way that remittances are allocated by households may affect the social value of a given remittance flow.

The rate of investment of remittance income will be high when:

- Remittance flows are viewed by the household as transitory rather than permanent and thus should be saved (and invested) rather than spent.
- The sender conditions the remittance on it being spent for particular purposes, which are more likely to involve investment than current consumption. Examples include education or the purchase of new farm machinery.
- The remittance is targeted (or "tagged") to household members more likely to use the funds for investment purposes (women rather than men).[25]
- Households practice a form of mental accounting with their overall budget, with remittances being disproportionately put in accounts set aside for investment purposes.[26]

On the other hand, some of the literature already reviewed suggests reasons to expect that the marginal propensity to invest remittance income will be low when (a) remittances are targeted to poor households that are struggling to meet subsistence needs and (b) they are targeted to credit-constrained households that are experiencing adverse consumption shocks.

The empirical challenge in identifying the causal effect of remittances on investment is that remittances are likely to be correlated with the extent of *opportunities* for investment, thereby biasing the estimated remittance effect. That correlation could be positive or negative. When more enterprising households are the ones sending migrants *and* the ones with substantial investment opportunities, high remittances will be wrongly associated with high investment. On the other hand, to the extent that households send migrants when investment opportunities are absent at home, then high remittances will be wrongly associated with low investment. The empirical solution is to find a source of variation in remittances that is plausibly unrelated to household investment opportunities.

Measuring the impact of remittances on investment—either in physical or in human capital—is not easy. Household budget surveys are best suited for this purpose, but most of the existing surveys either do not record data on international remittances or are poorly designed. Since remittances are fungible, it is difficult to isolate their effects from those of other sources of income. Simply asking how remittances are spent is unlikely to reveal the true marginal effect on spending, because remittances, even when used for investment purposes, may free up the marginal dollars for consumption spending.[27]

Remittances can lead to investments in education and health

Some of the clearest evidence for remittance-induced investments comes from work on human capital. The dramatic depreciation of the Philippine exchange rate during the Asian financial crisis increased remittances from Filipino migrants (because from the migrants' perspective, exchange-rate depreciation raised the relative price of their own consumption in the destination country compared with consumption by household members back home), leading to greater child schooling, reduced child labor, and increased educational expenditure in origin households (Yang 2004).[28] In El Salvador, remittances are estimated to reduce the probability of children leaving school by 10 times the effect of other sources of income in urban areas and by 2.6 times in rural areas (Cox Edwards and Ureta 2003).[29] They speculate that remittances have a disproportionate influence on schooling expenditures because the migrant has made it a condition for the financial support. Mexican children in households with migrants completed significantly more schooling, with the

largest impact (an additional 0.89 years of schooling) for girls in households where the mother has a low level of education (Hanson and Woodruff 2003).

Health status is both an important component of human capital and a central element of well-being in its own right. Unfortunately, the effect of migration on the health of family members remaining behind—notably children—is poorly understood. Migration from Mexico is associated with lower (by 3 percent) infant mortality and higher birth weights of children left behind (Hildebrandt and McKenzie 2005). The positive health effects come through increased access to health-related knowledge as well as through increased household wealth. Notwithstanding these encouraging outcomes, the authors caution that the impact of migration on child health is quite nuanced, with migration associated with lower measures of preventive health care such as breast-feeding and vaccinations.[30] De and Ratha (2005) find that in Sri Lanka, remittance income has a positive and significant impact on the weight of children under five; this result is especially strong for female-headed households. However, the health impact of absenteeism of one of the parents is negative.

Remittances can encourage entrepreneurship

There has been a marked shift from the belief that migrants are unlikely to establish new business enterprises in their countries of origin (either upon return or through remittance financing) to the view that migration encourages entrepreneurship. Large receipts of remittances from the United States are associated with a greater likelihood of productive investment in Mexico (Massey and Parrado 1998).[31] A survey of 6,000 small firms in 44 urban areas in Mexico shows that remittances are responsible for almost 20 percent of the total capital in urban micro-enterprises (Woodruff and Zenteno 2001). The share rises to one-third for the 10 states with the highest rates of United States–bound migration.

Remittances also appear to ease credit constraints on new business formation in the Philippines (Yang 2004). The effect of exogenous increases in remittance income on the probability of entering into entrepreneurship is larger for low- to middle-income households, which are the ones most likely to face credit constraints. Policies that facilitate easy exit and reentry for migrants may encourage increased involvement in remittance-funded investments or enterprises.

Remittances are often invested by recipient households

Contrary to the conventional wisdom that remittances tend to be "frittered away" by recipient households, recent work has estimated that a large proportion of remittance income is saved. Only 12 percent of net increments to expenditure by rural Egyptian households were allocated to consumption, with large propensities to invest in the construction and repair of houses, and in agricultural or building land (Adams 1991). This relatively high propensity to invest is assumed to result from households treating remittance receipts as temporary income flows, which forward-looking households save (and invest) rather than consume. These findings are largely confirmed in a later study of Pakistani households (Adams 1998).[32] In Guatemala, remittance-receiving households are found to have *lower* marginal propensities to consume and a higher propensity to invest in education, health, and housing than other households (Adams 2005c).

It should be noted that some survey results for a number of Latin American countries point to much higher propensities to consume remittance income (see, for example, IADB-MIF 2004). The percentages of remittances spent on household expenditures are 78 percent in Mexico, 77 percent in Central America, and 61 percent in Ecuador, while spending on real estate and education is low. However, surveys of how income from a particular source is spent tend to be unreliable, because monies from different sources are considered

perfect substitutes by the household. In contrast, studies such as Yang (2004) econometrically estimate expenditure propensities given exogenous changes in remittance income, so that the estimates should be less susceptible to the fungibility problem. A second explanation for the different results is that the econometric studies measure *marginal* propensities, whereas the direct surveys measure *average* propensities. It is the marginal propensity that is of interest when we consider the expenditure effects of policies that increase remittance flows.[33]

The role of remittances in funding investment has recently been questioned in a macroeconomic paper by Chami, Fullenkamp, and Jahjah (2005), who find that remittances tend to be negatively associated with economic growth. This countercyclical behavior of remittances is consistent with the evidence discussed above that remittances respond to adverse household shocks. But the observation that remittances tend to move countercyclically does not necessarily obviate their role in funding investment. The micro studies we reviewed point to remittances as both smoothing consumption and providing funds for investment. Moreover, the increased flow of remittances in the face of adverse shocks may allow households to sustain funding for key investments in areas such as business working capital, education, and health care.

The evidence reviewed in this chapter suggests that remittances play multifaceted roles in poverty reduction, consumption smoothing, and investment, with the balance of roles varying by time and place.

Annex 5A.1 Poverty simulation model: description and results

The poverty change model assumes that a particular measure of poverty (say the fraction of the population with incomes below $1 per day) is a function of descriptive parameters of the income distribution, such as the mean and the Gini coefficient. Building on

Ravallion (1997), we assume that there is a constant growth elasticity of poverty reduction, but we allow that elasticity to vary with the initial level of inequality.[34] We call this a conditional constant elasticity specification. Specifically, the poverty measure, P, is given by,

$$P = AY^{-\beta(1-I)},$$

where Y is per capita income (measured as mean survey income or consumption), I is the measure of inequality (which we take to be the Gini coefficient), and A and β are parameters. Differentiating the poverty equation and writing it in rate-of-change form yields our basic poverty change model,

$$\frac{dP}{P} = -\beta(1-I)\frac{dY}{Y} + \beta \ln Y \, dI$$

This equation can be interpreted as saying that the rate of poverty change depends on a

Table 5A.1 Effect of removing remittances on the poverty headcount rate

Country	Survey year	Poverty headcount rate ($1 a day, PPP, $1993)	Remittances as share of GDP (%)	Change in headcount rate (Gini = 0)	
				Using per capita GDP	Using survey mean income
Armenia	1998	13	5	2	4
Azerbaijan	2001	4	2	0	0
Bangladesh	2000	36	4	5	13
Bolivia	1999	14	1	0	1
Botswana	1993	31	2	1	3
Burkina Faso	1998	45	3	3	4
Colombia	1999	8	2	0	0
Côte d'Ivoire	1998	16	1	0	1
Ecuador	1998	18	3	2	3
Egypt, Arab Rep.	2000	3	3	0	1
El Salvador	2000	31	13	10	41
Gambia, The	1998	54	7	9	12
Georgia	2001	3	6	0	0
Guatemala	2000	16	3	1	2
Honduras	1999	21	6	3	4
India	2000	35	3	3	23
Kenya	1997	23	3	2	2
Lao PDR	1997	26	2	2	4
Lesotho	1995	36	44	29	34
Mali	1994	72	6	10	17
Mexico	2000	10	1	0	1
Moldova	2002	22	19	13	21
Mozambique	1997	38	2	2	2
Nepal	1996	39	1	1	2
Nicaragua	2001	45	2	3	13
Pakistan	1999	13	2	1	2
Panama	2000	7	2	0	0
Paraguay	1999	15	4	1	2
Peru	2000	18	1	1	2
Philippines	2000	16	8	3	10
Senegal	1995	22	3	2	3
Sierra Leone	1989	57	3	3	4
Sri Lanka	1996	7	6	1	3
Swaziland	1996	8	6	1	1
Tajikistan	1999	14	6	3	3
Uganda	1999	85	4	9	40
Yemen, Rep.	1998	16	19	10	7

Source: World Bank staff estimates.
Note: Remittance share is 1995 for Sierra Leone. Estimates are based on poverty reduction model.

measure of inequality-adjusted growth and an income-adjusted change in inequality.[35]

To estimate the relationship, we utilize the dataset assembled by Adams and Page (2005). The observations relate to spells between comparable nationally representative household surveys. For a given spell, we have data for the initial and final values of poverty, inequality, and per capita income.[36] The estimated equation for the headcount measure of poverty is reported in the table in box 5.1 in the main text. Similar results were found for the poverty gap measure.

The next step is to simulate the effect of removing remittances on the poverty measure under various assumptions about how remittances affect inequality. The proportionate increase in per capita income due to remittances is given simply by the share of remittances in GDP multiplied by the ratio of per capita GDP to mean survey income/consumption.[37] It is important to emphasize that the simulated poverty-increasing effect of removing remittances applies to the latest year for which a survey is available for that country, and thus different years are being used for different countries. Care should thus be taken in making comparisons about the importance of remittances in reducing poverty across different countries. Where the headcount rate is below 2 percent we do not attempt to estimate the poverty change effect of remittances.

Table 5A.1 shows results on the poverty headcount when remittances are removed (assuming there is no impact of remittances on inequality) for 37 countries where remittances are above 1 percent of GDP and where the poverty headcount rate is greater than 2 percent at the outset.

Notes

1. This represents a significant shift from the traditional earlier pessimism about the role of remittances in development. For example, Papademetriou and Martin (1991) emphasize how migration increases the dependence of emigration countries that are unable "to regulate or channel remittances," while Jacobs (1984) states that remittances "did nothing to convert stagnation to development" in abandoned regions.

2. Since data on what the migrant was earning before leaving are typically unavailable, the lost domestic income is estimated or imputed based on observed characteristics of the migrant and on knowledge of how those characteristics are rewarded in the domestic economy.

3. In the Sri Lanka Integrated Survey 1999–2000, nearly a third of households receiving remittances did not report having a migrant member overseas. It is possible that those households received remittances from their extended family; it is also possible that they received remittances from friends (De and Ratha 2005). The literature also notes third-party remittances in other countries (see, for example, Yang 2004 for the Philippines). A survey of African diasporas in Belgium found that more than one member in a typical migrant household sent regular remittances and that each remitter might send remittances to different recipients.

4. This situation is akin to the second counterfactual (a decline in remittances but no change in migration and hence household income) discussed at the outset. To the extent that a decline in remittance income may encourage households to devote more labor hours to domestic income-generating activities, the total decline in household income and the consequent poverty effect may be smaller than assumed in the simulation, a point made in Adams (2004a).

5. If we adopt the other extreme assumption—that remittances are not included in household income—the results can be interpreted with a simple reversal of the sign, which gives the reduction in poverty that would result if remittances were included.

6. As higher poverty increases the incentive to migrate, the ordinary least squares (OLS) estimates of the impact of remittances and stock of migrants are biased downward. On the other hand, when credit-constrained poor families do not have the resources to send migrants, the OLS coefficients are biased upward as poorer countries send fewer migrants. To deal with the bias, Adams and Page (2005) allow for remittances and emigrant stock variables in their regressions, using measures of international distance, government stability, and levels of education.

7. The poverty *depth* is the average shortfall below the poverty line expressed as a fraction of the poverty line (or simply the poverty gap ratio); and poverty *severity* is the squared poverty gap ratio. A key feature of this severity measure is that it is sensitive to the distribution of income among the poor (Foster, Greer, and Thorbecke 1984).

8. Stark, Taylor, and Yitzhaki (1986) found that a 1 percent increase in international remittances leads to

a 0.14 percent increase in the Gini coefficient in the case of Mexican villages with a short migration history; but in other villages with a long migration history, the Gini coefficient actually declines by 0.01 percent. Taylor (1992), McKenzie and Rapoport (2004), and Taylor, Mora, and Adams (2005) also find negative effects on the Gini in the case of Mexico.

9. Nearly 40 percent of households in a representative sample in Ghana receive remittances, of those remittances, 4 times as many households receive internal than international remittances (Adams 2005b). Households receiving internal remittances are disproportionately poor, indicating the importance of internal remittances in reducing poverty. Households surveys in Europe and Central Asia also show that in a number of countries (Albania, Kosovo, Moldova, and Tajikistan, for example) a large number of households receive remittances, many in rural areas (World Bank 2005).

10. Research has also shown that the inclusion of remittance-induced, indirect effects on income—such as income-induced reductions in nonmigrant labor supply or increases in entrepreneurial income due to the relaxation of credit constraints—can change the direction of the inequality effect.

11. The authors experiment with various instruments for location-specific migration levels in their regressions. The instruments include the historic (1924) state-level migration rate and unemployment rates for the U.S. state that includes the city that is the likely destination for migrants from a particular Mexican location.

12. This study imputes the counterfactual income by calculating the income from equivalent activities at home. In the bottom two deciles, remittance income is offset by the counterfactual loss of income from migration, whereas in the top two deciles, remittance income falls short of the counterfactual loss of income.

13. See, for example, Banerjee and Newman (1993).

14. See, for example, Alesina and Rodrik (1994) and Persson and Tabellini (1994).

15. The New Economics of Labor Migration (NELM) emphasizes that (a) migration is often better viewed as a family rather than an individual decision; (b) risk management and provision of credit are seen to play a central role in migration and remittance decisions; and (c) migration is often seen as a response to the failure of markets for insurance and credit (Taylor 1999). Rosenzweig (1988, p. 1167) highlights the informational problems that undermine crucial markets and emphasizes how ties of common experience, altruism, and heritage "enable families to transcend some of the informational problems barring the development of impersonal markets."

16. See also Stark and Lucas (1988).

17. Rainfall is used as an instrument for provincial income in establishing the covariance pattern.

18. Simple cross-sectional estimates of how remittances respond to hurricane damage will be biased downward if more risk-averse households are more likely to send migrants as a general insurance strategy *and* are more likely to take actions to reduce the risk of costly damage to the home. They will be biased upward if households with more vulnerable dwellings are more likely to send migrants *and* more likely to suffer hurricane damage. An additional complication is moral hazard, where insured (remittance receiving) households have less incentive to avoid risky behavior. Clarke and Wallsten (2004) deal with the potential endogeneity problem by using the average damage done in the neighborhood as an instrument for household-specific damage.

19. They cannot reject the null hypothesis that *all* of an exogenous decline in income is matched by an increase in remittances.

20. There is a disincentive to work if remittances are conditioned on low income. Conversely, if remittances are conditioned on domestic labor supply—"I will help you if you help yourself"—there is an added incentive to work. From the migrant's perspective, there is some similarity with the challenges faced by governments in providing social assistance without creating poverty traps and dependency. A traditional "welfare" model conditions remittances on household income, whereas the modern "workfare" model attempts to condition remittances on household effort in an attempt to avoid putting the household in a trap where working makes little economic sense. However, from the strict welfare perspective of the standard model, *any* distortion to the labor supply of the remaining members—negative or positive—reduces the welfare gain from the remittance.

21. See Layard, Nickell, and Jackson (1991) for a discussion of supply-side constraints on employment.

22. See Cooper (1999) for an introduction to multiplier effects under increasing returns where the outputs in different sectors are "strategic complements."

23. These values are assumed to be expressed in units of current consumption.

24. As examples, consider that the social return from human capital investments is greater than the private return due to knowledge spillovers (Moretti 2003); the social return from investments in vaccination is greater than the private return due to the spillover of reduced disease contagion (Miguel and Kremer 2001); and that the social return from entrepreneurship is greater than the private return due to externalities from demonstration effects about where a country's comparative advantage might actually lie (Hausmann and Rodrik 2002).

25. See Bourguignon and Chiappori (1992) and Browning and others (1994) for treatments of collective decision making in the "nonunitary household." Duflo (2003) demonstrates that pensions received by women in South Africa have a larger impact on the weight and height of girls than of boys living in the household. In other words, how that income is spent depends on who receives it. Using data from the Côte d'Ivoire, Duflo and Udry (2004) show that where husbands and wives farm different plots of land, the effect of rainfall shocks that differentially affect the plots has implications for the composition of household expenditure. They consequently reject the hypothesis of "full insurance" within the household.

26. See Thaler (1990) for a discussion of mental accounting.

27. Adams 2005a. See also Swaroop and Devarajan (2000) for a discussion of the fungibility problem in the context of evaluating the impact of official flows.

28. This is a useful test of the allocation of remittances between consumption and savings if the depreciation-induced change in remittances is independent of household investment opportunities.

29. This finding is subject to the problem of identifying whether remittances increase schooling or whether households with migrants are more likely to use additional income for schooling. The authors argue that remittances are closer to a randomly assigned transfer, particularly for political exiles whose migration is less likely to be correlated with household factors that affect the likelihood of human-capital investment.

30. Again, it is difficult to separately identify the impact of migration on health outcomes. Individuals from households with poor health status may not be well enough to make a difficult border crossing; the most prosperous and healthy households may find that local opportunities outweigh those yielded by a risky illegal move; or adverse shocks may affect both migration decisions and health status. Hildebrandt and McKenzie's (2005) empirical solution to this identification problem is to instrument for migration using the historic migration rate for the migrant's community.

31. Remittances sent during a household head's absence do not affect the likelihood of starting a new business; rather the resources accumulate and are available as seed capital after an adjustment period following the migrant's return. This delay may explain why contemporaneous surveys miss the business funding effect.

32. Likewise, Yang (2004) finds no evidence that aggregate household consumption expenditures were affected at all by the remittance-inducing exchange-rate shocks he studies, which contrasts with the significant positive effects he finds for education spending, adult labor supply, and capital investments.

33. On the other hand, the exogenous changes in remittance income that are used to identify the expenditure propensities in studies such as Yang (2004) are likely to be viewed by the household as temporary, leading the forward-looking households to invest rather than consume. These estimates would then provide a poor guide to the expenditure effects of policies that led to more sustained increases in remittance flows—for example, policies that permanently lower the cost of sending remittances.

34. Bourguignon (2003) uses a highly flexible functional form with multiple interactions between the key variables to estimate the relationship between poverty reduction, growth, and changes in inequality. Here we make stronger assumptions about the functional form of the relationship as a first pass in estimating the poverty-reducing effect in a relatively simple poverty-reduction model.

35. We actually take a slightly less restrictive version of this equation to the data by allowing for an intercept and allowing the coefficients on the two explanatory variables to differ. We also allow for the change in inequality to enter in separately, but the coefficient on this variable is insignificantly different from zero.

36. Observations where the initial and/or final poverty measure for the interval is zero are excluded. We also exclude observations from the Eastern Europe and Central Asian region due to concerns about comparable measurement during post-communist transition.

37. The growth in per capita income is given by $\Delta Y/Y$. Denoting per capita remittances as R, and letting the absolute change in per capita income equal the level of per capita remittances (that is, $\Delta Y = R$), then the growth rate of income due to remittances is simply R/Y. Since we use mean survey income/consumption as our measure of per capita income, R/Y is conveniently calculated as $(R/Y^{GDP}) \times (Y^{GDP}/Y)$, where the first term is equal to remittances as a share of GDP, and the second term is the ratio of per capita GDP to mean survey income.

References

Adams, Richard. 1989. "Worker Remittances and Inequality in Rural Egypt." *Economic Development and Cultural Change* 38(1): 45–71.

———. 1991. "The Economic Uses and Impact of International Remittances in Rural Egypt." *Economic Development and Cultural Change* 39(4): 695–722.

———. 1998. "Remittances, Investment, and Rural Asset Accumulation in Pakistan. *Economic Development and Cultural Change* 41(1): 155–73.

———. 2004a. "Remittances and Poverty in Guatemala." Policy Research Working Paper 3418. World Bank, Washington, DC.

———. 2004b. "Economic Growth, Inequality and Poverty: Estimating the Growth Elasticity of Poverty." *World Development* 32(12): 1989–2014.

———. 2005a. "International Remittances and the Household: Analysis and Review of Global Evidence." Paper presented at the Plenary Session of the African Economic Research Consortium, May 29, Nairobi.

———. 2005b. "Remittances and Poverty in Ghana." Unpublished paper. World Bank, Washington, DC.

———. 2005c. "Remittances, Household Expenditure and Investment in Guatemala. In *International Migration, Remittances, and the Brain Drain*, ed. Caglar Ozden and Maurice Schiff. Washington, DC: World Bank.

Adams, Richard, and John Page. 2005. "Do International Migration and Remittances Reduce Poverty in Developing Countries?" *World Development* 33(10): 1645–69.

Adelman, I., and J. E. Taylor. 1992. "Is Structural Adjustment with a Human Face Possible?" *Journal of Development Studies* 26: 387–407.

Alesina, Alberto, and Dani Rodrik. 1994. "Distributive Politics and Economic Growth." *Quarterly Journal of Economics* 109(2): 465–90.

Banerjee, Abhijit, and Andrew Newman. 1993. "Occupational Choice and the Process of Economic Development." *Journal of Political Economy* 101(2): 274–98.

Barham, Bradford, and Stephan Boucher. 1998. "Migration, Remittances, and Inequality: Estimating the Net Effects of Migration on Income Distribution." *Journal of Development Economics* 55: 307–31.

Bourguignon, Francois. 2003. "The Growth Elasticity of Poverty Reduction: Explaining the Heterogeneity across Countries and Time Periods." In *Inequality and Growth: Theory and Policy Implications,* ed. Theo Eicher and Steven Turnovsky. CES-IFO Seminar Series. Cambridge, MA: MIT Press.

Bourguignon, Francois, and Pierre-Andre Chiappori. 1992. "Collective Models of Household Behavior: An Introduction." *European Economic Review* 36: 355–64.

Browning, Martin, Francois Bourguignon, Pierre-Andre Chiappori, and Valerie Lechene. 1994. *Journal of Political Economy* 102(6): 1067–96.

Chami, Ralph, Connel Fullenkamp, and Samir Jahjah. 2005. "Are Immigrant Remittance Flows a Source of Capital for Development?" *IMF Staff Papers* 52(1): 55–81.

Clarke, George, and Scott Wallsten. 2004. "Do Remittances Protect Households in Developing Countries Against Shocks? Evidence From a Natural Disaster in Jamaica." Unpublished paper. World Bank, Washington, DC. November.

Coate, Stephen, and Martin Ravallion. 1993. "Reciprocity without Commitment: Characterization and Performance of Informal Insurance Arrangements." *Journal of Development Economics* 40: 1–24.

Cooper, Russell. 1999. *Coordination Games.* Cambridge: Cambridge University Press.

Cox Edwards, Alejandro, and Manuelita Ureta. 2003. "International Migration, Remittances, and Schooling: Evidence from El Salvador." *Journal of Development Economics* 72(2): 429–61.

De, Prabal, and Dilip Ratha. 2005. "Remittance Income and Household Welfare: Evidence from Sri Lanka Integrated Household Survey." Unpublished paper. Development Research Group, World Bank, Washington, DC.

de Brauw, Alan, J. Edward Taylor, and Scott Rozelle. 2001. "Migration and Incomes in Source Communities: A New Economics of Migration Perspective from China." Unpublished paper. Department of Agricultural and Resource Economics, University of California-Davis. October. www.agecon.ucdavis.edu/aredepart/facultydocs/Taylor/migration_income.pdf.

Duflo, Esther. 2003. "Grandmothers and Granddaughters: Old-Age Pensions and Intrahousehold Allocation in South Africa." *World Bank Economic Review* 17(1): 1–25.

Duflo, Ester, and Christopher Udry. 2004. "Intrahousehold Resource Allocation in Côte D'Ivoire: Social Norms, Separate Accounts, and Consumption Choices." NBER Working Paper 10498. National Bureau of Economic Research, Cambridge, MA.

Ellerman, David. 2003. "Policy Research on Migration and Development." World Bank Policy Research Working Paper 3117. August.

Fafchamps, Marcel. 2004. *Market Institutions in Sub-Saharan Africa: Theory and Evidence.* Cambridge, MA: MIT Press.

Foster, James, Joel Greer, and Erik Thorbecke. 1984. "A Class of Decomposable Poverty Measures." *Econometrica* 52(3): 761–66.

Funkhouser, Edward. 1992. "Migration from Nicaragua: Some Recent Evidence." *World Development* 20(3): 1209–18.

Gustafsson, Bjorn, and Negatu Makonnen. 1993. "Poverty and Remittances in Lesotho." *Journal of African Economies* 2(2): 49–73.

Hanson, Gordon, and Christopher Woodruff. 2003. "Emigration and Educational Attainment in Mexico." Working Paper. University of California-San Diego.

Hausmann, Ricardo, and Dani Rodrik. 2002. "Economic Development as Self Discovery." NBER Working Paper 8952. National Bureau of Economic Research, Cambridge, MA.

Hildebrandt, Nicole, and David McKenzie. 2005. "The Effects of Migration on Child Health in Mexico." Policy Research Working Paper 3573. World Bank, Washington, DC.

IADB-MIF (Inter-American Development Bank, Multilateral Investment Fund). 2004. "Sending Money Home: Remittance to Latin America and the Caribbean." Washington, DC. May.

IMF (International Monetary Fund). 1995. "Migrant Remittances, Labor Markets, and Household Strategies: A Comparative Analysis of Low-Income Household Strategies in the Caribbean Basin." *Social Forces* 74(2): 633–55.

IMF. 2005. *World Economic Outlook.*

Jacobs, Jane. 1984. *Cities and the Wealth of Nations: Principles of Economic Life.* New York: Random House.

Layard, Richard, Stephan Nickell, and Richard Jackman. 1991. *Unemployment: Macroeconomic Performance and the Labour Market.* Oxford: Oxford University Press.

Lucas, Robert. 1987. "Emigration to South Africa's Mines." *American Economic Review* 77(3): 313–30.

Lucas, R.E.B. 2004. "International Migration to High Income Countries: Some Consequences for Economic Development in the Sending Countries." Unpublished paper. Boston University.

Lucas, Robert, and Oded Stark. 1985. "Motivations to Remit: Evidence from Botswana." *Journal of Political Economy* 93: 901–18.

Martin, Philip, and Thomas Straubhaar 2002. "Best Practices to Reduce Migration Pressures." *International Migration* 40(3): 5–23.

Massey, Douglas, and Emilio Parrado. 1998. "International Migration and Business Formation in Mexico." *Social Science Quarterly* 79(1): 1–20.

McKenzie, David, and Hillel Rapoport. 2004. "Network Effects and the Dynamics of Migration and Inequality: Theory and Evidence from Mexico." BREAD Working Paper 063. Harvard University, Cambridge, MA. www.cid.harvard.edu/bread/papers2.htm.

Miguel, Edward, and Michael Kremer. 2001. "Worms: Education and Health Externalities in Kenya." NBER Working Paper 8481. National Bureau of Economic Research, Cambridge, MA.

Papademetriou, Demetrious, and Philip Martin. 1991. "Introduction." In *The Unsettled Relationship: Labor Migration and Economic Development*, ed. Demetrious Papademetriou and Philip Martin. New York: Greenwood.

Morduch, Jonathan. 1994. "Poverty and Vulnerability." *American Economic Review* 84(2): 221–25.

Moretti, Enrico. 2003. "Human Capital Externalities in Cities." NBER Working Paper 9641. National Bureau of Economic Research, Cambridge, MA.

Paulson, Anna. 2000. "Insurance Motives for Migration: Evidence from Thailand." Unpublished paper. Northwestern University.

Persson, Torsten, and Guido Tabellini. 1994. "Is Inequality Harmful for Growth." *American Economic Review* 84(3): 600–21.

Ravallion, Martin. 1997. "Can High-Inequality Developing Countries Escape Absolute Poverty?" *Economic Letters* 56: 51–57.

Rosenzweig, Mark R. 1988. "Risk, Implicit Contracts, and the Family in Rural Areas of Low Income Countries." *Economic Journal* 98(393): 1148–70.

Rosenzweig, Mark R., and Oden Stark. 1989. "Consumption Smoothing, Migration, and Marriage: Evidence from Rural India." *Journal of Political Economy* 97(4): 906–26.

Seabright, Paul. 2004. *The Company of Strangers: A Natural History of Economic Life.* Princeton: Princeton University Press.

Sen, Amartya. 1973 (rev. 1997). *On Economic Inequality.* Oxford: Clarendon.

———. 1976. "Real National Income." *Review of Economic Studies* 43(1): 19–39.

Stark, Oded, and Robert Lucas. 1988. "Migration, Remittances, and the Family." *Economic Development and Cultural Change* 36(3): 465–81.

Stark, Oded, J. Edward Taylor, and Shlomo Yitzhaki. 1986. "Remittances and Inequality." *Economic Journal* 96(383): 722–40.

Swaroop, Vinaya, and Shantayanan Devarajan. 2000. "The Implications of Foreign Aid Fungibility for Development Assistance." In *The World Bank: Structure and Policies*, ed. Christopher Gilbert and David Vines. Cambridge: Cambridge University Press.

Taylor, J. Edward. 1992. "Remittances and Inequality Reconsidered: Direct, Indirect, and Intertemporal Effects." *Journal of Policy Modeling* 14(2): 187–208.

———. 1999. "The New Economics of Labor Migration and the Role of Remittances." *International Migration* 37(1): 63–86.

Taylor, J. Edward, and Philip Martin. 2001. "Human Capital: Migration and Rural Population Change." In *Handbook of Agricultural Economics*, ed. Bruce L. Gardner and Gordan C. Rausser New York: Elsevier Science.

Taylor, J. Edward, Jorge Mora, and Richard Adams. 2005. "Remittances, Inequality, and Poverty: Evidence from Rural Mexico." Research Program on International Migration and Development. DECRG. Mimeo. World Bank.

Taylor, J. Edward, and T. J. Wyatt. 1996. "The Shadow Value of Migrant Remittances, Income, and Inequality in a Household-Farm Economy." *Journal of Development Studies* 32(6): 899–912.

Thaler, Richard. 1990. "Anomalies: Saving, Fungibility, and Mental Accounts." *Journal of Economic Perspectives* 4(1): 193–205.

Wodon, Quentin, Diego Angel-Urdinola, Gabriel Gonzalez-Konig, Diana Ojeda Revah, and Corinne Siaens. 2002. "Migration and Poverty in Mexico's Southern States." Regional Studies Program, Office of the Chief Economist for Latin America and the Caribbean, World Bank, Washington, DC.

Woodruff, Christopher, and Rene Zenteno. 2001. "Remittances and Microenterprises in Mexico."

Unpublished paper. Graduate School of International Relations and Pacific Studies, University of California–San Diego.

World Bank. 2005. "Remittances in Europe and Central Asia: Size, Distribution, and Impact." ECA Migration Study, Europe and Central Asia Region, World Bank, Washington, DC.

Yang, Dean. 2004. "International Migration, Human Capital, and Entrepreneurship: Evidence from Philippine Migrant's Exchange Rate Shocks." Research Program on International Migration and Development. DECRG. Policy Research Working Paper 3578. World Bank.

———. 2005. "Coping with Disaster: The Impact of Hurricanes on International Financial Flows, 1970–2001." Unpublished paper. Gerald R. Ford School of Public Policy, University of Michigan.

Yang, Dean, and HwaJung Choi. 2005. "Are Remittances Insurance? Evidence from Rainfall Shocks in the Philippines." Research Program on International Migration and Development. DECRG. Mimeo. World Bank.

Yang, Dean, and Claudia Martinez. 2005. "Remittances and Poverty in Migrants' Home Areas: Evidence from the Philippines." In *International Migration, Remittances, and the Brain Drain,* ed. Caglar Ozden and Maurice Schiff. Washington, DC: World Bank.

6

Reducing Remittance Fees

Following the discussion in chapters 4 and 5, on the macro- and microeconomic importance of remittances, chapter 6 focuses on a specific policy issue: reducing remittance costs and strengthening the financial infrastructure that supports remittances. Reducing the cost of personal remittances is the most promising area of policy intervention for several reasons. First, it will stanch a drain on the resources of poor migrants and their families back home. Second, it will increase flows through formal channels, especially banks. Third, it will improve financial access for the poor in developing countries.

Cost is usually not an issue in large remittances (made for the purpose of trade, investment, or aid), because, as a percentage of the principal amount, it tends to be small. But for small, personal transfers, remittance costs are high—unnecessarily so. Providers of remittance services in the formal sector typically charge a fee of 10–15 percent of the principal amount to handle the small remittances typically made by poor migrants.[1] High fees place a financial burden on the migrant remitters and on the recipients of the remittances, who receive a smaller amount of the much-needed funds sent by their family members.

Major international banks tend to focus on large-value remittance services rather than on services for migrants. Poor migrants may feel uneasy about using a major bank for remittance services; they tend to prefer smaller financial institutions, money transfer operators

(MTOs), or informal channels, such as a friends, family members, export-import firms, and transport companies.

The main messages of this chapter are as follows:

There is significant scope to reduce the fees on remittance services, especially for the small transfers typically made by poor migrants. Remittance transaction costs are often significantly lower than the fees that most customers pay. Reducing transaction fees will increase the disposable income of poor migrants and increase the incentives to remit (as the net receipts of beneficiaries increase). It may also significantly increase annual remittance flows to developing countries. Cross-border payments for retail trade, investment, and pension benefits (typically defined in foreign currency) would also increase in response to a reduction in remittance fees.

A weak competitive environment in the remittance market, lack of access to technology-supporting payment and settlement systems, and burdensome regulatory and compliance requirements all tend to keep fees high. Competition in the remittance market could be increased by lowering capital requirements on remittance services and opening up postal, banking, and retail networks to nonexclusive partnerships with remittance agencies. Disseminating data on remittance fees and establishing a voluntary code of conduct for fair transfers would improve transparency in remittance transactions. In countries with exchange controls, efforts to align the official and the market exchange rates would reduce the foreign-exchange spread in remittance transactions.

Reducing remittance costs and improving access to the financial system for migrants and their families will do more to encourage the use of formal channels than will regulation of so-called informal services. While regulation is necessary for curbing money laundering and terrorist financing, overregulation of informal services may conflict with the objective of reducing remittance costs.

Expanding migrants' access to banking services may enable remitters to bundle remittances and thereby take advantage of the lower fees available for larger remittances. This would require expanding the banking network, allowing domestic banks from origin countries to operate overseas, providing identification cards to migrants, and facilitating the participation of savings banks, credit unions, and microfinance institutions in providing low-cost remittance services. Remittances, in turn, can be used to support financial products—such as deposits, loans, and insurance—for poor people, and to contribute to the financial development of the recipient economy.

The plan of this chapter is as follows. The first section describes remittance fees and costs in various remittance channels. It shows (a) that remittance fees paid by customers are high for smaller transactions, especially in low-volume corridors; (b) that the cost of providing remittance services need not be so high; and (c) that remittance flows to developing countries would increase if remittance costs were reduced. The next section examines the factors underpinning remittance fees—market competition, regulations, payment infrastructure, and technology—and suggests policies for reducing costs and fees. This section also briefly discusses the recommendations of the international Financial Action Task Force (FATF) to prevent misuse

of remittance systems for criminal purposes. The last section discusses complementarities between remittances and other financial products such as loans, deposits, and insurance. Finally, an annex to the chapter briefly describes the historical evolution of three major remittance service providers (Western Union, MoneyGram, and Bank of America) to provide a perspective on the remittance market.

Remittance fees and costs

The remittance industry consists of formal and informal fund transfer agents. Major competitors include a few large global players, such as the major money transfer operators (MTOs) and banks, as well as hundreds of smaller participants that serve niche markets in specific geographic remittance corridors. The informal fund transfer agents include friends, family, and unregistered MTOs such as *hawala* dealers and trading companies.

The price of a remittance transaction includes a fee charged by the sending agent (typically paid by the sender when initiating the remittance transaction) and a currency-conversion fee for delivery of local currency to the beneficiary in another country. (A stylized remittance transaction is presented in annex 6A.1.) Some smaller MTOs require the beneficiary to pay a fee to collect remittances, presumably to account for unexpected exchange-rate movements. In addition, remittance agents (especially banks) may earn an indirect fee in the form of interest (or "float") by investing funds before delivering them to the beneficiary. The float can be significant in countries where overnight interest rates are high.[2] Many recipients spend considerable time and travel considerable distances to collect remittances. These costs typically are not included in the price.

Remittance fees are high, regressive, and nontransparent

Remittance fee pricing is complex, and rarely are senders informed about the full and precise price of a remittance transaction. Fees may be as high as 20 percent of the principal, depending on the remittance amount, channel, corridor, and transaction type. The average price is reported to have been around 12 percent of the principal in 2004 (Taylor 2004; Kalan and Aykut 2005). Prices are believed to have declined recently but are still very high in low-volume corridors. Currency-conversion charges are even less transparent than remittance fees; they, too, vary depending on the competitor, corridor, and channel, ranging from no charge in dollarized economies to 6 percent or more in some countries (Orozco 2004; Hernández-Coss 2004; Kalan and Aykut 2005).

Major MTOs such as Western Union and MoneyGram apparently charge higher remittance fees than banks and other financial institutions that offer remittance services to attract migrant customers (table 6.1). Informal channels such as *hawala* are reported to be cheaper than formal services. Some heavily traveled remittance corridors, such as United States–Mexico and South Africa–Mozambique, are much cheaper than others. Urgent transactions delivered in minutes cost much more than next-day transfers, and electronic transfers cost more than bank checks or drafts, because they also clear much faster than the latter.

The fee amount also depends on the remittance amount. Average remittance fees, as a percentage of money sent, decline rapidly as the transaction size increases, indicating scale economies and the potential advantage of bundling remittances—that is, the advantage of sending more funds, but less frequently. According to one firm's fee schedule, the cost of sending money from Belgium to Africa drops from 21 percent to below 4 percent as the transaction amount increases from 40 euros to 900 euros (figure 6.1). Similarly, the cost of remittances from the United States to Mexico (through the major MTOs) is more than 10 percent for $100, but less than 3 percent for $500 (figure 6.2).

In recent years, remittance fees have declined in high-volume corridors in response to several factors. First, global and regional MTOs have intensified their competition in mature corridors (United States–Latin America, for example), as new competitors have been attracted by high and growing remittance volumes. In the United States–Mexico corridor, for example, remittance fees have dropped nearly 60 percent since 1999 (box 6.1).[3] Second, Bank of America and

Table 6.1 Approximate cost of remitting $200
Percent of principal amount

	Major MTOs	Banks	Other MTOs	*Hawala*
Belgium to Nigeria*	12	6	9.8	—
Belgium to Senegal*	10	—	6.4	—
Hong Kong, China, to the Philippines	4.5	—	—	—
New Zealand to Tonga ($300)	12	3	8.8	—
Russia to Ukraine	4	3	2.5	1–2
South Africa to Mozambique	—	1	—	—
Saudi Arabia to Pakistan	3.6	0.4	—	—
United Arab Emirates to India	5.5	5.2	2.3	1–2
United Kingdom to India	11	6	—	—
United Kingdom to the Philippines	—	0.4–5.0	—	—
United States to Colombia	—	17	10	—
United States to Mexico	5	3	4.7	—
United States to Philippines	1.2–2.0	0.4–1.8	—	—

Source: Brocklehurst 2004; Orozco 2004; Gibson, McKenzie, Rohorua 2005; Hernandez-Coss 2004; Ratha and Riedberg 2005; Kalan and Aykut 2005; Andreassen and others 2005.
*World Bank survey of African diasporas in Belgium.
Note: Figures do not include currency-conversion charge.
— Data not available.

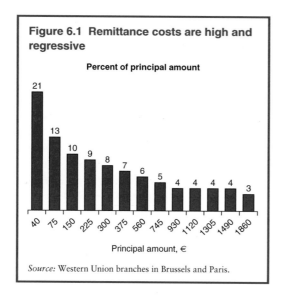

Figure 6.1 Remittance costs are high and regressive

Percent of principal amount

Source: Western Union branches in Brussels and Paris.

policies to improve transparency in remittance transactions (as in the United Kingdom), provide financial training to migrants (as in the Philippines), and establish bilateral initiatives (such as the Partnership for Progress between the United States and Mexico) have helped reduce remittance costs.

These positive developments remain the exception. In most corridors, particularly the low-volume corridors, remittance fees continue to be very high. In the New Zealand–Tonga corridor, for example, fees are about three times as high as those in the United States–Mexico corridor. The wide gap between remittance fees and costs shows that both should be reduced.

other banks in source countries are using minimal transfer fees to attract migrant accounts, while a growing number of banks in recipient countries (including ICICI and Bancomer) are competing for remittance customers. Third, the use of Internet-based technology for messaging and advanced clearing and settlement has reduced the cost of remittance transactions. In some countries, new remittance tools have emerged, based on cell phones (see box 6.6) and smart cards. Finally, government

The cost of a remittance transaction appears to be far lower than the price

Service providers' remittance costs appear to be much less than the fees charged to customers. Domestic transfer fees are only a fraction of the cross-border remittance fees (net of the currency-conversion charge). The cost of a domestic automated clearinghouse (ACH) payment in the United States is one-third of a cent. Domestic transfers using Visanet cost 2 cents per transaction, as opposed to 51 cents

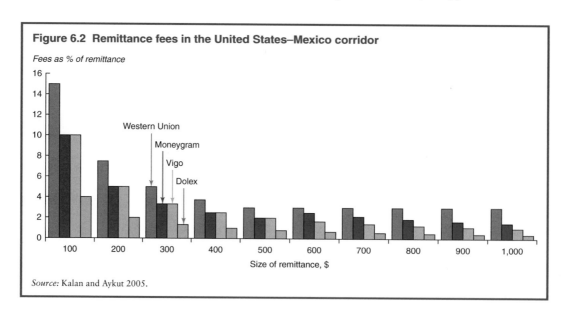

Figure 6.2 Remittance fees in the United States–Mexico corridor

Fees as % of remittance

Western Union

Moneygram

Vigo

Dolex

Size of remittance, $

Source: Kalan and Aykut 2005.

Box 6.1   Decline in remittance costs in the United States–Mexico corridor

The cost of sending $300 from the United States to Mexico declined nearly 60 percent between 1999 and 2005—from $26 to $11 (according to PROFEC data, see figure). The decline can be traced to greater competition. Prices generally remained stagnant when one MTO dominated the transmission service through exclusive contracts with distributors. Practitioners inside the industry cite the breakup of these exclusivity contracts and the entry of new competitors—especially banks—into the corridor as key events leading to a steady decline in prices.

Starting with Citibank's acquisition of Banamex in 2001—a $12.5 billion deal reportedly motivated by the attractiveness of Banamex's remittance business, U.S. banks have increased their stake in the United States–Mexico remittance market in the past two years. Being able to use the *matricula consular* identification card to establish identity when opening an account has helped this process. The card is

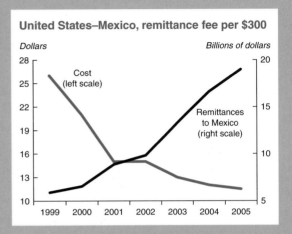

accepted as a valid identity document in 32 U.S. states, more than 1,000 police stations, 409 cities, 125 counties, and 280 banking institutions.

per transaction for international transfers (Brocklehurst 2004). In some corridors, fees for international remittances are as low as $1.80 per transaction (London-Manila), which hints at a falling lower bound for the cost of remittances. The fact that some banks have been offering free remittance services as loss-leaders to attract new business suggests that the actual cost of remittances is modest. Courier services that offer remittances also charge small fees for this additional service. Finally, industry cost estimates as well as other calculations presented below suggest that remittance costs are not very high.

The cost of providing remittance services varies with the business model used by the service provider. Western Union, MoneyGram, and Vigo use agents who pay all operating costs in exchange for their franchise and a commission on sales. In the "branch" model used by Dolex and many of the smaller

regional MTOs, the fixed and operating costs associated with each branch are paid by the MTO. By leveraging existing businesses on a commission basis, the agency model is much less capital-intensive than the branch model and can be expanded rapidly through partnerships, but it has higher variable costs.[4] In both models, relatively high fixed costs are associated with transaction-processing operations, compliance with regulatory requirements, marketing, and administration.[5]

Data on MTOs' costs of providing remittance services are hard to obtain. However, an analysis of profitability of the market leaders[6] using publicly available financial statements suggests that remittance costs are significantly lower than the fees charged to customers. Western Union has sustained operating margins that are at least 50 percent higher than other MTOs and industry peers in the payments and electronic processing market (table 6.2).[7] Its operating profit *per remittance transaction* may have averaged $8 to $9 in 2004. This is consistent with an earlier annual report (Western Union 2000) that put the company's operating profit at $684 million (or 30 percent of its $2.3 billion revenue). The operating profitability of the other major market players (MoneyGram and Dolex) has been in the range of 15–20 percent (table 6.2). A very simple model for Western Union (which assumes that agency commission costs are 35 percent of revenues after deduction of fixed costs and that all other costs are fixed costs) suggests that average transaction fees could be reduced by as much as one-third while maintaining operating margins within the same range as those of other major MTOs and peers. Reducing these operating profits to zero would provide a rough estimate of the break-even cost for these firms. Such an exercise reveals that the break-even fee for Western Union is probably around $9 per transaction and would fall below $5 if the volume of transactions were to double (box 6.2). Although it would be unreasonable to suggest that any company reduce its prices to cost, this simple model does appear to indicate that there is considerable latitude for reductions in transaction fees within the higher-priced corridors.

A more direct way of estimating the cost of a remittance transaction in a hypothetical MTO is to add up plausible cost components,

Table 6.2 Operating profits of major MTOs
Percentage of revenue

	2004
First Data Corporation, Western Union money transfer operations[a]	32
MoneyGram money transfer operations	15
Global Payments money transfer operations, including Dolex[b]	20
Peer group average[b]	18

Source: Yahoo Finance Database financial summaries; Kalan and Aykut 2005; Piper Jaffray Equity Research; MoneyGram International.
a. 90 percent Western Union; 50–55 percent non-United States/Canada consumer-to-consumer money transfers.
b. Includes American Express, Total System Services, DST Systems, Sunguard Data Systems, and Fiserv. These companies are not directly comparable to the MTOs as they are not necessarily in the money transfer business.

such as staff to process the transaction and provide security, rental of the premises, fixed costs (including franchise licensing), the cost of network and technology, and administrative costs for regulatory compliance.[8] This methodology yields a cost estimate of $5.50 for the first remittance transaction (table 6.3). Because most remittance transactions tend to be repetitive—the same amount is remitted from the same location to the same beneficiary—the cost for subsequent transactions drops to $3.60 (less staff time is required). It drops to under $3 per transaction if electronic processing is used.

Admittedly, the calculations in table 6.3 are based on a theoretical model of a basic

Table 6.3 Estimating the cost of a remittance transaction
Cost in dollars

	First transaction	Subsequent transaction	Electronic processing	Explanation
Sending staff	2.50	0.83	0.50	10 minutes of staff time at $15 per hour
Receiving staff	0.17	0.17	0.17	10 minutes of staff time at $1 per hour
Fixed costs	0.27	0.27	0.27	$40 million system cost recovered over 10 years; 2,000 branches with 20 transactions per day
IT, telecommunications	0.60	0.60	0.60	1 minute international phone call
Rent	1.50	1.50	1.50	$30 rent per day; 20 transactions per day
Administrative costs	0.50	0.50	0.50	Compliance, general overhead
Total costs	5.54	3.60	2.94	

Source: Ratha and Riedberg 2005.

Box 6.2 Estimating remittance industry costs

Remittance industry costs are difficult to obtain. Isolating the cost of remittance services is difficult in the case of financial institutions that provide other services as well. Estimating costs is not easy even in the case of dedicated remittance service providers because of the differences in the quality and reliability of remittance services (only some providers give customers legal redress). In Remittance industry costs, therefore, we have used publicly available information on Western Union, the largest MTO that is also a publicly listed company.

We used a simple model to estimate a break-even fee for Western Union's international money transfer operations. The model suggests that for Western Union's operating margins on its international money transfers to drop to the peer group average of 17.8 percent (table 6.2), the average transaction fee would have to be lowered from $22.90 to $15.30 (column 2 of the table below)—very close to the company's current fee in several U.S. corridors. The model also indicates that the break-even fee at which the operating profit becomes zero is $9.30 (column 3). This price is in the same range as MoneyGram's standard flat price in the U.S. corridors. A sensitivity analysis using this model suggests that the break-even fee would be $6.50–$7.00 if agency commissions were 25 percent, and around $11 if commissions were 45 percent.

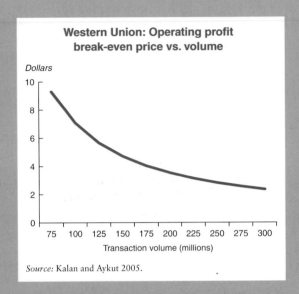

Western Union: Operating profit break-even price vs. volume

Source: Kalan and Aykut 2005.

The figure illustrates how the break-even fee shown in the table decreases as the number of transactions increases. If transaction volume doubled from the current 76 million to 150 million, the lowest fee at which the international operation would remain profitable would be $4.74.

	2004 data	Calculation assuming peer group margin of 18%	Calculation assuming break-even margin
Operating margin (operating profit over revenue) (%)	30	18	0
Operating profit per transaction (revenue minus costs) ($)	8.8	3.9	0.0
Costs ($)	20.4	17.7	15.7
Agency commission, 35% of fee	8.0	5.3	3.3
Fixed costs	12.4	12.4	12.4
Revenue ($)	29.3	21.6	15.7
Foreign-exchange commission	6.4	6.4	6.4
Fee	22.9	15.3	9.3

Source: Western Union financial statement for 2004.
Note: Reflects 76 million transactions in 2004. Fixed costs include marketing, administration, depreciation, and amortization, agency start-up, and other unidentified costs. Figures may not add up due to rounding errors.

remittance transaction that does not capture the global network and diversified services provided by major MTOs. Moreover, the model's assumptions are subject to considerable uncertainties, the greatest of which is that average costs would be higher if the number of transactions were smaller. It is worth noting, however, that many independent agents provide remittances as a side business: for them, fixed and variable costs could be significantly lower than for dedicated remittance service providers. Indeed, there may be a case for providing free remittance services in order to draw customers for other products and services, as practiced by certain banks.

Remittance costs should continue to fall under the influence of increased competition and better technology. Large MTOs may have considerable latitude to reduce fees while maintaining reasonable profit margins. In corridors where costs have already fallen significantly, further decline may be modest; but elsewhere there is scope for significant decline, especially with the volume of transactions rising rapidly.

Reducing remittance fees will increase remittance flows to developing countries

Reducing remittance fees would increase the disposable income of remitters, encouraging them to remit more. It also might encourage smaller and more frequent remittances. And lower prices in a particular channel might encourage remitters to shift from other channels—notably informal ones.

The degree to which a fee reduction would result in an increase in flows depends on the purpose of the remittance. At one extreme, where the purpose is to meet a specific need—payment for tuition, a medical emergency, a social ceremony, or the purchase of a gift item—the amount of remittance may not be sensitive to the remittance fee. At the other extreme, remittances by a poor, cash-strapped remitter may be highly cost elastic. Similarly, remittances meant for investment are likely to be cost elastic. In reality, most remittance transactions fall between these two extremes. Even when remittances are driven by altruism, they will tend to be cost elastic, as evidenced by the literature on charity, which shows that people tend to donate more as the cost of donating declines (box 6.3).

In a recent survey of Senegalese migrants in Belgium, two-thirds of the migrants said they would send more if the cost of sending went down. In a survey of Tongan migrants in New Zealand, 30 percent of remitters said they would increase the amount of remittances by 0.74 percent (on average) if costs fell by 1 percent (Gibson, McKenzie, and Rohorua 2005). That survey found the overall cost-elasticity of

---

Box 6.3   Even charitable donations are sensitive to cost

Charitable donations and bequests, like altruistic remittances, increase when the costs of such actions decline. In one of the best-known early studies of the responsiveness of gift-giving to tax deductions, Feldstein and Taylor (1976) estimated a price elasticity of the amount given of -1.3.[a] Although this finding has been challenged on the ground that gift-giving responds more to temporary changes in the cost of giving (Glenday, Gupta, and Pawlak 1986), the general agreement is that people give more when it costs less to do so (Cordes 2001). The literature on charitable bequests reaches a similar conclusion. Bakija, Gale, and Slemrod (2003) estimate a price elasticity of -2.14 for charitable bequests.

---

[a]In the United States, taxpayers can deduct the amount of charitable contributions from their income for tax purposes. Thus, Feldstein and Taylor (1976) view an increase in the income tax rate as a decline in the price of charitable donations.

remittances with respect to the fee (averaging the elasticity over those who would increase remittances and those who would not) to be –0.22. Based on this estimate, Gibson and others (2005) calculate that lowering the fixed cost of sending money through banks and MTOs from New Zealand and Tonga to competitive levels in the world market would result in a 28 percent increase in remittances from existing remitters. It might also induce some nonremitters to start remitting.[9]

If the cost elasticity (–0.22) of the New Zealand–Tonga study were applicable to all developing countries, a reduction in remittance cost from 12 percent to (say) 6 percent could result in an 11 percent increase in annual remittance flows to developing countries. One caveat to this calculation is that the cost elasticity applies only to high-cost corridors, which also tend to have low volumes. In corridors where the remittance cost is already low, further decreases may not increase flows. For example, a fee reduction by a major MTO may not produce much effect if a major part of the flows is already moving through low-cost informal channels. This is confirmed by the World Bank survey of Senegalese migrants in Belgium; half of the respondents who paid remittance fees of 20 percent or more said they would send more if costs were halved; not even one-fourth of those who paid less than 10 percent said they would send more (table 6.4). Almost 75 percent of the Senegalese migrants who send money through the large MTOs said that

they would send more if the costs were lowered, a result confirmed by findings from a World Bank survey of the Nigerian diaspora in Belgium.

An indirect implication for cost elasticity may be drawn from Yang's (2004) finding of an elasticity of 0.6 for remittance receipts denominated in Filipino pesos with respect to the peso–dollar exchange rate. Applying this elasticity to a remittance transaction of $150, if the remittance fee were halved from (say) 12 percent to 6 percent, remittance receipts would rise by 3.6 percent, or $5.4, while the remittance fee would decline from $18 to $9.31.[10] If the same elasticity were to apply to the entire flow of remittances to developing countries, remittance receipts, in response to a halving of costs would increase significantly, by more than $5 billion using only recorded flows, and more than $8 billion using both recorded and unrecorded flows.

Reductions in remittance fees would also be likely to increase other cross-border retail flows such as transfers from public and private institutions to individual beneficiaries (pensions, child-care payments), small-value payments in exchange for goods and services, acquisitions of assets, and debt servicing.[11] In more developed countries, migrant remittances are only a small share of retail payments, which, in turn, are a fraction of wholesale payments. But in developing countries, especially in smaller and poorer countries, remittances are a significant source of funding in relation to the size of the economy and, therefore, of the retail payment system. A reform of the retail payment system to facilitate remittances would probably benefit other (not easily quantifiable) components of retail payments.

Based on the evidence presented above, notably the finding that the cost elasticity of remittances is negative, policies that aim to lower remittance costs by increasing access to banking services, promoting competition, and disseminating information have the potential to provoke sizeable increases in remittance flows to developing countries.

Table 6.4 Remittances are more cost-elastic when costs are higher

Cost (% of principal)	% of respondents who would remit more	
	Senegal	Nigeria
1–9	23	64
10–19	50	67
20 and above	50	83

Source: World Bank Survey of Senegalese and Nigerian diasporas in Belgium.

Factors underpinning high remittance fees

What accounts for high transaction costs in the remittance business? Are they related to large sunk costs, regulatory measures that restrict competition, or the lack of access to low-cost public infrastructure (such as payments systems)? Do exchange controls, country risks, or other specific factors keep the cost of cross-border transfers higher than those of domestic transfers?

Before answering these questions, it is worth noting some general findings from a cross-country regression analysis of remittance fees (Freund and Spatafora 2005). Remittance fees tend to be higher in corridors in which bank concentration is high and competition low (as reported in chapter 4, table 4A.2.2). They tend to be lower in more developed financial sectors (proxied by the ratio of deposits to GDP) in the recipient country and in dollarized economies and other economies that present low exchange-rate risk. Greater credit risk[12] reduces the willingness of agents to provide remittance services. Finally, high wages at the recipient end (as proxied by domestic output) are associated with more costly remittance services. These results, which should be treated as indicative rather than conclusive, suggest that measures to increase competition among remittance-service providers and to reduce financial risk and exchange-rate volatility are likely to reduce the transaction costs associated with remittances.[13]

Several factors related to conditions in the corridor and in the sending and receiving countries have significant impacts on remittance pricing. Two corridor-related factors that have a significant impact on price are the (potential) level of competition in the corridor and special arrangements with postal systems to handle distribution.

A high level of competition may considerably reduce remittance prices in a corridor. The level of competition in a corridor can be proxied by remittance volume, since high-volume corridors attract more competi-

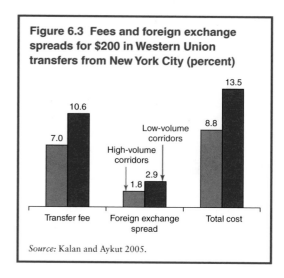

Figure 6.3 Fees and foreign exchange spreads for $200 in Western Union transfers from New York City (percent)

Source: Kalan and Aykut 2005.

tors, particularly small niche players that compete primarily on price. The relatively lower prices in high-volume corridors, such as United States–Mexico and Saudi Arabia–India, can be ascribed in part to the presence of regional and smaller players, in addition to the major MTOs (and in part to scale economies). The remittance prices of the global market leader, Western Union, are significantly lower in the high-volume U.S. corridors than elsewhere (figure 6.3).[14]

High volume in a corridor does not always guarantee high competition, however. *Exclusive* access to an extensive distributional network (such as a post office network) may distort competition in the corridor. Using post offices as money transfer agencies can give an MTO a significant advantage, because the postal system almost always offers the most extensive distribution networks in both sending and receiving countries, particularly in rural areas. Exclusive arrangements with postal systems have been employed by the two largest MTOs, Western Union and MoneyGram.

Exclusive arrangements can block or bar entry by small competitors and may thus allow the company that enjoys the arrangement to maintain a high price premium. Moreover, exclusive arrangements with the post office, typically a trusted and ubiquitous presence, may facilitate price leadership and

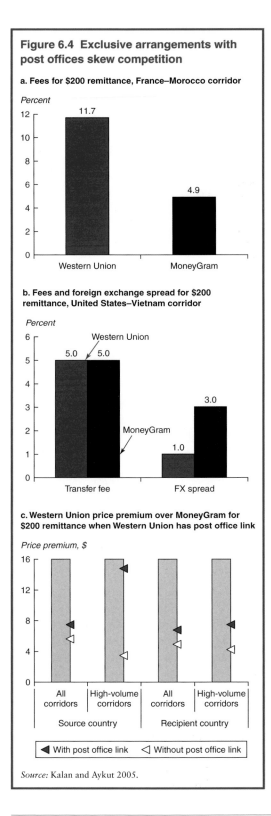

Figure 6.4 Exclusive arrangements with post offices skew competition

a. Fees for $200 remittance, France–Morocco corridor

Percent

11.7 — Western Union

4.9 — MoneyGram

b. Fees and foreign exchange spread for $200 remittance, United States–Vietnam corridor

Percent

Western Union
MoneyGram

Transfer fee: 5.0 / 5.0
FX spread: 1.0 / 3.0

c. Western Union price premium over MoneyGram for $200 remittance when Western Union has post office link

Price premium, $

	All corridors	High-volume corridors	All corridors	High-volume corridors
	Source country		Recipient country	

◀ With post office link   ◁ Without post office link

Source: Kalan and Aykut 2005.

price signaling—thereby raising the fee structure across the board. For example, arrangements with the postal systems in France and Morocco may help explain Western Union's ability to charge significantly higher fees in that corridor than its major competitor, MoneyGram (figure 6.4a). However, in the United States–Vietnam corridor, where MoneyGram has such an arrangement, Western Union lowers its price to the same level as MoneyGram's, whereas MoneyGram charges higher foreign-exchange commissions (figure 6.4b).

At the global level, Western Union's price premium over MoneyGram's fees, even in high-volume corridors, appears to be significantly higher when the company has a link with the postal system in either the sending or receiving country (figure 6.4c).[15] On the other hand, when MoneyGram, which almost always offers lower prices than Western Union, has the agency relationship with the post office, its strong distribution advantage forces Western Union to lower its prices to compete in the corridor.

Other factors that appear to have an impact on corridor pricing include active participation of banks, credit unions, or other nonbank financial institutions in the remittance market; cultural and geographic commonality with a group of countries that includes one highly competitive, high-volume corridor with lower prices; the size of informal transfer network in the corridor; and government policy initiatives within the corridor.

Regulatory and policy decisions have a significant effect on remittance costs. In a recent survey of providers of remittance services in the United States, 40 percent of those surveyed cited the process of getting a license as the chief barrier to their operation, followed by building a compliance system (figure 6.5). In the United States, remittance service providers are supervised by state departments of consumer affairs and banking. Not all states have specific regulations on remittances. And registration requirements vary widely from state to state (annex 6A.2). To set up a money transfer

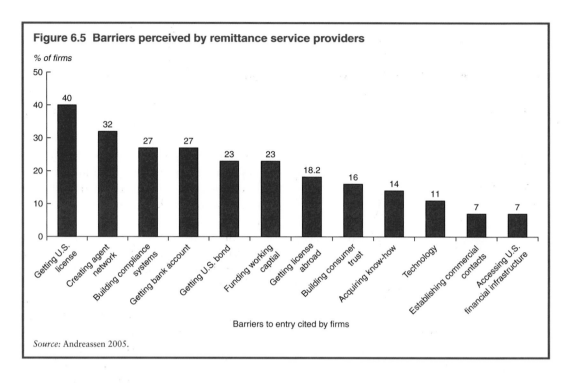

Figure 6.5 Barriers perceived by remittance service providers

% of firms

Barriers to entry cited by firms

Source: Andreassen 2005.

business with offices in all 50 states would require net worth and bonds of more than $5 million (Ratha and Riedberg 2005). Although bond and capital requirements protect consumers and deter fraudulent practices, the wide variation in requirements from state to state, mirrored in wide variances among countries, can be confusing and costly, thereby discouraging competition from new, smaller players. Many countries, including France, Italy, and the Russian Federation, require a provider of remittance services to be a fully licensed bank or financial institution. Only recently did Germany allow remittances to be conducted under a financial institution license instead of under banking regulations. Costly and stringent licensing requirements, like bond and capital requirements, discourage the entry of smaller players that could provide effective competition in many remittance corridors.

Regulating informal remittances may raise costs

Since the terrorist attacks of September 11, 2001, authorities in many countries have adopted more stringent regulations and stepped up enforcement of existing rules governing the transfer of foreign exchange.[16] An increasing number of countries are requiring MTOs to register with the authorities and to report transactions on a regular basis. These regulatory requirements have raised the cost of fund transfers to the remittance service providers, which tend to pass them on to customers.

National requirements center on the registration of transfer businesses, application of know-your-customer procedures, detailed record-keeping, and frequent reporting. "Money service businesses" in the United States must maintain a list of their agents and make the list available to the Financial Crimes Enforcement Network (FinCEN) upon request. Operating such a business without registering it is a crime. The introduction of the USA Patriot Act in late 2001 tightened the know-your-client requirements for fund transfers. In addition, U.S. financial institutions are required to comply with the recommendations of the international Financial Action Task Force to Prevent Money Laundering (FATF

2005), which are incorporated into U.S. regulations, and to comply with the sanctions list maintained by the Treasury Department's Office of Foreign Assets Control.

Since early 2005, correspondent bank accounts of hundreds of money service businesses in the United States have been closed by banks for fear that they may be targeted by authorities for servicing customers regarded as "high-risk." The wave of closures can be traced to a June 2004 notice from the Office of the Comptroller of Currency that "[s]ome national banks also provide banking services to foreign [money service businesses], a line of business that can carry significant money laundering risks."[17] Clear guidance on how to assess risks and spot suspicious activity is lacking.

Some argue that the users of informal remittance channels face a great risk of fraud and default. Requirements for bonds, capitalization, auditing, reporting, and disclosure can shield consumers from excessive fees, fraud, or other losses. At the same time, trust and self-regulation, characteristics of informal remittance networks such as *hawala*, *hundi*, *padala*, *fei chien*, and others, have proven effective in protecting customers against losses, although they are by no means immune to fraud. Moreover, their low cost, speed, reach, and convenience of informal door-to-door remittance services remain extremely competitive compared with the inefficiencies of formal operators (Ballard 2005; El Qorchi, Maimbo, and Wilson 2003; Maimbo and Passas 2005). Law enforcement cases from all continents show that formal and informal remittance channels are both susceptible to criminal abuse.[18]

The regulatory regime governing remittances must strike a balance between curbing money laundering, terrorist financing, and general financial abuse, and facilitating the flow of funds through efficient formal channels. Policies that encourage formal operators to imitate the best practices of informal transfer systems will benefit poor migrants. Strengthening the formal remittance infrastructure by offering the advantages of low cost, flexible hours, expanded reach and language, and increasing efforts to identify and regulate the unregulated sector, would effectively facilitate remittance flows while preserving their integrity.

Policies to reduce remittance costs

Measures to reduce remittance costs should aim to improve the efficiency of remittance transactions by (a) enhancing market competition to reduce high profit margins; (b) helping remittance service providers' access to new payments technology; and (c) devising ways to encourage remitters to send larger amounts (table 6.5). As a way to enhance competition, governments can encourage postal systems and other state-owned distribution alternatives to open their networks to multiple MTO partnerships on a nonexclusive basis. In addition, they should avoid overregulation, excessive monitoring, or reporting requirements that could drive out smaller competitors that lack the economies of scale to absorb the cost of compliance.

Developing a shared network would be a powerful way to increase competition. Cooperation on infrastructure and competition in service provision would allow network benefits to accrue to the consumer.[19] The technology required to set up a payment-processing infrastructure with large capacity is no longer an expensive proposition. A functioning payment infrastructure could be extended to a new country at a minimal cost and in a matter of weeks.[20] There have been some attempts to set up shared networks in the remittance-source countries (for example, the United States–Mexico FedACH system, box 6.4). Also some governments in remittance-receiving countries have facilitated the establishment of payment networks that are shared by savings banks, credit unions, and microfinance institutions operating in poor and remote areas (for example, BANSEFI in Mexico[21] and Apex Link in Ghana).[22]

Table 6.5 Policies to reduce costs, regulate informal providers, and provide remittance-linked financial services

	Source country	Recipient country
Reducing costs		
Increase competition	X	X
Avoid exclusive arrangements	X	X
Harmonize regulation and capital requirements (same policy for all players)	X	
Introduce and harmonize electronic payment systems (card-based products)	X	
Improve data on corridors	X	X
Voluntary code of conduct	X	X
Bundling of transactions	X	X
Regulating informal providers		
Make formal sector operations more convenient and user friendly	X	X
Improve banking access	X	X
Leveraging remittances		
Improve banking access	X	X
Encourage microfinance institutions and credit unions to provide remittance services	X	X

Another way to address the issue of high fees in the remittance industry would be to develop best-practice guidelines for remittance service providers. Several such guidelines have been issued by Credit Union National Association, Inter-American Development Bank, and World Savings Bank Institute, which urge service providers to disclose fees, exchange rates, and the time of delivery. At the end of 2004, the World Bank and the Bank for Committee on Payment and Settlement Systems (CPSS) set up a task force, with participation from the IMF, to develop voluntary principles for remittance service providers, regulators, and supervisors for improving transparency in the market (box 6.5).[23]

Such guidelines would have to be voluntary. Central banks generally are not willing to impose such guidelines or to cap remittance fees and foreign-exchange commissions. A recent survey (de Luna Martinez 2005) revealed that in only 9 of 40 countries—Brazil, Bulgaria, Indonesia, Pakistan, Philippines, Russian Federation, Thailand, Tunisia, and República Bolivariana de Venezuela[24]—did central banks even have the legal power to do so. All 40 central banks indicated that even if they had the power to limit fees, they would not do so, preferring to leave fee-setting to financial institutions in response to market competition.[25]

Raising consumer awareness through financial literacy efforts and publicizing information on costs (as Mexican authorities have done through the PROFECO initiative) will strengthen competition among remittance service providers. In April 2005, Britain's Department for International Development

---

Box 6.4 United States–Mexico FedACH

United States–Mexico automated clearinghouse was created as part of the U.S.-Mexico Partnership for Prosperity to reduce the cost of sending remittances between the two countries. In 2002, the central banks of the United States and Mexico undertook a cooperative effort to link their automated clearinghouse (FedACH) systems. The cross-border service began operating in February 2004. Today, approximately 23,000 payments are sent from the United States to recipients in Mexico through this channel each month. The cost of a remittance transaction is just $0.67; the exchange-rate spread is only 0.21 percent. Since July 2005, the cross-border service has made funds available to a recipient on the first business day after a payment is originated.

But FedACH has not been as popular with the banking community as was expected. It suffered from some technical weaknesses—for example, insufficient coding flexibility for certain remittances. Also, major international banks that earn significant remittance fees from their own proprietary payment systems and from foreign-exchange commissions have been slow to join FedACH. And other cross-border ACHs between the United States and Canada and between the United States and Europe have had similar difficulty attracting participation from banks.

Box 6.5 The World Bank/CPSS task force on general principles for international remittance systems

At the end of 2004, the World Bank and the Bank for International Settlements' Committee for Payment and Settlement Systems (CPSS) convened a task force, with members from central banks of sending and receiving countries, international financial institutions, and development banks, to address the need for international policy coordination in remittance systems. The task force is expected to issue general principles for international remittance systems in the first half of 2006. The purpose of the principles is to promote a sound, efficient, and competitive market in remittance services. The recommendations of the task force are expected to cover market environment, consumer protection and transparency, market infrastructure, and public policy.

(DFID) launched a website that provides information on remittance costs and options in several countries.[26]

Assisting remittance service providers to adopt new payment systems technology and instruments would help lower their service costs. Some technologically advanced methods of sending transfers already exist. Card-based instruments, such as stored value cards (similar to phone cards), credit cards, and debit cards, are now frequently used to send remittances to urban locations that have access to card-processing machines. Systems such as iKobo.com use the Internet to make remittances. PayPal and other services move money between virtual accounts, although they do not (yet) focus on immigrants' transfers. Similar technology has been adapted by an operator in the Philippines to send fast—and reportedly cheap—remittances using a cell phone (box 6.6).

Migrant workers need easier access to the formal financial system

Improving migrant workers' access to banking services could reduce transaction costs, and at the same time, help to develop the financial system in the countries where remittances are received. Sending and receiving countries alike could support migrants' access to banking by providing them with the means to establish their identity.

In receiving countries, the factor that exerts the greatest effect on remittance costs (and on the choice of remittance channel) is the reach of the remittance agent's distribution network. Recipients in rural areas underserved by banks may have to pay high costs for receiving remittances, especially through formal channels. Partnerships between remittance operators and institutions that have wide networks in rural areas (such as post offices) would help reduce such costs.[27] In countries where residents are allowed to hold foreign currency deposits, permission to deliver remittances in U.S. dollars (or the same foreign currency sent by the remitter) would significantly reduce (if not eliminate) the exchange rate spread on remittances (as seen in the case of dollarized economies such as El Salvador).

Remittances and financial institutions

Banks and smaller financial institutions, such as credit unions and microfinance institutions, can deliver convenient and possibly low-cost, remittance services in developing countries, especially in rural areas. In contrast to cash transactions, remittances channeled through bank accounts may encourage savings and enable a better match for savings and investment in the economy. Remittances, in turn, can be used to support business and consumer loans, insurance, and other financial products for remittance recipients.[28] Some institutions are exploring ways to target remittances to specific uses such as school fees or medical

Box 6.6   Smart's phone-based remittance system in the Philippines

The largest mobile phone company in the Philippines, Smart Communications, has developed an innovative remittance system based on cell-phone text messaging. Cell phones are widespread in the Philippines, in use by at least 30 percent of the 84 million Filipinos. A standard Smart remittance works like this: A Filipino in Hong Kong, China, deposits money to be remitted with one of Smart's remittance partners, which then sends a text message to the beneficiary in the Philippines, informing him or her of the transfer. The remittance is credited into a Smart Money "electronic wallet" account by any Smart mobile customer. The money can be withdrawn from an ATM using the Smart Money cash card, which can also be used as a debit card for purchases. Smart's partners in the Philippines—among them McDonald's, SM malls, SeaOil gas stations, 7-Eleven

stores, and Tambunting pawn shops—will also pay out cash to Smart customers.

Smart has already formed remittance partnerships with Travelex Money Transfer; Forex International Hong Kong; Dollar America Exchange in California; CBN Grupo in Greece, Ireland, Japan, Spain, and the United Kingdom; New York Bay Remittance; and Banco de Oro Bank in Hong Kong, China.

The system's simplicity keeps fees down. Fees at origination vary from country to country. In Hong Kong, China, it is about $2. In the Philippines, it is 1 percent plus the cost of the text message.

The Smart system also appears to be secure. The use of different PINs for the cell phone and the Smart account make it difficult for a thief to access the funds. An ID is required when collecting cash.

---

bills. Others are exploring insurance products, for example, to ensure a stable flow of income to the remittance beneficiary in the event that the sender suffers an income shock.

Credit unions in El Salvador, Guatemala, Honduras, Nicaragua, Mexico, and Jamaica that are members of the World Council of Credit Unions (WOCCU) encouraged WOCCU to establish the International Remittance Network (IRnet) in July 1999 to facilitate remittance flows from the United States to Latin America. That initiative has lowered remittance costs by raising customer awareness of remittance fees and by generating some competition in the remittance market. To send up to $1,000, IRnet charges a flat $10—much less than the fees charged by major MTOs. Besides fee income, IRnet institutions hope to use remittances to build relationships with customers. It is reported that 14–28 percent of nonmembers who visited WOCCU-affiliated credit unions to transfer funds eventually opened an account; 37 percent of credit union members saved a part of their remittance receipts (Grace 2005).

Smaller nonbank financial institutions face challenges in entering the remittance market because of regulatory constraints—such as licenses for transactions involving foreign exchange and access to national payment systems. For prudential reasons, access to payment and settlement systems is typically restricted to well-capitalized and well-established banking institutions. Microfinance institutions and smaller institutions generally must enter into corresponding banking relationships with commercial banks[29] and with international remittance providers (such as the IRnet or the major MTOs).

A survey of central banks found that 35 of 40 developing-country authorities were not enthusiastic about allowing small financial institutions to have access to clearing and settlement systems (de Luna Martinez 2005). Central banks appear to believe that most nonbank financial institutions in developing countries lack the technological infrastructure required to participate directly in clearing and settlement systems. Also, central banks believe that giving nonbank financial institutions direct access to central banks' clearing and settlement systems may not help reduce the remittance fees charged by those institutions. According to the survey, only five countries—Azerbaijan, Belarus, Bolivia, Philippines, and Thailand—are contemplating granting access for clearing and settlement systems to a few large nonbank financial institutions (mostly post offices).

Even if microfinance institutions were to offer remittance services, they might face restrictions on taking deposits and offering loan and insurance services, again for prudential reasons. Given these constraints, sources of funds for such institutions tend to be expensive and their capacity to offer financial products limited.

Annex 6A.1 A stylized remittance transaction—structure, players, instruments

A typical remittance transaction takes place in three steps: (1) initiation of remittances by a migrant sender using a sending agent, (2) exchange of information and settlement of funds, and (3) delivery of remittances to the beneficiary. In step 1, the migrant sender pays the principal amount of the remittance to the sending agent using cash, check, money order, credit card, debit card, or a debit instruction sent by e-mail, phone, or Internet. In step 2, the sending agency—which may be an MTO, bank, or other financial institution, money changer, or merchant (gas station, grocery store)—then instructs its agent in the recipient's country to deliver the remittance. In step 3, the paying agent makes the payment to the beneficiary. In most cases, there is no real-time fund transfer; instead, the balance owed by the sending agent to the paying agent is settled periodically according to a mutually agreed schedule. Settlement usually occurs through commercial banks acting through the national clearing and settlement system. A portion of informal remittances is settled through goods trade.

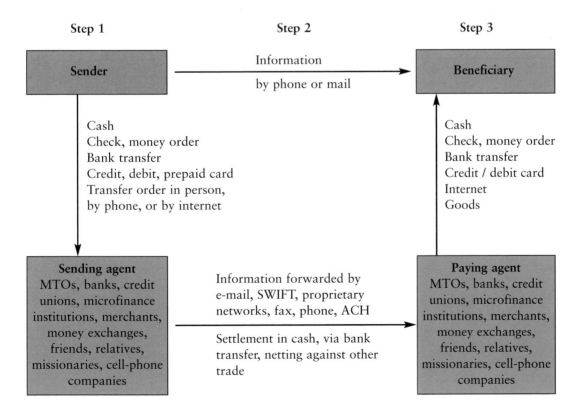

| Step 1 | Step 2 | Step 3 |

Sender → Information by phone or mail → **Beneficiary**

Cash
Check, money order
Bank transfer
Credit, debit, prepaid card
Transfer order in person, by phone, or by internet

Cash
Check, money order
Bank transfer
Credit / debit card
Internet
Goods

Sending agent
MTOs, banks, credit unions, microfinance institutions, merchants, money exchanges, friends, relatives, missionaries, cell-phone companies

Information forwarded by e-mail, SWIFT, proprietary networks, fax, phone, ACH

Settlement in cash, via bank transfer, netting against other trade

Paying agent
MTOs, banks, credit unions, microfinance institutions, merchants, money exchanges, friends, relatives, missionaries, cell-phone companies

Annex 6A.2 Licensing and registration requirements for remittance service providers

Country	Net worth($)	Audited financials required?	Bond	Comment
United States[27]				
California	Min. $500,000 in equity	If available	Discretionary depending on size of business. Min. $200,000.	Fee $5,000 plus $50 per agent
Florida	100,000 plus $50,000 per location up to $500,000	Yes	1% of annual turnover, max $250,000; can be set at $500,000 in exceptional circumstances; may be waived upon request	Application fee $500 plus $50 per agent; renewal $1,000 plus $50 per agent up to $20,000.
Illinois	Depending on locations: 1 = $35,000 25+ = $500,000	Yes	Greater of $100,000 or the average daily outstanding for 12 months, maximum $2,000,000	Fee $100 Licensing + $100 $10 per location; $100 renewal
Massachusetts	None	No	$50,000 (or 2x amount of outstanding transactions)	Fee $250
New Jersey	(1) Min. $100,000 plus $25,000 per location (or agent) in NJ up to $1,000,000 (2) $50,000 for foreign money transmitter plus $10,000 per location (or agent) up to $400,000		(1) Not less than $100,000 and not more than $1,000,000 (2) Foreign remitters: depending on business volume, $25,000 to $100,000; commissioner may require up to $900,000 In general: investments not less than outstanding payment instruments; this can be waived by the commissioner	Application fee $1,000 Licensing fee up to $4,000 Biennial fee $25 per location up to max. of $5,000
New York	Liquidity equivalent to outstanding payments	Yes, 2 years	$500,000 unless the superintendent lowers the amount	Fee $500 Licensing + $1,000 investigation.
Pennsylvania	$500,000		$1,000,000	Application fee $1,000 Renewal fee $300
Texas	$25,000 per location up to $1,000,000	Yes	$100,000 for first location, $50,000 for each additional, max. $400,000	Fee $500 licensing + $2,500 investigation fee
Virginia	$100,000–$1,000,000 as determined by the commission		$25,000–$1,000,000 as determined by the commission	Licensing fee $500 Renewal fee $750
Wisconsin	"Suitable to conduct business" Should not be lower than $10,000	No	$10,000 for 1st location + $5,000 for each additional Max. $300,000	Fee $500 license (annual) + $300 investigation + $5 per location (annual)
Canada	None	No	None	Reporting threshold: Can$3,000 STR and CTR above Can$10,000
France	Min. €2,400,000 plus capital to cover first year's expenses	Yes, 3 years	None	Full bank license; the ownership structure must be adequate AML procedures scrutinized
Germany (federal legislation)	€125,000 capital Net worth must be sufficient to cover exposures	Yes	None	Reporting threshold: €2,500 STR; AML laws must be followed; 2 managing directors must have suitable backgrounds

Annex 6A.2 *(continued)*

Country	Net worth($)	Audited financials required?	Bond	Comment
Italy	€750,000	Yes	None	Reporting threshold: €12,500 STR; the license is only required by the service provider, not by his agents
United Kingdom	None	No	None	Register normal business; Moneys may not be held for more than 3 days, as a bank license (deposits) would be required in this event

Source: For United States, www.rubinsanchez.com; Canadian Bankers Association; French Central Bank, Banque de France, Comité des Etablissements de Crédit et des Entreprises, d'Investissement (CECEI), Committee for Credit Institutions and Investment Companies; German Financial Supervisory Board, Bundesanstalt für Finanzdienstleistungsaufsicht; Italian Law 106; Bank of England.
Note: Licensing and registering approaches may differ. See FATF Typologies Report (FATF 2005). STR = suspicious transaction report; CTR = currency transaction report; SAR = suspicious activity report; AML = anti-money laundering.

Annex 6A.3 A brief history of some remittance service providers

This annex describes the historical role of three key providers of remittance services—Western Union, MoneyGram, and Bank of America. The intention is to shed light on their business strategies.

Western Union

Western Union descended from the New York and Mississippi Valley Printing Telegraph Company, originally formed by a group of businessmen in Rochester, New York, in 1851. The Western Union Telegraph Company was subsequently formed in 1956 following the acquisition of several competing telegraph systems. Having completed the first transcontinental telegraph line by 1861, the telegram network started providing the Western Union Money Transfer service nationally by 1871.

Historically, Western Union has been involved in a wide range of telecom and other products. These included introducing the New York Stock Exchange stock ticker in 1866, offering a nationwide standard time, introducing teletypewriters in 1923, offering the first intercity fax service, and launching the telex. It also launched the first domestic communications satellite, Westar I in 1974.[30] Today, Western Union is primarily a remittance company.

Western Union has always followed the strategy of developing its own proprietary products. For money transfers, Western Union has developed its own software and network of exclusive agents. It has been able to develop this network by being the first truly global remittance company. Currently its network comprises slightly more than 220,000 locations in about 195[31] countries (including the network of its subsidiary Orlandi Valuti). The growth rates in Western Union's international remittance transactions (excluding Mexico) were 32 percent, 25 percent and 24 percent for the years 2002, 2003, and 2004, respectively.

MoneyGram

The MoneyGram money transfer service was started in 1988 by Integrated Payment Service, a U.S.–based division of First Data Corporation (FDC), a data processing company owned by American Express at the time of inception.[32] FDC divested its MoneyGram operation in December 1996 through an initial public offering of its common stock to comply with the company's agreement with the Federal Trade Commission as part of a merger with FFMC.

In 1998, Travelers Express, a division of Viad Corp. acquired MoneyGram. On June 30, 2004, the Travelers Express business was spun off from Viad Corp.,[33] and became an independently traded company called MoneyGram International, Inc. Travelers Express and MoneyGram Payment Systems, Inc. continue as operating companies under this new corporate umbrella.

Whereas Western Union insists on a strategy of exclusive partnership with its agents, MoneyGram allows its agents to represent other remittance companies as well, as shown by its partnership with the World Council of Credit Unions and Bancomer Transfer Services.

Bank of America

Bank of America (BoA) was established in 1929 as an outgrowth of the merger between the Bank of Italy and the Bank of America, Los Angeles. California became the fastest-growing state after World War II, with the highest use of checking accounts. To cope with the transaction volume, the bank invested heavily in information technology and is generally credited, together with GE and SRI, with inventing modern centralized bank operations; BoA has a number of financial transaction processing technologies, such as automatic check processing, account numbers, and Magnetic Ink Character Recognition (MICR), and, based on these technologies, credit cards linked directly to individual bank accounts. Because of the efficiency of these technologies, BoA had significantly lower administrative costs than other banks and was able to expand further, until it was the world's largest bank by the early 1970s.

In 1959, BoA invented the bank credit card, the BankAmericard, which changed its name to VISA in 1975. A consortium of other California banks founded Master Charge (now MasterCard) in order to compete with the BankAmericard.

BoA offers remittance services along with regular savings and loan products to its customers. It has a banking relationship with 44 percent of all Hispanic households; it opened more than 1 million checking accounts for Hispanic customers in 2004. The bank offers remittances under the SafeSend brand to its customers wishing to send money to Mexico. In early 2005, it announced that it would eliminate the $10 transfer fee for all checking account holders for remittances from the United States to Mexico to attract new business from migrant customers.

Notes

1. Western Union reports an average fee of 6–8 percent and an additional foreign exchange spread of 2 percent on its global remittance services. The average size of a Western Union remittance (covering personal remittances as well as small business-to-business remittances), however, is around $700, much higher than the average transaction size (under $200 reported in household surveys of migrants by, for example, a Pew Hispanic Center study on Mexican migrants in the United States and a Genesis Analytics study on South Africa). A World Bank survey of African diaspora in Belgium found that the average monthly remittances were 154 euros in the case of Senegalese migrants, 126 euros for Nigerian migrants, and only 78 euros for Congolese migrants.

2. For example, if a Brazilian bank received remittances on October 11, 2004, delayed payment to the beneficiary for two weeks, and invested the funds in the overnight money market, it would earn a float of 2.85 percent (IOM 2005). Humphrey, Keppler and Montes-Negret (1997) note widespread use of floats by banks, especially in the Russian Federation.

3. Some banks have announced even more aggressive price cuts recently. Bank of America, for example, eliminated fees for United States–Mexico remittances, to attract customers from the Mexican migrant community. Banks have also been providing free remittance services in some other corridors as well. It is worth noting, however, that there are hidden fees—account maintenance fees, minimum balance requirements, taxes on interest income—involved in such transactions besides the cross-selling of loan and deposit products.

4. According to the Piper Jaffray *Global Money Transfer Report* (2005), Western Union has said that it

can add a new agency for $1,000–$1,500 (the cost of setup, terminal, software, and training), while Dolex requires $12,000–$15,000 to establish a new branch.

5. In the case of banking institutions (also gas stations and grocery stores), remittance services may be cross-subsidized by other product lines, which renders remittance costs hard to determine.

6. The leading MTOs are Western Union, with a reported 13 percent market share, and MoneyGram, with a 3 percent market share. Vigo and Dolex are the third and fourth largest MTOs, respectively, with about a 2 percent combined market share. See Aite (2005) for their U.S. market shares.

7. Western Union has sustained high margins by taking the initiative to enter underserved markets, building a strong distribution network, and leveraging its brand name. Overall, the company has provided remittance services to millions of individuals in previously underserved markets.

8. This methodology is similar to that suggested by Humphrey, Keppler, and Montes-Negret (1997) for pricing payment services. These calculations do not include the costs of advertising and security.

9. This analysis is less conclusive with respect to the sensitivity of remitters to exchange-rate commissions. Migrants do have fairly accurate knowledge of the exchange rate used by their remittance operator, but they may be less informed about the premium involved in this rate. The estimate of cost-elasticity from the New Zealand study is based on responses from a small random sample of new Tongan migrants to questions about how they would react to a potential change in costs. It was not based on actual reactions.

10. This example assumes no change in the exchange rate.

11. There is no standard definition of a retail payment. Here it is defined as a transaction originated by, or payable to, an individual, the counterparty being an individual, a firm, or a government agency. It also includes frequent, small-value business-to-business payments. See also BIS (1999).

12. As measured by the International Country Risk Guide, credit risk is based on foreign debt as a percentage of GDP, foreign debt service as a percentage of exports of goods and services, current account as a percentage of goods and services, the import cover of international reserves, and exchange-rate stability.

13. The regression that generated these results is based on remittance fees from a single large MTO, so the results are not representative of costs in the remittance industry as a whole. Also the low R^2 suggests that the regression does not fully explain the cost structure.

14. The remittance price estimates provided by Western Union and MoneyGram on their Web sites often differ from the actual transfer fees. For this study, we gathered remittance price data by visiting Western Union and MoneyGram agents in Washington, New York, Brussels, Paris, London, and Singapore and by calling agents in other cities in various parts of the world. At various points, seven individuals were collecting remittance fee data in various corridors (for example, North America to Latin America and Asia, the EU to Africa and South Asia, the Gulf to South Asia, Eastern Europe to Central Asia, and East Asia to Southeast Asia). We collected daily foreign exchange data (for Western Union transfers to a broad range of countries from the United States and the United Kingdom and for Moneygram transfers from the United States to the same countries) on four consecutive business days in early June and calculated the FX spread by comparing these data to the exchange rates quoted on Bloomberg.

15. Lack of competition has been a persistent problem in this industry. In December 1996, MoneyGram was spun off from First Data Corporation, the holding company of Western Union, as part of an agreement with the U.S. Fair Trade Commission. See the annex for a history of remittance service providers.

16. In July 2005, the European Commission proposed that banks in the European Union be required to register the name, address, and bank account of anyone making an international money transfer. The requirements, which the commission hopes will come into force in January 2007, are the latest EU response to terrorism following the bombings in London on July 7, 2005.

17. OCC Advisory Letter 2004-7, www.occ.treas.gov/ftp/advisory/2004-7.doc.

18. Abuses include money laundering, the transfer of corrupt payments, payment of human smuggling fees, tax evasion, customs offenses, violations of currency controls, subsidy frauds, smuggling, illegal arms sales, and funding of terrorism. International trade is subject to many of the same abuses, but it is widely recognized that efforts to curb them must not interfere unduly with vital trade.

19. This is easier said than done, however, because major remittance service providers that have invested in their own proprietary networks and used them to expand their market share may not willingly share them. Furthermore, even if a shared network were developed with public funding, it may not easily gain participation by key banks and financial institutions (box 6.4). Federal Reserve Bank (2004, pp. 33–37) lists major proprietary payment networks.

20. Visa reported that in 2004 it set up a Visanet system in Iraq within eight weeks and for less than $200,000 (Brocklehurst 2004).

21. BANSEFI has a commercial alliance (L@Red de la Gente) with 62 regulated saving banks and MFIs operating mostly in areas where commercial banks

have no presence. This network provides a common platform for collecting and distributing financial products; for example, it facilitates migrant remittances as well as government transfers for pension and social and education programs, and it offers savings accounts and mortgage and consumer loans, small business lending, and health insurance products to the poor. Its IT network is aimed at offering the advantage of scale economies to its members.

22. Apex Bank in Ghana was set up (with support from the government and the World Bank) to provide banking services in rural areas. The Apex Bank has developed Apex Link, a domestic funds-transfer scheme among 75 rural and community banks. The Apex Bank is also collaborating with some financial institutions for the payment of foreign inwards remittances through the rural and community banks to beneficiaries in the rural areas.

23. The International Remittance Protection Act proposed by U.S. senator Paul Sarbanes in September 2004 marks an effort to improve disclosure of fees and exchange-rate commissions in remittance transactions.

24. In the European Union, the fees that financial institutions charge their customers for money transfers between EU countries cannot be higher than the fees charged for domestic money transfers.

25. In some cases, consumer rights legislation has enabled customers to challenge price gouging. In 2002, Western Union paid $30 million to settle two class-action suits stemming from its use of different exchange rates for converting remittances than the rates it received in the international money market (Aite 2005).

26. The related websites are www.profeco.gob.mx and www.sendmoneyhome.org.

27. For example, BANSEFI and Apex Link (as mentioned earlier).

28. This correspondent banking relationship between MTOs and some commercial banks, which had been working smoothly for a long time, came under pressure recently because of a misunderstanding of the know-your-customer rules. More than 300 small MTOs that collected remittances and then wired them through a correspondent bank were told in February 2005 that such transfers were no longer permitted. On March 30, 2005, FinCEN, FDIC, the Federal Reserve, and the Office of the Comptroller of Currency issued a joint statement that such transactions were indeed legitimate.

29. Source: www.rubinsanchez.com, representing the legislations for the different states of the United States.

30. Historical data on Western Union from www.westernunionalumni.com/history.htm.

31. PR Newswire, February 1, 2005.

32. See www.sec.gov/divisions/investment/noaction/firstdata011304.htm. In 1992, AmEx and First Data completed an initial public offering that resulted in approximately 40 percent of the common shares of First Data being held by the public. Over the next five years, AmEx sold its remaining shares to third parties, and by 1997 AmEx had no reportable ownership interest in First Data.

33. Source: www.MoneyGram.com.

References

Aite Group. 2005. "Consumer Money Transfers: Powering Global Remittances." www.aitegroup.com.

Andreassen, Ole. 2005. "Remittance Service Providers in the United States: How Remittance Firms Operate and How They Perceive Their Business Environment?" Unpublished paper. Washington, DC: World Bank.

Bakija, Jon M., William G. Gale, and Joel B. Slemrod. 2003. "Charitable Bequests and Taxes on Inheritances and Estates: Aggregate Evidence from across States and Time." *American Economic Review Papers and Proceedings* 93(2): 366–70.

Ballard, Roger. 2005. "System-Security in Hawala Networks: An Analysis of the Operational Dynamics of Contemporary Developments." Unpublished paper. Centre for Applied South Asian Studies, University of Manchester.

BIS (Bank for International Settlements). 1999. "Retail Payments in Selected Countries: A Comparative Study." Committee on Payment and Settlement Systems, Basel.

Brocklehurst, Stuart. 2004. "Sending It Home: How a Card Payment System Can Facilitate Remittances to Help Developing Economies." Presentation at Barcelona Forum 2004–HMI World Congress, September 1–5, Barcelona. www.mhicongress.org/.

Cordes, Joseph. 2001. "The Cost of Giving: How Do Changes in Tax Deductions Affect Charitable Giving?" Emerging Issues in Philanthropy Seminar Series, Urban Institute, Washington, DC. www.urban.org/UploadedPDF/philanthropy_2.pdf.

de Luna Martinez, Jose. 2005. "Workers' Remittances to Developing Countries: A Survey with Central Banks on Selected Public Policy Issues." Policy Research Working Paper 3638. World Bank.

DFID (Department for International Development). 2005. "Sending Money Home? A Survey of Remittance Products and Services in the United Kingdom." London. www.sendmoneyhome.org.

El Qorchi, M., S. Maimbo, and J. Wilson. 2003. "Informal Funds Transfer Systems: An Analysis of the Informal Hawala System." IMF Occasional Paper 222. International Monetary Fund, Washington, DC.

FATF (Financial Action Task Force Against Money Laundering). 2005. "Money Laundering and Terrorist Financing Typologies, 2004–2005." Paris. June. www.fatf-gafi.org.

Federal Reserve Bank of Chicago. 2004. "Global Electronic Payments." April.

Feldstein, Martin, and Amy Taylor. 1976. "The Income Tax and Charitable Contributions." *Econometrica* 44(6): 1201–22.

Freund, Caroline, and Nikola Spatafora. 2005. "Remittances: Costs, Determinants, and Informality." Background paper prepared for this report. World Bank.

Gibson, John, David J. McKenzie, and Halahingano Rohorua. 2005. "How Cost-Elastic Are Remittances? Estimates from Tongan Migrants in New Zealand." Background paper prepared for this report. World Bank, Washington, DC.

Glenday, Graham., Anil K. Gupta, and Henry Pawlak. 1986. "Tax Incentives for Personal Charitable Contributions." *Review of Economics and Statistics* 68(4): 688–93.

Grace, David. 2005. "Exploring the Credit Union Experience with Remittances in the Latin American Market." In *Remittances and Development: Development Impact and Future Prospects*, ed. Samuel Maimbo and Dilip Ratha. Washington, DC: World Bank.

Hernández-Coss, Raúl. 2004. *The U.S.-Mexico Remittance Corridor: Lessons on Shifting from Informal to Formal Transfer Systems.* Washington, DC: World Bank.

Humphrey, David B., Robert Keppler, and Fernando Montes-Negret. 1997. "Cost Recovery and Pricing of Payment Services: Theory, Methods, and Experience." World Bank Working Paper 1833. Washington, DC.

IMF. 2005a. *Approaches to a Regulatory Framework for Formal and Informal Remittance Systems: Experiences and Lessons.* Washington, DC.

———. 2005b. *World Economic Outlook: Globalization and External Imbalances,* April 2005, Washington, DC.

IOM (International Organization for Migration). 2005. *World Migration 2005.* Geneva.

Kalan, George, and Dilek Aykut. 2005. "Assessment of Remittance Fee Pricing." Background paper prepared for this report. World Bank, Washington, DC.

Orozco, Manuel. 2004. "The Remittance Marketplace." Unpublished paper. Pew Hispanic Center. June.

Maimbo, Samuel M., and Nikos Passas. 2005. "The Regulation and Supervision of Informal Funds Transfer Systems." In *Remittances and Development: Development Impact and Future Prospects,* ed. Samuel Maimbo and Dilip Ratha. Washington, DC: World Bank.

Passas, Nikos. 1999. "Informal Value Transfer Systems and Criminal Organizations: A Study into So-Called Underground Banking Networks." The Hague, Ministry of Finance.

Piper Jaffray. 2005. "Global Money Transfer Report."

Prahalad, C. K. 2005. *The Fortune at the Bottom of the Pyramid: Eradicating Poverty through Profits.* Philadelphia: Wharton School Publishing.

Ratha, Dilip, and Jan Riedberg. 2005. "On Reducing Remittance Costs." Unpublished paper. Development Research Group, World Bank, Washington, DC.

Taylor, John B. 2004. "Remittance Corridors and Economic Development: A Progress Report on a Bush Administration Initiative." Remarks presented at the Payments in the Americas Conference, Federal Reserve Bank of Atlanta, October 8.

Western Union. 2000. *Annual Report.* Greenwood Village, CO.

Yang, Dean. 2004. "International Migration, Human Capital, and Entrepreneurship: Evidence from Philippine Migrants' Exchange Rate Shocks." Research Program on International Migration and Development. DECRG. Policy Research Working Paper 3578. World Bank.